EVOLUTION, POLITICS AND CHARISMA

CU00951932

Evolution, Politics and Charisma: Why Do Populists Win? shines compelling new light on the way in which the systematic targeting and manipulation of human physiology remain a cornerstone of all populist political campaigns. Readers wishing to make sense of the populist juggernauts of Trump and Brexit and of the cyclical and formulaic nature of the rise and fall of charismatic populism will find this book particularly appealing.

Elesa Zehndorfer begins by presenting a highly applied explanation of the critical importance of political physiology, physiology theory, neuroscience and evolutionary biology in populist charismatic politics. She later eloquently explains how manipulation of physiological variables (such as heightened testosterone and dopamine) renders the political rally one of the most powerful weapons in a populist leader's campaign. Weber's seminal conceptualization of charisma 'in statu nascendi' and Hyman Minsky's insightful theories of cyclical boom-and-bust scenarios are then juxtaposed alongside physiological theory to greatly amplify our understanding of the powerful biological antecedents of charismatic populism. These theoretical observations are then applied directly to recent high-profile populist campaigns – including the 2016 Trump Presidential campaign and early Presidency – and the Brexit Referendum, to elucidating and compelling effect.

Ultimately, *Evolution, Politics and Charisma* paints a clear evolutionary picture of the way in which politics is an emotional – not a rational – process, where our emotions are continually targeted to great, and strategic, effect, and where the most recent intersection of technology and physiology has driven the greatest surge in populism ever seen across the Western hemisphere since the 1930s. Acknowledging this reality opens up exciting vistas in our understanding of the true power of charismatic populism and provides answers as to how its seductive and often dangerous power can be effectively resisted.

Elesa Zehndorfer was awarded her PhD from the School of Sport, Exercise and Health Sciences at Loughborough University, UK, in 2006. Recently awarded Quora Top Writer 2018 and 2017, Dr Zehndorfer is also a Thought Leader for Hartford Funds, Research Officer for the high-IQ society British Mensa and author of three other books, also published by Routledge: *The Physiology of Emotional and Irrational Investing: Causes and Solutions* (2018); *Charismatic Leadership: The Role of Charisma in the Global Financial Crisis* (2015); and *Leadership: A Critical Introduction* (2014).

EVOLUTION, POLITICS AND CHARISMA

Why Do Populists Win?

Elesa Zehndorfer

Routledge
Taylor & Francis Group

NEW YORK AND LONDON

First published 2019
by Routledge
52 Vanderbilt Avenue, New York, NY 10017

and by Routledge
2 Park Square, Milton Park, Abingdon, Oxon OX14 4RN

Routledge is an imprint of the Taylor & Francis Group, an informa business

© 2019 Elesa Zehndorfer

British Library Cataloguing in Publication Data
A catalogue record for this book is available from the British Library

Library of Congress Cataloging-in-Publication Data
Names: Zehndorfer, Elesa, author.
Title: Evolution, politics and charisma : why do populists win? /
Elesa Zehndorfer.
Description: Abingdon, Oxon ; New York, NY : Routledge, 2019. |
Includes bibliographical references and index.
Identifiers: LCCN 2018046369| ISBN 9781138625037 (hbk) |
ISBN 9781138625044 (pbk) | ISBN 9780429460234 (ebk)
Subjects: LCSH: Populism. | Biopolitics. | Behaviorism (Political science) |
Charisma (Personality trait)--Political aspects. |
Polarization (Social sciences)--Political aspects. |
Demonstrations--Political aspects.
Classification: LCC JC423 .Z46 2019 | DDC 320.56/62--dc23
LC record available at https://lccn.loc.gov/2018046369

ISBN: 978-1-138-62503-7 (hbk)
ISBN: 978-1-138-62504-4 (pbk)
ISBN: 978-0-429-46023-4 (ebk)

Typeset in Bembo
by Taylor & Francis Books

FOR HENRY AND CLEMENS

CONTENTS

FIGURES

ACKNOWLEDGEMENTS

I first wish to extend a tremendous debt of gratitude to my Editor, Natalja Mortensen, whose belief in, and support for, the book have made the writing of this manuscript possible. I am also extremely grateful to my publisher Taylor & Francis who have now supported me through the publishing of four books.

Many thanks are due to my husband Clemens for his constant and invaluable encouragement and to my family and friends for giving me the time and encouragement to write when I needed it most. My son Henry has inspired me throughout and it is to him, as always, that I owe the greatest thanks!

I wrote my previous book (*The Physiology of Irrational and Emotional Investing: Causes and Solutions*) against a backdrop of great political change. I owe a great deal to the website Quora for awarding me Top Writer 2017 and 2018, in its facilitation of posts and debates via which I was able to shape, define and explore theoretical arguments, and for the ideas and insights that it led to, which ultimately led to the writing of this book. Interacting with passionate Trump supporters, liberals, Republicans, centrists and political observers from around the world indispensably guided my observations in theoretical and practical ways, for which I shall be forever grateful.

I also want to honour and acknowledge the memory of a couple of special people – my late Jewish great-uncles Sammy and Stanley, who both spent time in POW camps, from which they both bravely escaped, before being re-captured. The pathos of populism revolves around the construction of false heroes and revolutionaries, yet the heroism of those two was real, so I recalled and felt motivated by their story often. Similarly, the stories of Alan and Ghalib Kurdi[1] – and every child who has suffered at the hands of populist agendas – moved me greatly in moving towards the successful completion of this manuscript.

Finally, I remain hugely inspired by my two childhood heroes, the anti-Apartheid activist Steve Biko and *Daily Dispatch* Editor Donald Woods. It is quite something to have real heroes like them to look up to, particularly during a time when freedom of the press is once again emerging as a valuable and contentious commodity.

Note

1 The image of 3-year-old Alan Kurdi, a Syrian refugee, who tragically died whilst trying to cross the Mediterranean Sea with his family in 2015, made headlines around the globe.

INTRODUCTION

Populism is not the solution ... creating psychosis is not the cure.

– Pope Francis[1]

Interest in populism has exploded in recent years, facilitated by the ascension of populist leaders to positions of power in North America, Europe, Africa and the Middle East. Yet populism remains a remarkably misunderstood phenomenon (e.g. Barth, 2016).[2] Former US Vice President Joe Biden's timely warning of the rise of pre-war fascist-style populist 'strongmen'[3] in times of economic and political uncertainty clearly echoes fears that we are living through a new, populist era of 'demagogues and charlatans'.[4] We are currently witnessing a spike in populism that has not been rivalled since the 1930s,[5] necessitating a thorough and committed analysis of the way in which a new era of populism is made manifest. It is a timely and powerful warning, and one that subsequently directs the chapters of this book.

This book is unique in that it provides the first extensive, applied analysis of the foundational role of evolutionary and physiological variables in the cyclical, formulaic and powerful rise of populism. Extensive utilization of scientific and academic theory accompanies a detailed observation of current events, including the 2016 US Presidential Election, the British Brexit Referendum, the rise of Italy's Five Star Movement, Russia's interference in US politics, and the charismatic anti-populist approach of France's Emmanuel Macron.

The readers' journey begins with Chapter 1 ('The Ninety-Eight Percent'), a compelling introduction to the relatively youthful, emergent field of political physiology. Chapter 2, discussing the seductive power of populist rhetoric ('The Political Rally') uncovers the roller coaster dopamine highs, excitation-transfer and endocrinological lows of the populist political rally, whilst Chapter 3 ('Nature versus the Election Cycle') shines a light on the role of the weather and other natural variables in influencing our political behaviours. Chapter 4 ('The Physiology of Polarization') uncovers the powerfully monetizable and weaponizable nature of polarizing, right-wing rhetoric, whilst Chapter 5 ('The Life Cycle of Charismatic Populism') provides a clear and prescient take on the manipulation of evolutionary and endocrinological variables at every step of a charismatic populist's rise and fall. Chapter 6 ('Political Animals and Animal Spirits') explores the role of the economy in furthering the populist political agenda, engaging ably with an analogous reference to Keynes's *animal spirits* [6] to provide a taxonomy of irrational voting behaviours.

Notes

1 Official statement made on World Refugee Day, 2018, by Pope Francis.
2 Barth, M. 'What Investors Misunderstand about the Politics of Rage'. *Financial Times* online. Retrieved from: www.ft.com/content/58f0ef02-a4bf-11e6-8898-79a99e2a4de6
3 Wintour, P. 'Demagogues and Charlatans Are Stoking Fear, Says Joe Biden'. *The Guardian* (22 June 2018) online edition.
4 Wintour, P. 'Demagogues and Charlatans Are Stoking Fear, Says Joe Biden'. *The Guardian* (22 June 2018) online edition.
5 See Bridgewater Developed World Populism Index (Dalio, Kryger, Rogers & Davis, 2017, p. 1).
6 Keynes, J.M. (1936). *The General Theory of Employment, Interest and Money*. New York: Harcourt, Brace and Company.

1

THE NINETY-EIGHT PERCENT

The insights generated by neuroscience permit the study of politics to be anchored on as scientific foundation for the first time.

- *Friend & Thayer, 2013, p. 72*

In his Presidential Farewell Address of 1796,[1] George Washington warned of the dangers of a two-party state that might pit voters against each other in an 'alternate domination of one faction over another, sharpened by the spirit of revenge, natural to party dissension, which in different ages and countries has perpetrated the most horrid enormities'. Washington went on to warn of 'a frightful despotism' that could cause 'ill-founded jealousies and false alarms' and could open 'the door to foreign influence and corruption, which find a facilitated access to the government itself through the channels of party passions'.

Washington's words portended the current FBI investigation into Russian interference in the 2016 US Presidential Elections and echoed the words of American lawyer and founding father John Adams, who referred to a division of the nation into two great parties as the greatest potential evil that could face the US Constitution.[2]

Political physiology offers a timely and fascinating support to the words of Washington and Adams, explaining the evolutionary and physiological bases for their concerns. It is an explanation that inspires and forms the very bases of this chapter.

The Ninety-Eight Percent

It is possible, 98% of the time, to accurately predict the partisan affiliation of a voter (Ahn et al., 2014) when voters are shown non-political, emotion-invoking images. Given that at least 80% of the US population are partisan (Schreiber, 2012; Westen, 2007), we can reasonably conclude that over 80% of Americans are therefore already 'prejudiced in favor of a particular cause'[3] when it comes to political preferences, and that, as partisans, the 98% statistic represents a unique window into our emotional receptiveness to the appeals of our own party (e.g. McDermott, 2009; Tingley, 2011). We really think and vote with our emotions, and it is statistics such as these that betray the fundamentally emotional nature of man as a 'political animal'.[4]

If 80% of Americans are partisan, they are already 'wired' to reject data that don't fit into their positive image of a politician or party. We know that 'The brain registers the conflict between data and desire and begins to search for ways to turn off the spigot of unpleasant emotion' (Westen, 2007, p. xiii), explaining much about our proclivity to choose a side. It is a practice unique to *homo sapiens* that allows us to engage wholly in politics as emotional, not rational, voters, betraying evolutionary instincts to herd, to belong, to be led more powerfully by hedonism than rationality, and to achieve a physiologically comfortable homeostatic, eustatic state.[5]

Whilst it has taken over a century for modern academic thought to discard assumptions of rationality and begin to embrace the idea that we really might be closer to Aristotle's *political animals* (Aristotle, 4th century BC/1996) than we would at first have liked to admit, the scientific doors of discovery have been truly thrown open – by way of the advances in functional magnetic resonance imaging (fMRI) technology, for example – to embrace the role of evolution in shaping and defining our political behaviours. We are now at a point where we are, for the first time, able to discover the 'biological origins of political behavior', ushering in a veritable 'renaissance' in political thought (Friend & Thayer, 2013, p. 72). It is for this reason that the remainder of this chapter now constitutes a compelling and enjoyable ride through the recent advances in one of the most exciting new fields in academia – political physiology.

Political Junkies: An Introduction to Political Physiology

Aristotle and Plato provided some of the first recorded discussions of how biology influences political behaviour as far back as 400 BC, reflecting the role of hedonism in shaping our day-to-day decisions and actions. We know, for example, that:

> Allusions to biological influences on human politics are as old as the Greek philosophers. Plato's metaphor of bronze, silver, and gold, developed in 'The Republic' is an early analogue to later suggestive work on the genetic bases of human behavior.
>
> *(Somit & Peterson, 2011, p. 3)*

Those genetic influences are why partisanship can make us feel good. So good, in fact, that it could be likened to a drug, where recognizing a charismatic politician whom we enjoy listening to, watching a bombastic viral campaign video, attending a rally, or just seeing the logo of our preferred party releases dopamine and oxytocin in our brains: 'These reward circuits overlap substantially with those activated when drug addicts get their "fix", giving new meaning to the term political junkie' (Westen, 2007, p. xiv).

Political scientist and bestselling author Drew Westen likens the emotions that underpin political voting choices to a wild horse, where the reason-based circuitry also engaged in decisions is best represented by a bareback rider; whilst reason can try to tame emotion, it is far less powerful, ultimately, than the beast that it is trying to control. As is the case with Aristotle's *political animal*, it has been said that 'Conventional political reasoning (path c–g–i) can only occur in the context of hot cognition' (Kraft, Lodge & Taber, 2015, p. 127). Hot cognition, in this context, describes the heady emotions that fire up and drive our cognitive decisions, regardless of how rational we might otherwise think them to be. It is a process attributable to our unique evolutionary hardwiring: 'The capacity for rational judgement evolved to augment, not replace, evolutionarily older motivational systems ... Reason can prod, regulate, and offer direction, but on its own it is pedestrian' (Westen, 2007, pp. 62–63).

When it comes to a *homo sapiens* brain, all of our decisions, whether conscious or unconscious, rational or emotional, are 'affectively charged' (Kraft et al., 2015, p. 127). The 'John Q. Public Model' (Kraft et al., 2015; Lodge & Taber, 2013), for example, charts the process whereby first affective, and then cognitive, processing, triggered by an external stimulus (e.g. a tweet by a politician), triggers unconscious biased, motivated reasoning. In short, it remains unclear how fully we can control the 'cognitive monster' of unconscious processing (Bargh & Chartrand, 1999) – but we know that emotions always play a defining part. It is ultimately this *hot cognition* that has made us the political animals that we are today.

Partisanship: The Madness of Crowds

In an American study of partisanship behaviours, brain scan data were used to predict politically-motivated judgements (in this case, relating to human rights violations), with politically partisan decisions exhibited 84% of the time (Westen, 2007, p. 111). This led to the powerful observation that voters are able to forgive – or condone – egregious moral and ethical acts on the basis of their partisan standing; as noted by the researchers, 'even when we handcuffed people to the data with titanium cognitive cuffs, they managed, Houdini-like, to free themselves from any constraints of reality through the power of emotion' (Westen, 2007, p. 111). Partisanship is dangerous because it encourages and normalizes the practice of discounting potentially high-quality data in favour of thought processes that align with our previously held political beliefs. In a review of empirical studies published in 2015 (Kraft et al., 2015), for example, it was found that 'Partisans ... systematically denigrate, depreciate, and counterargue evidence that is contrary to their political views but accept uncritically the supportive evidence' (p. 122). Propaganda and denigrating partisan content, as we now know, characterized the US 2016 Presidential Elections, leading to a surge in populist-focused research, such as the Harvard report 'Partisanship, Propaganda, and Disinformation: Online Media and the 2016 U.S. Presidential Election' (Faris et al., 2017).

The Political Battlefield

Voters on each side of the ideological battlefield demonstrate strong partisan tendencies, with none of us immune to the practice of bending the facts to suit our ideological position. It has been said, for example, that

> None of the circuits involved in conscious reasoning were particularly engaged. Essentially, it appears as if partisans twirl the cognitive kaleidoscope until they get the conclusions they want ... Everyone from executives and judges to scientists and politicians may reason to emotionally biased judgements when they have a vested interest in how to interpret 'the facts'.
>
> *(Westen, cited in* Science Daily, *2006, para. 5)*

In evolutionary, survival-focused terms, this approach suddenly makes more sense, given that the ability to reason appears to be a relatively recent development in the *homo sapiens* brain: 'Organisms survived for millions of years without consciousness and without the faculty philosophers have extolled for 2,500 years as reason' (Westen, 2007, p. 88). As a result, our far more powerful emotional processor still takes control of a lot of our decision-making, without us even realizing it: 'Emotions provide a compass that lead us toward or away from things, people or actions associated with positive or negative states' (Westen, 2007, p. 88). It provides valuable insight as to why charisma, channelled through the conduit of populist discourse (see Chapter 5 for greater depth) remains such a powerful weapon. It is also why Francis Bacon (2014, n.p.), as far back as 1620, noted that when we have formed an opinion, facts to the contrary are deemed ignoble variables that the brain 'either neglects and despises ... in order that by this great and pernicious predetermination the authority of its former conclusions may remain inviolate'. It has taken around 400 years for the scientific community to catch up with Bacon's sentiments.

We are designed, evolutionarily, to try to attach to a source of comfort when threatened, rather than rationalizing that threat. It has been reported, for example, that there appears on average to be an innate advantage in preferring attachment over cognition for managing anxiety. This preference is because physiologically the arousal of anxiety is regulated more quickly through the 'lower' limbic region and brainstem regions than through the 'higher' cortex regions managing cognitive functions.

(A. Stein, 2017, p. 83)

Aristotle famously defined man as a quintessentially 'political animal' (*zoon politikon*)[6] more than 2,000 years ago. The emergent field of political physiology (e.g. Wagner et al., 2015) has opened the floodgates in continuing to explore the evolutionary and neurological bases that explain why we vote as we do (e.g. Alford, Funk & Hibbing, 2005; Balzer & Jacobs, 2011; McLean et al., 2011), laying bare the physiological and cognitive processes that shape our political actions:

> Rather than believing those with political views opposing ours are lazily uninformed or wilfully obtuse, political tolerance could be enhanced and cultural conflict diminished if it is recognized that at least part of our political differences spring from subconscious physiological and cognitive variations that lead people to experience the world in fundamentally different ways and therefore to believe that fundamentally different political policies are appropriate.
>
> *(Dodd et al., 2012, p. 648)*

Politics versus Reason

Neurological studies inform us that we process data emotionally, not rationally (e.g. Ballmaier et al., 2004), an idea understood ably by Cambridge Analytica, the political offshoot of SCL Elections, whose parent company, SCL, has, for many years, specialized in the field of military psychological operative techniques.

As stated by Managing Director Mark Turnbull of Cambridge Analytica – a major player in recent populist-driven political campaigns:

> the two fundamental human drivers when it comes to taking information on board effectively are hopes and fears, and many of those are unspoken and even unconscious – you didn't know that was a fear until you saw something that just evoked that reaction from you … our job is to get, is to drop the bucket further down the well than anybody else to understand what are those really deep-seated underlying fears, concerns. It's no good fighting an election campaign on the facts, because actually it's all about emotion.[7]

Fear and anger are powerful mobilizers that drive an electorate to the polling booths, a phenomenon that is revisited at length in later chapters.

Homeostasis

One great driver of emotional voting, of the 'forgivability of an action' (Westen, Blagov, Harenski, Kilts & Hamman, 2006, p. 1956) that allows us to re-tweet a news story despite its questionable source or excuse the malfeasant acts of a favoured politician, reflects a tendency to engage in 'avoidant and escape conditioning' (Westen et al., 2006, p. 1956) that ultimately meets our need for physiological balance, or homeostasis. Basal, healthy homeostasis, or eustasis, represents the healthiest point of a U-shaped dose-response curve (Figure 1.1), where allostasis (or cacostasis; defective homeostasis) represent sub-optimal, harmful states that our central nervous system (CNS) immediately seeks to resolve. One well-known response that reflects the body's need for homeostasis is the 'fight-or-flight' response that emboldens us to remove, or run from, a threat, lowering stress hormones that have flooded our body and returning us to a more balanced state.

It is a physiological reflex that can also direct political decisions. Chasing eustasis, for example, can lead us to seek out '*emotionally preferable conclusions*' (Westen et al., 2006, p. 1947) that cause us intellectual confusion and stress – discrediting unwanted data as 'fake news', for example – to remove cognitive conflict (e.g. Rada, Mark & Hoebel, 1998). This need to reconcile 'data and desire' (Rada et al., 1998, p. 1951) is reflected in engaging in motivated political action (e.g. Westen et al., 2006, p. 1956), itself reflective of our ongoing, short-term need for mental and physical equilibrium.

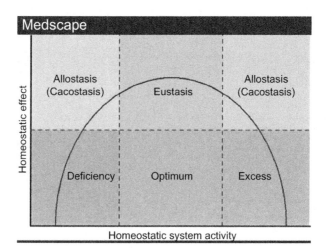

FIGURE 1.1 Stress and disorders of the stress system
Source: *Nature Reviews Endocrinology* © 2009 Macmillan Publishers Limited.

As far back as 1884 (James, 1884), there has been the idea that the body's perpetual drive for, and immediate need to achieve, physiological homeostasis forms a primary motivator for action. Evolutionary biology tells us the crucial role that homeostasis – our perpetual pursuit of physiological balance – ultimately plays in everything that we do, where 'the political ramifications of our evolution-shaped genetic tendencies become more startling' (Friend & Thayer, 2013, p. 75).

An Appetite for Fear and Risk

Research reflects a 'biphasic' model of emotional reaction where emotional responses are governed either by 'appetitive' responses (the Behavioural Activation System, or BAS), or by 'defensive' responses (the Behavioural Inhibition System, or BIS) (Gray, 1972; Gray, 1981). Together these responses direct voluntary (or somatic) and involuntary (or autonomic) nervous system activity, representing proximate causes of behaviour (Dodd et al., 2012). Cambridge Analytica's Managing Director Mark Turnbull's words, cited above, thus represent an explicit desire to target and manipulate BAS and BIS to actualize preferred political outcomes. This can be achieved most effectively through the use of disturbing content (e.g. characterization of immigrants as rapists and gang members) as aversive stimuli constitute a particularly powerful motivator:

> On the whole, people are risk-sensitive in that their physiological responses and cognitive attention are heightened by aversive stimuli, a pattern that makes sense from an evolutionary point of view. ... physiological and cognitive responses to aversive images outstrip those to appetitive images.
>
> *(Dodd et al., 2012, p. 641)*

Thus, we begin to see why right-wing populism has emerged so strongly as an advertising strategy in recent years; stimulating anger, fear and disgust represents the fastest way to reach voters on an evolutionary level and build their trust.

Germophobes, Pathogens and Politics

Disgust is 'a fundamental emotion linked to the evolutionary need to avoid environmental pathogens and toxic substances' (Balzer & Jacobs, 2011, p. 1298). It is a powerful director of moral judgements, creating a kind of 'behavioral immune system' (Balzer & Jacobs, 2011, p. 1299) that leads to the rejection of perceived pathogens, including perceived violations of moral or ethical societal norms (e.g. homosexuality). Conservative ideologues appear more receptive to divinity- and community-focused ethical messages (Haidt & Hersh, 2001, pp. 206–207) which we can see reflected in the US Republican Party's strategy of forging close bonds with the Evangelical Christian Movement and in invoking religion and faith-based constructs frequently in their campaigns. Religion often emphasizes the 'proper use of the human body' (Haidt & Hersh, 2001, p. 208) which provides a powerful pathogen-invoking response to the idea, for example, of homosexuality as a sin.

Donald Trump is, by his own admission, a germaphobe,[8] who favours drinking through straws to avoid contamination and has commented on the potentially germ-spreading practice of shaking hands as barbaric. Trump would fit well into the characterization of an individual who is *particularly sensitive to stimuli that evoke disgust*' (Ahn et al., 2014; Inbar, Pizarro & Bloom, 2012; Terrizzi, Shook & Ventis, 2010). Interestingly, ideological differences have been linked to a greater disgust response, where a 'variation in ideology may be strongly linked with disgust-related biases'. Research indicates that conservative ideologues tend to exhibit 'a greater negativity bias than those who endorse more politically liberal beliefs' (Oosterhoff, Shook & Ford, 2018, p. 227) where 'conservatives are more likely than liberals to experience disgust in response to specific behaviours that violate ideals of purity' (Inbar, Pizarro & Bloom, 2009, pp. 715–716). Research using skin conductance and self-report measures support this idea, particularly in relation to a marked disgust bias amongst conservative ideologues, with researchers stating that 'it is quite remarkable that involuntary physiological responses to non-political stimuli exert such an effect' (Smith, Oxley, Hibbing, Alford & Hibbing, 2011, e25552).

We can see immediately why political advertising campaigns targeting conservative ideologues heavily utilize anti-immigrant rhetoric as it provides a powerful way to exploit disgust-reactive responses. For those voters who 'fear change, dread disorder, are intolerant of nonconformity, and derogate reason' (McClosky, 1958, p. 40), alongside a more pronounced response to disgust and pathogen-related fear, an immigrant-targeting, negative campaign might prove very successful.

We can also observe a pattern of behaviours relating to deference to science (Blank & Shaw, 2015), a practice far more prevalent amongst liberal ideologues (e.g. Bolsen, Druckman & Cook, 2014), and a greater desire for punitive action amongst conservatives, demonstrated by a study of the willingness of voters to support legal reforms based on the incorporation of new neuroscientific evidence that would have led to potential reductions in the sentences of felons (Shen & Gromet, 2015). We know that 'skepticism seems to be stronger among conservatives than liberals' (Kraft, Lodge & Taber, 2015, p. 121), a scepticism mediated in part by a tendency to be less open to new information and experience (De Neve, 2013). Interestingly, voters who drift towards conservative ideologies are motivated by values of ingroup/loyalty, authority/respect and purity/sanctity that liberal ideologues do not seem to possess (Caprara, Schwartz, Capanna, Vecchione & Barbaranelli, 2006; Haidt & Graham, 2007; Mondak, 2010; Schwartz, 2010).

Lust and Disgust

In a nod to hedonic theory, the intriguingly-named 'lust–disgust axis' shines further light on the role of pleasure and pain – in this context, conceptualized as lust and disgust – as 'the original building block of all emotions' (Smith et al., 2011, p. 1). The aforementioned axis explains how conservative ideologues tend to be more receptive to negative affect messages, responding with greater force (disgust) than liberal ideologues to negatively framed triggers, giving greater weight to negative-focused messages, and recalling negative data more readily (Mills et al., 2016; Shook & Fazio, 2009). A tendency to respond more strongly to perceived risk, to feel threatened more readily and to feel fear far more easily (Schreiber et al., 2013) underscore the broad-ranging neurological differences across the political right and left: in sum, these conservative individuals feel more 'easily victimized, easily offended, indecisive, fearful, rigid, inhibited, relatively over-controlled and vulnerable' (Block & Block, 2005, p. 395).

Recalling that *homo sapiens* was designed to live in a relatively unsafe, pathogen-dense environment, before the advent of medicinal care or sanitation of any kind, the reader can see that these impulses (particularly when co-existing with more adventurous 'liberal' ideologues) would have, in ancient times, been invaluable in protecting oneself, family, offspring and community. However, in the days of modern populist campaigns, which target the 'lust–disgust' axis so effectively, these evolutionary strengths make the voter more vulnerable to manipulation, particularly in the context of micro-targeted, race-based messages of fear, and reasons to vote for the party that will save them and remove the threat.

This kind of fear response, as previously mentioned, held great evolutionary benefits and should not be viewed as a neural weakness; quite the opposite, given its survival – maximizing outcomes. In physiological terms, 'the aversive in life appears to be more physiologically and cognitively tangible to some people and they tend to gravitate to the political right' (Dodd et al., 2012, p. 647). What does this mean for how voters interact with the political system, exactly? It appears, interestingly, that voters who react more strongly to the aversive in life are also more anxious, and this anxiety might lead them to process political data more emotionally. As A. Stein (2017) states:

> there appears on average to be an innate advantage in preferring attachment over cognition for managing anxiety. This preference is because physiologically the arousal of anxiety is regulated more quickly through the 'lower' limbic region and brainstem regions than through the 'higher' cortex regions managing cognitive functions.
>
> *(A. Stein, 2017, p. 83)*

In short, it is easier to manage anxiety emotionally than rationally.

An Emotional Monopoly

Political scientist Drew Westen (2007) states that 'Republicans … have a near monopoly in the marketplace of emotions' (p. 36), but why? The Republican Party has made a decades-long commitment to investing millions of dollars in think-tanks and research into the power of emotion in mobilizing their base, leading to the observation that 'Republicans understand what the philosopher David Hume recognized three centuries ago: that reason is a slave to emotion, not the other way around' (Westen, 2007, p. 15).

It is a valid observation, reflecting distinct neural differences amongst individuals that can exert a notable effect on their vulnerability to different kinds of emotional political appeals. One area of the brain, the amygdala, plays a fascinating role.

As stated by Kraft et al., (2015, p. 129), 'Initial affective responses to a stimulus enter the decision stream before any and all conscious deliberations and thereby influence all down-streaming processes'. In other words, we process data emotionally and largely unconsciously before we are conscious of making any rational, analytic decision about it. This becomes really interesting if we consider, for example, that 'individuals with larger amygdala are more inclined to integrate conservative views into their belief systems' (Kanai, Feilden, Firth & Rees, 2015, p. 678).

In other words, we favour a more liberally or conservatively inclined message based in part on our genetic ability to process risk, but we are not consciously aware of this affective bias. A negative affect message stressing the risks of granting a safe home to asylum seekers would appeal, for example, to voters whose denser amygdala predisposes them to experiencing sensations of fear and disgust:

> political conservatism [is] a form of motivated social cognition; people embrace social conservatism in part "because it serves to reduce fear, anxiety, and uncertainty; to avoid change, disruption and ambiguity, and to explain, order and justify inequality among groups and individuals".
>
> *(Jost, Glaser, Kruglanski & Sulloway, 2003, p. 340)*

A positive affect message stressing the ethical virtues of granting a safe home to asylum seekers would, conversely, appeal to the more liberally-inclined. It can lead to a situation where 'some on the right view those on the left as hedonists who ignore pressing issues while some on the left view those on the right as doomsayers who obsess over constructed threats and problems' (Jost et al., 2003, p. 340).

It has been said that 'the primacy of amygdala function during stressful events makes evolutionary sense because in a fight-or-flight context survival depends upon "reflexive and instinctual behaviour," not deliberate cost-benefit calculations' (McDermott, 2004, p. 697, cited in Friend & Thayer, 2013, p. 77). Some voters possess a denser amygdala, which can expose a voter to a greater vulnerability to emotional appeals, particularly negative ones, and to a greater receptivity to charismatic appeal. Given that charisma emerges with the greatest force in situations of uncertainty (see Chapter 5 for greater depth), it is unsurprising to see a dominant use of negative affect-based, charismatically-delivered content in recent Republican political strategies that play on the fact that differences in 'political orientation [are] associated with psychological processes for managing fear and uncertainty' (Kanai et al., 2011, p. 678). Voters with a denser amygdala are potentially more likely to be drawn to fear-based messages, such as those exemplified by right-wing populist campaigns; 'The amygdala has many functions, including fear processing. Individuals with a large amygdala are more sensitive to fear' (Kanai et al., 2011, p. 678).

Liberal ideologues are not receptive to negative affect messages, but are still receptive to emotion, particularly optimistically-charged appeals. Conservative ideologues might still respond favourably to both (as 8.4 million voters demonstrated in the context of an Obama-Trump swing in 2016). Democrat Conor Lamb's campaign for the Pennsylvania special election in March 2018, for example, played on liberal ideals of unity whilst simultaneously addressing conservatively-minded preferences for nationalism as expressed through militaristic involvement, and inferred masculinity ('My only bias is the one they taught us in the Marines: a bias for action'). His campaign easily won over the negative, divisive rhetoric of his Republican rival Rick Saccone ('I was Trump before Trump was') and flipped a seat won easily by Trump in 2016. Research tells us that rational incentives alone are unable to win over voters; 'Research on the role of the limbic system suggests that dependence on rational incentives is unlikely in itself to resolve … fears and hatreds' (Blank, 2011, p. 220).

Lamb's message of unity exemplifies the power that can be realized in combining charismatic appeal with a recognition of the drivers of conservative and liberal concerns, and challenges the wisdom that 'many Democrats have come to associate emotional appeals with demagoguery' (Westen, 2007, p. 44). A failure to recognize the uniting potential of an approach like Lamb's risks handing far greater power to opponents who far more willingly engage with the power of evolutionarily appealing, emotionally-driven campaigns.

Half Genetic

It would be a big mistake to believe that conservative and liberal voters are somehow pre-ordained at birth to choose a specific political affiliation based only on, say, the density of their amygdala. Instead we need to recognize that, whilst these broad neural differences undoubtedly play a decisive role in many voters' lives and choices, they are far from being the decisive factor. We can say instead that 'Brain structure can exhibit systematic relationships with an individual's experiences and skills, can change after extensive training, and is related to different aspects of conscious perception' (Kanai et al., 2015, p. 679). Donald Woods, CBE, Editor of the South African Apartheid-era *Daily Dispatch* newspaper, provides an interesting example.

Whilst studying as a young man to become a lawyer at the University of Cape Town, Woods was initially in favour of government policies based on segregation of blacks and whites. Over the course of his life he was to emerge as one of the most powerful anti-Apartheid voices to emerge from South Africa, his story made famous in the film *Cry Freedom*. The movie was based on the manuscript for the book *Biko* that Woods smuggled out of the country. The book played a vital role in shining a light on the murder in detention of peaceful activist and intellectual Steve Biko and played a key role in bringing the horrors of Apartheid to the eyes of the world. It is a story that illustrates the complex web of social, genetic and environmental forces that ultimately act to shape and reshape our political values.

As noted by researchers, 'The political ideology of individuals is, on average, about half determined by genes' (Alford et al., 2005, p. 87), with studies generally reflecting the idea that there are, at any given moment, many complex political forces at play that influence our political values and decisions: 'Human behaviour emerges from the interaction and interplay of genes, socialization and environmental stimuli, working through ontogenetic neurobiological processes embedded in an evolutionary framework' (Hatemi et al., 2011, p. 281).

Uncertainty and Ambiguity

Voters who fall on the right side of the political spectrum are less ambiguity-tolerant than their left-wing counterparts (Amodio, Jost, Master & Yee, 2007) which might lead to a more willing tolerance of racial stereotypes. For example, 'implicit negative associations to a social group may result in an automatic emotional response when encountering members of the groups' (Cunningham, Raye & Johnson, 2004, p. 811). The creation of racial categories appears to prime even unprejudiced minds to stereotype on racial grounds (Fiske, 2002), with brain imaging studies demonstrating a human proclivity to react emotionally (via amygdala activity) to 'out-group' faces (Phelps, 2001). If geared towards the right audience, the development of racist beliefs via the systematized targeting of evolutionary fears (e.g. familial safety) is, biologically speaking, a relatively easy target.

The manipulative nature of politicized agendas that weaponize race really moves to the foreground if one considers that 'no part of the human cognitive architecture is designed to specifically encode race' (Kurzban, Tooby & Cosmides, 2001, p. 15387). It remains a clear truth that voters whose genetics predispose them to negative affect and charismatic appeals are relentlessly targeted by modern-era political campaigns that seek to win their loyalty by stoking fears around the concept of race. Liberal ideologues, it seems, are far less targeted in this way, although at times, the practice of voter suppression appears to emerge as a relatively successful strategy within this group (see Chapter 4 for more depth).

High levels of stress are a threat to homeostasis; for example, 'Neurobiological evidence shows that with increasing levels of stress, there is a decrease in prefrontal functioning and increased limbic-striatal level responding, which perpetuates low behavioral and cognitive control.'[9] This means that the body often favours an immediate, emotionally-driven 'fight-or-flight' response as it is most likely to ensure our survival. The reason that cognitive control is low in this instance is because cognitive reasoning takes longer and might, in former Palaeolithic times, fatally slow down our reactions when faced with danger. It disempowers us in political scenarios, however, as it inhibits our ability to seek and be open to new data, and to rationally and objectively analyse that data. The Dunning Kruger Effect, for example, explains that 'those with limited knowledge in a domain suffer a dual burden: Not only do they reach mistaken conclusions and make regrettable errors, but their incompetence robs them of the ability to realize it' (Kruger & Dunning, 1999, p. 1121). It can also heighten receptiveness to authority and authoritarian structures that provide a deliverance from negative affect-driven pathogenic-focused threats. Right-wing populist voters, for example, seem to 'support adherence to social norms and avoidance of out-group members, such as collectivism, right-wing authoritarianism, and religious fundamentalism' (Oosterhoff et al., 2018, p. 228).

Resistance to Change

Another way in which greater anxiety can manifest itself in political voting scenarios is via a resistance to change (Jost et al., 2003) and a 'belief that the world is dangerous and threatening' (Oosterhoff et al., 2018, p. 234), increased perception of risk where it does not exist (McEwen, 1998), a generally impaired ability to moderate risk (Coates, Gurnell & Sarnyai, 2010) and even an addiction to the source of stress itself. Modern right-wing political parties routinely exploit these tendencies, creating and fuelling security fears of dangerous 'out-groups' (Weber's demonized 'other'; see Kalberg, 1980) such as immigrants. Research shows, for example, that specific advertising and campaign appeals are 'likely to be differentially effective for those on the political right and those on the political left' (Dodd et al., 2012, p. 648), with right-wing populist appeals concentrating on fear and anger invocation that leads to the secretion of glucocorticoids (stress hormones), directs emotions, blunts cognitive processing capabilities (De Kloet, 2000), and negatively affects the parts of the brain (e.g. hippocampus) responsible for effective decision-making (Coates et al., 2010).

Low IQ or Low Effort?

A common misnomer in political discourse is the idea that voters across the ideological spectrum can somehow be demarcated by intelligence. There is no truth to this belief, although low effort did seem to emerge as a differentiator. Conservative ideologues displayed more low-effort thought as compared to more liberally-ideologic voters (Eidelman, Crandall, Goodman & Blanchar, 2012), most likely a reflection of explicit, long-term exposure to the negative affect, fear-inducing messages so characteristic of right-wing populist appeals, alongside greater bias, characteristic of the 'out-group' focus of the aforementioned (Jost et al., 2003; Kraft et al., 2015; Nisbet, Cooper & Garrett, 2015; Talhelm et al., 2012).

Serotonin and Voter Turnout

It is possible that a neurotransmitter, serotonin (5-HT), also exerts an interesting effect on political behaviours such as our likelihood to turn out to vote (e.g. Fowler & Dawes, 2008). Location matters; a recent study even found that right-of-centre parties fared better when the polling booth was stationed in a church (Berger, Meredith & Wheeler, 2008; Rutchick, 2010), an interesting idea given the close relationship between the US Republican Party and the Evangelical Christian Movement. A decreased level of 5-HT has also been found to lead to greater aggression and inability to control impulses (Masters & McGuire, 1994), leading to intellectual or physical altercations online or in person (e.g. Siever, 2008, p. 435). Individuals who possess higher-than-average basal and reactive testosterone levels might be more at risk of engaging in violence following exposure to inflammatory right-wing rhetoric: 'high-testosterone subjects are much more likely to engage in unprovoked attacks against their opponents than their lower-testosterone counterparts' (McDermott, Johnson, Cowden & Rosen, 2007, p. x), with a link between testosterone and amygdala activation shining a potentially elucidating light on the vagaries of 'trolling' and other derogatory social media-based behaviour.

Social Media, Social Provocation?

There appears to be a correlation between testosterone and amygdala activation (Derntl et al., 2009), with a reduction in self-regulation and impulse control evident following social provocation of some kind (Mehta & Beer, 2010). An estimated 140 million Facebook users were exposed to right-wing populist, generally pro-Trump propaganda during the 2016 US Presidential Campaign, much of it aggressive and divisive in nature. Propaganda created by Russian operatives as part of a campaign of Russian political interference[10] was designed to innervate a voter's 'fear circuit' in the prefrontal cortex (Coccaro, McCloskey, Fitzgerald & Phan, 2007) using sophisticated micro-targeted appeals tailored to the psychological profile of each individual voter. The appeals are powerful; when the prefrontal cortex does not adequately moderate impulses that derive from the limbic region, it can lead quickly to aggression (Glenn, Raine & Shug, 2009) which we see exhibited continually on online, partisan-driven forums and social media outlets. It also facilitates 'in-group' pride and 'out-group' demonization (e.g. Harris & Fiske, 2006, p. 852). In recent studies, for example, fMRI scans recorded lower mPFC (medial prefrontal cortex) activity in the brains of individuals who believed the ethnic or 'other' group to be less valuable than their own. The research is valuable as mPFC activation reflects the ability to engage in social cognition – in other words, to recognize an out-group as people, not objects (Mitchell, Banaji & Macrae, 2005; Harris & Fiske, 2006, p. 847). Dehumanization plays a vital step in conflict, war and

genocide (see Chapter 4 for more depth) and plays a central role in the effectiveness of right-wing populist strategies. We can see evidence of this kind of
dehumanizing instinct in the context of continued support for a policy of
forced incarceration and familial separation of babies and young children from
their parents along the US–Mexican border.

Blue Brains

We know that substantial differences exist in the cognitive styles of liberals and
conservatives (e.g. Jost et al., 2003). What is also interesting is that the impact of
genes can be moderated by environmental variables; the effect of a variant of a
dopamine receptor on political behaviour can, for example, be mediated by the
effects of friendship (Settle, Dawes, Christakis & Fowler, 2010). We know that
liberal voters are more comfortable with ambiguity (Amodio et al., 2007) and that
significant differences can be traced to regions of the brain known as the amygdala and the anterior cingulate cortex; 'the association of gray matter volume of
the amygdala and anterior cingulate cortex with political attitudes that we
observed may reflect emotional and cognitive traits of individuals that influence
their inclination to certain political orientations' (Kanai et al., 2011, p. 678).

The amygdala also plays a vital role in mediating emotional memory and prejudice
(Coccaro et al., 2007; Morrison, Allardyce & McKane, 2002), which might explain
the vastly different divisions that we currently can observe, from empirical research,
between Democratic and Republican partisan voters in the context of race.

Dopamine and Democrats

Genetic dopamine levels appear to exert a significant effect on an individual's attitude to risk, and on his or her general emotional state (Sapra, Beavin & Zak, 2012).
Adolescents with fewer dopamine receptors make riskier decisions (Steinberg,
2010); dopamine generally exerts a profound effect on financial decision-making
behaviour (Knutson & Bossearts, 2007), and even plays a role in trading and gambling addictions (traders with high DRD4 – dopamine receptor D4 – levels, for
example, are less likely to trade in volatile markets; and dopamine levels, as a
whole, may be able to assist in predicting one's success as a trader: 'two genetic
alleles that affect DA [dopamine] are associated with success at trading stocks on
Wall Street' [Sapra et al., 2012, p. 5]). The length of dopamine alleles (a genetic
variant of dopamine that different individuals are born with) also influences DRD4
activity, where a decrease in DRD4 activity can be seen to be closely associated
with 'novelty seeking, attention deficit hyperactivity disorder, and substance abuse'
(Sapra et al., 2012, p. 2). The reframing of politics as entertainment and as a pleasurable, sensation-seeking activity (see Chapter 3 for more depth), when combined
with the novelty-seeking, quick attentional requirements of social media interactions – might consequently appeal most to this kind of genetic profile.

Humour as Resistance

Jonathan Guyer of the Institute of World Affairs recently spent a month in Istanbul researching the work of Turkey's satirists operating under President Recep Tayyip Erdoğan. His research led him to comment that 'Political satire is maybe the most radical outlet for criticism of the government' (cited in Hills, 2016, para. 2). It is a power recognized by oppressive regimes; in 2016, for example, an aggressive group of Erdoğan's supporters broke into the *LeMan* magazine offices following a recent unsuccessful coup against Erdoğan's rule, incensed at the way in which their leader had been portrayed in the magazine's satirical cartoons. Guyer noted that 'Every cartoonist I interviewed in Turkey told me that 2016, irrespective of the recent coup and crackdown, has been the most difficult year for cartoonists on record' (cited in Hills, 2016, para. 7), going on to comment that around 1,500 people (cartoonists as well as celebrities and journalists) were under investigation for insulting President Erdoğan. His belief was that cartoonists were doing a good job of holding the President to account.

From a biological perspective, satire is powerful – it taps into charisma, creates positive affect, raises dopamine and serotonin (Harvard Medical School, 2010), and stimulates oxytocin when presented in the form of 'in-jokes'. Take Barack Obama's response to personal criticisms made towards him by Donald Trump on a Jay Leno show – a classic satirical play which not only entertains, but requires a more empowering level of cognitive gymnastics in order to get the joke: 'The trouble between Donald and me began', said Obama, 'when we were kids growing up together in Kenya and my team always beat his team at soccer. He never got over that'.[11]

Saturday Night Resistance

In the United States, *Saturday Night Live* (*SNL*) can be considered a *de facto* voice of humour-based resistance, with Alec Baldwin's take on President Trump already a mainstay of comedic history. But long before Donald Trump's ascension to the White House, Steven Colbert, American award-winning political satirist, plied his trade as a humorous resister to right-wing rhetoric and the dangers of charismatic populism.

Colbert's in-character comment that 'The truthiness is, anyone can read the news to you. I promise to feel the news at you' (Peyser, 2012) really hits at the heart of the charismatic, affect-dependent nature of populism; it isn't news that he is selling, but how to feel (quoted in Westen, 2007, p. 104, taken from *The Colbert Report*). Stephen Colbert's character was inspired in part by Bill O'Reilly, the anchor for the high-rating Fox News show, *The O'Reilly Factor*. *The Colbert Report* really hit a nerve, reporting, at its peak, a viewership of 1.5 million per show, four times a week.

Interestingly, a recent Pew Research Report (Gottfried & Anderson, 2014) cited both *The Colbert Report* and Jon Stewart's satirical *The Daily Show*, rating their viewers as better informed in political affairs than individuals who gathered their information principally from more traditional news sources. Stephen Colbert and

Jon Stewart both received prestigious George Foster Peabody Awards for their powerful contributions to news and journalism. Stephen Colbert's SuperPAC parody, 'Americans for a Better Tomorrow', raised $1 million and raised awareness of the dangers inherent in uncapped political funding enabled by a 2010 Supreme Court vs. Citizens United ruling.

Similarly, the Annenberg Public Policy Center reported that 'Americans for a Better Tomorrow'-themed segments of Colbert's show increased viewers' knowledge of PAC (political action committee) and $501(c)(4)^{12}$ campaign finance regulation more successfully than any other types of news media (Annenberg Public Policy Center, 2014). More recently, Colbert provided a strongly critical voice on the Charlottesville rally violence, with *The Atlantic magazine* (15 August 2017) running an article which stated that 'Colbert was doing what late-night comedians, more and more commonly, are doing: serving as arbiters, not just of humor but of morality' (Garber, 2017, n.p.).

A Different Kind of Humour

A 2017 study of 146 college students at Ohio State University found an interesting difference in how liberally- and conservatively-minded partisan voters processed satirical humour. Whilst Democrats reported that satire increased feelings of efficacy, Republicans felt undermined, a difference that the researchers attributed to differing views on authority. Professor Silvia Knobloch-Westerwick, the author of the study, commented subsequently that 'satirical news could be a gateway into more serious news use for people who aren't currently engaged in politics' (cited in Grabmeier, 2017, para. 16) which is obviously a trend that we have seen evidenced earlier in the Colbert case.

Alison Dagnes, a political science professor at Shippensburg University in Pennsylvania, notes that satire has to be anti-establishment to *be* satire, perhaps explaining why it is generally less well-received by conservative ideologues. Perhaps it is also because satire is viewed as a left-wing vehicle, though data do not support this; a 2010 study (Warner & McGraw, 2012), for example, carried out over an 8-month period, recorded every political joke told about a political figure on *The Tonight Show* with Jay Leno, *The Late Show* with David Letterman, *Late Night with Jimmy Fallon* and *The Daily Show* with Jon Stewart. Data reflected that 9% of political jokes were directed at Barack Obama, with President Bush receiving a similar 10% over the same period in 2002.

Summary

Following the extreme right-wing Charlottesville rally in 2017, Stephen Colbert delivered a passionate monologue, criticizing what he viewed to be an assault on American values. His passion felt charismatic (see Chapter 5 for more in-depth discussion on the appeal of charisma), genuine and intuitively appealing as a result. It reflects the view (as stated by Westen, 2007) that, 'from the perspective of the passionate mind, candidates shouldn't be running on issues in the first place. Candidates should be running on principles' (p. 174). This highlights the need for truth, conveyed passionately, in positive political appeals, as passion allows us to connect emotionally with the underlying message. That message instantly becomes more powerful when combined with the rational appeal of the message itself, and passion conveys charisma. This is a strategy that has been missing in recent years from political strategies; 'If a strategist tells a candidate "avoid that issue", the candidate should avoid that strategist, because he or she doesn't understand how the brain works' (Westen, 2007, p. 189).

Whilst 'Political scientists ... have generally assumed, [by] contrast to science, that rational processing takes place independently of emotional processing' (McDermott, 2004, p. 693), neuroscience and evolutionary biology tell us a different story: that 'emotion is part of rationality itself' (McDermott, 2004, p. 693). If we look at the Stephen Colbert ratings, we can see that they have rocketed under Trump's Presidency, averaging 3.2 million viewers per show in 2017. Humour – particularly satire – a form of resistance that embodies this duality, is powerful indeed.

Notes

1 https://en.wikisource.org/wiki/Washington%27s_Farewell_Address
2 John Adams, Letter to Jonathan Jackson (2 October 1780), *The Works of John Adams*, vol. 9, p. 511.
3 Google dictionary definition.
4 Man is by nature a political animal – an idea first voiced by the philosopher Aristotle.
5 Homeostasis reflects our physiological need to achieve balance, with eustasis reflecting the state of happiness and contentment reached when homeostasis occurs. It partly explains our hedonic nature and tendency for short-term thinking. This is explained in more depth later in the chapter.
6 Gintis, H., van Schaik, C. and Boehm, C., 'Zoon Politikon': retrieved from: www.umass.edu/preferen/gintis/Zoon%20Politikon%20Published%20Version.pdf
7 As reported in the undercover investigation, 'Data, Democracy and Dirty Tricks', accessible at: www.channel4.com/news/data-democracy-and-dirty-tricks-cambridge-a nalytica-uncovered-investigation-expose
8 E.g. Sinclair, H. (2017). 'Trump Says He Is Scared of Germs and Needs to Drink from a Straw to Avoid Contamination'. *Newsweek* online edition. Retrieved from: www. newsweek.com/trump-scared-germs-needs-drink-straw-avoid-contamination-671730
9 Sinha, R. (2009). 'Chronic Stress, Drug Use, and Vulnerability to Addiction', p. 3. Originally published in *Annals of the New York Academy of Sciences*, October 2008, 1141, 105–130. Retrieved from: www.ncbi.nlm.nih.gov/pmc/articles/PMC2732004/pdf/ nihms-123829.pdf
10 See FBI Indictment, retrievable from: https://apps.npr.org/documents/document.htm l?id=4380489-Justice-Department-s-Internet-Research-Agency
11 E.g. 'Barack Obama Appears on the Tonight Show with Jay Leno'. *The Guardian* online. Retrieved from: www.theguardian.com/world/video/2012/oct/25/obama -tonight-show-jay-leno-video. Source: Reuters.
12 Section 501(c)4 of the US Tax Code carries significant ramifications for campaign financing; a brief instructive overview can be found in a Political Law Briefing located at: www.politicallawbriefing.com/2013/06/501c4s-why-all-the-fuss/

2

THE POLITICAL RALLY

I felt a sort of energy flow through me that I had never felt before — as if I was a part of something greater than myself[1]

When Christian Picciolino attended a Chicago Area Skinheads (CASH) rally for the first time, it represented the most transformative, powerful and seductive moment of his young life (Bentz & Seavy-Nesper, 2018). An instant convert to the skinhead group, Picciolino founded the successful skinhead rock group Final Solution and became one of CASH's leading recruiters. He recalled the charismatic power of music in enabling seductive 'promises of paradise', cautioning that 'music is a very powerful tool that the movement uses to inspire vulnerable young people into a very hateful social movement' (Bentz & Seavy-Nesper, 2018, n.p.).

The transformative influence of the CASH rally that Picciolino first attended is not uncommon, reflecting the heady excitation-transfer and endocrinologically-innervating roller coaster that attendees of right-wing populist rallies are subject to. The seductive and charismatic power of the event causes a deactivation of executive function (e.g. MRI studies of religious charismatic worshippers report a frontal inhibition of the brains of worshippers [Gruzelier, 2006], and a deactivation of executive function during a religious healing event [Schjoedt, Stødkilde-Jørgensen, Geerts, Lund & Roepstorff, 2011]). Just as religious worshippers felt that they trusted a charismatic healer more after a service, Picciolino felt drawn to CASH with the same strength of reverence. Just as religious worshippers experienced a stronger deactivation commensurate with the strength of their belief (Schjoedt et al., 2011, p. 125), Picciolino experienced increased feelings of reverence as his attendance at rallies increased. Reverent supporters of President Donald Trump, whose love of rallies is well known, will experience the same heady rush, and the same increased deactivation of executive function that accompanies charismatic, powerful, emotionally-imbued displays.

Rallies and Oaths

> Don't forget you all raised your hand, you swore. Bad things happen if you don't live up to what you just did.
>
> – *Donald Trump, Rally in Orlando, Florida, 2016*

Political rallies have traditionally played a sizeable role in populist political campaigns. It is difficult to understand the true power and intentions of the populist rally, however, before first developing an appreciation of populism itself. It is to this concept that we shall consequently turn.

Degrading Democracy

Populism has been referred to as 'a degraded form of democracy that promises to make good on democracy's highest ideals' (Müller, 2017, p. 6), offering little more than a fantasy (e.g. Achen & Bartels, 2016) or seductive metapolitical illusion.

Populists claim to be *critical of elites*, they are *anti-pluralist* (that is, they alone claim to represent 'the people') and that anyone who is not with them, is *against them and the people that they are fighting for*. Populism is necessarily simplistic ('populism is simple, democracy is complex' [Dahrendorf, 2003, quoted in Müller, 2017, p. 10]) because one of the key roles of populism is to reframe politics as a source of sensation-seeking. 'Make America Great Again' appeals directly, for example, to 'a helpless articulation of anxieties and anger by those longing for a simpler, "premodern" life' (Müller, 2017, p. 17). Populist rallies rely on the use of chants and slogans, from which utopian, simple promises, devoid of strategy, usually emerge; this ably reflects 'the frequently extreme contradiction between its heavenly or freedom-touting pronouncements and the grimly oppressive reality of life within the system' (A. Stein, 2017, p. 19).

Populism has been referred to as a 'political logic' as opposed to a belief system, whilst hedge fund Bridgewater Associates positions it as a

> political and social phenomenon that arises from the common man being fed up with 1) wealth and opportunity gaps, 2) perceived cultural threats from those with different values in the country and from outsiders, and 3) the "establishment elites" in positions of power, and 4) government not working effectively for them … In other words, populism is a rebellion of the common man against the elites and, to some extent, against the system.
>
> *(Dalio, Kryger, Rogers & Davis, 2017, p. 2)*

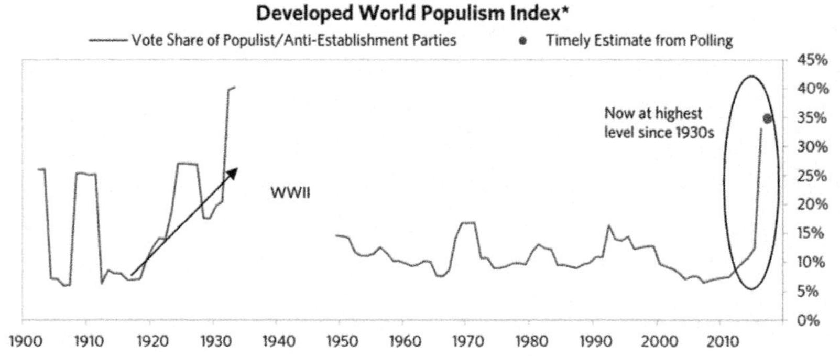

Developed World Populism Index*

──── Vote Share of Populist/Anti-Establishment Parties   ● Timely Estimate from Polling

FIGURE 2.1 Bridgewater Developed World Populism Index
Source: Dalio, R., Kryger, S., Rogers, J., & Davis, G., 'Populism: The Phenomenon'.
Bridgewater Daily Observations, 22 March 2017, p. 1. © 2017 Bridgewater Associates, LP. Permission granted.

Every populist who rose to power since the 1930s (Roosevelt, Huey Long, Father Charles Coughlin, Mussolini, Hitler, Ernst Thälmann, Franco, Mosley, Léon Blum, James Shaver Woodsworth and Getúlio Vargas) shared an environmental condition; nations characterized by very weak economies and (excepting the USA), political paralysis. Bridgewater's Developed World Populism Index paints a clear picture of a return to the populist surge of a pre-World War II world, with the current spike in populism unrivalled since that era (Figure 2.1).

Cashing In

Populist strategies focus on the creation of a central message of fear and anger. Picciolino experienced this phenomenon directly in his first CASH rally:

> it was the fear rhetoric ... I can tell you that every single person that I recruited or that was recruited around the same time that I did, up to now, up to what we're seeing today is recruited through vulnerability and not through ideology.
>
> *(Bentz & Seavy-Nesper, 2018, para. 9)*

As Müller (2017, p. 4) states, populists all share three key features: i) an initial period of seductive promises; ii) attempts to hijack the state apparatus; and iii) corruption, and clientelism (see Chapter 5 for greater depth). Political rallies, imbued with charisma, play a vital role in establishing the initially seductive promises and in demonizing the state, particularly because of the biological power of excitation-transfer (see later in the chapter) in amplifying the potency of the message. Populist rallies recorded for posterity and shared on social media offer an excellent means of perpetuating that simplistic fantasy, explaining in part why 'No US election campaign in living memory has seen as many invocations of "populism"' (Müller, 2017, p. 1) as the US Presidential Election of 2016. The formulaic quality of right-wing populist appeals, the sharing of simplistic, utopian messages and the ubiquity of the biological power of in-person rally attendance transcend ideologies, religions and cultures; anti-terror researcher J. M. Berger, for example, recently noted that 'The process and structure of radicalization and extremism are the same in different kinds of movements, even when the content of the extremist belief is different (such as with neo-Nazis and jihadists)' (cited in Graham, 2018a, para. 10). Whereas left-wing populism often invokes positive appeals to unity, right-wing populism always focuses on the aggressive demonization and dehumanization of out-groups. Both share a common theme of railing against an oppressive elite and speaking for the will of the people (the subsequent irony of populism's close relationship to authoritarianism is explored in greater depth in Chapter 5).

The Attraction of Political Rallies

The 'neuropsychological mechanism that may underlie effective emotional appeals' of a charismatic politician (Knutson, Wimmer, Kuhnen & Winkielman, 2008, p. 2) can be addictive. Weber (1904/1958, p. 22) characterizes charisma as a kind of religious authority, where the charismatic leader is endowed with superhuman powers. Whilst some voters (see Chapter 1, 'Blue Brains' for more depth) appear to be more susceptible to charismatic, populist appeals than others, we seem to possess a universal tendency to react more positively to candidates whom we find physically attractive.

When we find a person attractive, a specific pattern of affective brain activation occurs, which can lead to emotions of excitement or euphoria (Tingley, 2007). If the person also appears to be wealthy and popular, the amplification effect is substantial; in fact, there seems to be 'a substantial overlap between the neural representation of monetary and social reward' (Saxe & Haushofer, 2008, p. 164), leading to dopamine-enhancing, pleasurable effects for our brain. Wealth is viewed as an indicator of social standing, making it doubly attractive to us from an evolutionary perspective (Lea & Webley, 2006, p. 164). It also represents a kind of ubiquitous 'indicator of achievement, respect, and freedom or power' (section 4.4, in Lea & Webley, 2006, p. 179). For many voters, therefore, an attractive, wealthy politician becomes the 'gatekeeper' to all that the voter, personally, wishes to be, with those qualities acting as proxy-indicators of that individual's suitability for a politically powerful role.

Susceptibility to Appeals

When we pay for a ticket to attend a Tony Robbins seminar, for example, we know what we have signed up for. We walk into the event, the pumped-up music starts blaring from the speakers, the energy for the crowd is infectious and the motivation provided by Robbins engenders a kind of mass euphoria. The motivational messages begin, a flood of dopamine hits our brain, our executive processing centre shuts down as we become subsumed in the emotionality of the event, our testosterone rises, and amygdala-led passion motivates our behaviour (e.g. McDermott, 2004). The experience, for those that opt in to it, is generally pure entertainment and great value for money. In the right-wing populist political realm, however, the ubiquity of the rallygoers' predicted experience is unsettling.

Dopamine has been found to play a role in partisanship (Dawes & Fowler, 2009), with higher levels positively impacting liberal tendencies, when combined with exposure to friends and socializing amongst others of similar persuasion (Settle et al., 2010). But in individuals for whom dopamine and serotonin are deficient (e.g. due to depression, abuse of drugs, use of certain prescribed medications), we can expect to see higher rates of anxiety, depression, drug dependence, suicide, post-traumatic stress, metabolic disruption, aggression, fear, anger, poor memory and impaired learning ability (Hatemi et al., 2011; , Lipsky & Zhu, 2006; Lopez-Leon, Janssens & Ladd, 2008). The outcomes, when aggressively amplified by the bombastic rhetoric of charismatic rallies, can be frightening (the murder of counter-protester Heather Heyer, for example, at a neo-Nazi rally in Charlottesville, USA in 2017; or the assault on demonstrators at Trump rallies in 2016 – see later in the chapter) – particularly because lower genetic levels of serotonin and tryptophan are correlated with higher levels of aggression and greater impulsivity (Crockett, Clark, Hauser & Robbins, 2010). These genetic signals do not only lead to a greater mobilization to vote (Fowler & Dawes, 2008) but risk a greater propensity to violence and aggression if repeatedly targeted in political environments.

Animal Magnetism

In the 18th century, doctor Franz Mesmer described an unseen natural force ('*lebensmagnetismus*') that he believed could exert a hypnotic effect on believers. It is a concept that prompted Samuel Taylor Coleridge to comment disparagingly of the relatively young William Pitt (1759–1806), a 19th-century British Prime Minister, that 'The great political Animal Magnetist has most foully worked on the diseased fancy of Englishmen and thrown the nation into a feverish slumber' (Fulford, 2004, p. 1). Coleridge's use of the term appeared analogous to what we could now regard as charisma.

What he would make of Boris Johnson and Brexit is anyone's guess ('I can hardly condemn UKIP as a bunch of boss-eyed, foam-flecked euro hysterics, when I have been sometimes not far short of boss-eyed, foam-flecked hysteria myself.').[2] But just as American 19th-century journalist Ambrose Bierce described magnetism as 'Hypnotism before it wore good clothes, kept a carriage and asked Incredulity to dinner' (Bierce, 1911, p. 217), populism is also widely critiqued as a fantastical illusion. An illusion, yes, but a powerful one, amplified during a political rally to infinite levels if delivered with true charismatic appeal.

Addicted to Politics? Sensation-Seeking in Political Campaigns

> The total group effects of testosterone may be more than the sum of the effects in all the individuals separately.
>
> –Dabbs, 2000, p. 84

Populist rallies are charismatic, enjoyable, immersive events, designed to stimulate feelings of unity, exuberance and euphoria. The chanting of simplistic yet innervating populist slogans encourages the madness of crowds, exploiting our evolutionary tendency to herd (see Chapter 6, 'Political Behaviours: A Taxonomy of Irrational Voting Behaviours' for more depth). Framing the leader's role as a revolutionary is empowering, boosting testosterone, whilst the noble explanation of the right-wing populist as an ideologue spikes dopamine. It is pleasurable, after all, to feel as if you are part of a utopian movement that seeks to change your world.

It is for this reason that populist rallies appear so formulaic; because they target the same evolutionary and endocrinological responses. We therefore expect to see 'persistent features of discourse, which transcend individual texts, speakers or authors, situational contexts and communicative actions' (Heracleous & Barrett, 2001, p. 758; see also Jarzabkowski, Sillince & Shaw, 2010). One routinely formulaic rhetorical strategy focuses on the construction of *crisis rhetoric* which constructs a social reality (Smircich & Morgan, 1982) reminiscent of 1930s-era populism; demonization of out-groups, capitalization on a fear of economic uncertainty, and the mobilization of the populist voter as an ideological warrior against an ever-present threat.

From Populism to Pathos

Pathos represents one rhetorical pillar of persuasion,[3] describes an appeal to emotion (for example, recalling events that evoke feelings of national pride and nostalgia). *Ethos* refers to an appeal to ethical credibility, whereas *logos* represents an appeal to logic (Heracleous & Klaering, 2014). Populist pathos provides a powerful channel for the avalanche of endocrinological effects evoked by politicians at rallies, often engaging powerfully with the use of metaphor. Metaphors provide a necessarily distal (distant and vague) vision that suits a utopian discourse, appealing to voters across a disparate landscape (Hartog & Verburg, 1997), and have been reported as being used almost twice as often by successful US Presidents (Mio, Riggio, Levin & Reese, 2005). The use of root metaphors (an image, fact or narrative that shapes a voter's interpretation of reality) in populist rallies is profound, given that a rally targets a range of senses (e.g. music, imagery, use of alcohol, a sense of camaraderie when standing shoulder-to-shoulder); these metaphors are powerful, and thus become commonly invoked (Audebrand, 2010).

Apocalyptic Confrontations

Right-wing populist rallies also benefit from the perpetuation of crisis rhetoric, a unique form of pathos. As Müller opines:

> Populists in office continue to polarize and prepare the people for nothing less than … apocalyptic confrontation. They seek to moralize political conflict … a "crisis" can be a performance, and politics can be presented as a continual state of siege.
>
> *(Müller, 2017, pp. 42–43)*

The siege mentality is whipped up using charismatic appeals, a necessary and potent weapon given the fact that followers 'contagiously invest excessive faith in a leader's "vision"' (Bénabou, 2013, p. 444) (contagion in this context is explained later in the chapter in the form of biological excitation-transfer). Charisma crosses the boundaries of legitimate authority, and benefits from the *salience effect* (Hirshleifer, 2001, p. 1547) – a tendency for voters to rely excessively on the strength of information, as opposed to its weight. Again, a political rally amplifies these effects; an in-person display of fearless dominance, bombastic, charisma-imbued rhetoric, packaged up in an entertaining endorsement by a rock star or TV chat show host offer immense weight and appeal to the message itself. This can be problematic, of course, given the fact that 'anyone who hopes to rise to the top of an organization should have a solid dose of narcissism' (Kets de Vries, 2004, p. 188) – an idea revisited in depth in Chapter 5.

The power of charismatic rhetoric has been shown to be particularly powerful in conditions of uncertainty, and where negative feelings such as fear of persecution are present (Burns, 1978; House, 1977; House, 1996; House, Spangler & Woyke, 1991; Weber, 1924/1947). The reason that crisis rhetoric (Kiewe, 1994, p. 17) is so relevant to populists is that it amplifies profoundly the appeal of their message, with the link between rhetorical competence and charisma made clear in the academic literature (e.g. Heracleous & Klaering, 2014; Mio et al., 2005; Shamir, Arthur & House, 1994).

Crises Breed Charisma

US President Donald Trump's multitudinous deployment of root metaphors reflects a rhetorical reliance on pathos, where the construction of conflicts and wars is used to shape a crisis rhetoric amongst his base (e.g. trade wars with China, the EU, Canada). Klein and House (1995) state that *crises breed charisma* (p. 185), where the appeal of the charismatic leader is strongest at times of both uncertainty, and crisis (House, 1977; Rosenthal & Pittinsky, 2006; Shamir, House & Arthur, 1993). A populist's characterizations of wars, immigrant crises – or utopian futures – rest on 'a world of speculative make believe' (Galbraith, 1954/1988, p. 3, cited in Raines & Leathers, 2010, p. 541).

The invocation of crisis is powerful. Perceived anomie,[4] upheaval and crisis create feelings of helplessness amongst an electorate, which facilitates the emergence of a charismatic leader (Kets de Vries, 1988) – an idealized hero figure (Bass, 1985) who can rescue followers from their emotional distress. The greater the crisis, the greater the magnitude of an emotional disturbance; the greater the emotional disturbance, the greater the subsequent investment of some of this emotion in the charismatic hero (Bass, 1985; Pillai & Meindl, 1998).

Alpha Campaigns

Raised basal and reactive testosterone levels form part of a 'fight-or-flight' response, making us confident, emboldened and literally physically stronger. It can make us hypercompetitive, and the feeling can even be addictive (Kashkin & Kleber, 1989), making repeat ticket purchases for charismatic political rallies a likelihood. It reframes politics as entertainment, and sensation-seeking, but can be dangerous; it can amplify evolutionary mechanisms geared towards punishing contravenors of social norms, or actions that coerce expressions of explicit group conformity (de Quervain et al., 2004). One example of the latter is hazing – a ritualized and often brutal or humiliating initiation ceremony usually invoked in the first weeks of a fraternity, sorority or sports team membership (and which is now banned in many institutions).[5]

Right-wing populist rallies provide a source of androgenic priming, ramping up testosterone, and emboldening the rallygoer to engage in aggressive, risky acts. During a Donald Trump campaign rally in Dallas on 16 June 2016, for example, a rock was thrown at the head of a reporter. Trump supporters pepper-sprayed anti-Trump demonstrators outside a rally in San Diego on 28 May 2016. Pepper-spray was also used in an altercation at a Trump rally in Anaheim, California, on 26 April 2016, whilst in Bridgeport, Connecticut, an anti-Trump protester was pulled out of a venue in a chokehold. A protester was shoved in the face – twice – by a Trump supporter in Albany, New York, whilst another Trump protester in Tucson, Arizona, was punched and kicked at a Trump rally in March 2016. The perpetrator was arrested subsequently on an assault charge.

A black protester at a Trump rally in Fayetteville, North Carolina, was punched, with video footage showing the protester, and not the perpetrator, then being pulled to the ground by law enforcement officials. Trump campaign manager Corey Lewandowski allegedly grabbed a female reporter in Jupiter, Florida, in March 2016, while a black woman in Louisville, Kentucky, was surrounded and shoved around by white Trump supporters during a March 2016 rally. Rallygoers at a Trump rally in Las Vegas in December 2015 were filmed chanting '*Sieg heil*' and 'light the motherfucker on fire' – chants directed at a black protester who was, at the time, being forcibly removed from the venue. A similar event involved the punching and kicking of a black protester in Birmingham, Alabama, in November 2015. During a Trump rally in Miami on 23 October 2015, a Latino protester was reportedly kicked and knocked to the floor, whilst a *Time* magazine photographer was reportedly choked and slammed to the floor by a Secret Service agent in a rally in Radford, Virginia, in February 2016. Earlier, in November 2015, a Black Lives Matter protester was attacked by a number of Trump-rally attendees in Alabama, who punched and kicked him whilst shouting racist slurs. At a rally in Wisconsin, a 15-year-old girl was reportedly pepper-sprayed and sexually assaulted (Berenson, 2016).

These events are not limited to Trump rallies, but to any political rally that relies on right-wing populist rhetoric. The strategic utilization of root metaphors, the endocrinological wave accompanying rousing imagery, music and excitationtransfer (emotional contagion), utopian visions prevented by nothing more than a demonized minority (simplistically represented), and the charisma of the speaker combine with potentially devastating consequences.

Energy Flow

Christian Picciolino, the CASH member whose sentiments opened this chapter referred to an 'energy flow' that he felt coursing through his veins when he attended his first CASH rally, as illustrated in Figure 2.2 ('Energy Flow and ExcitationTransfer'). This energy flow is distinctly biological, and helps a charismatic politician

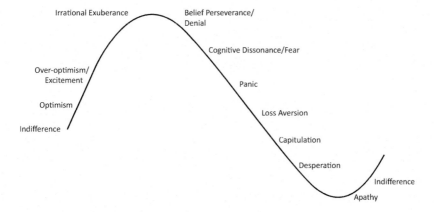

FIGURE 2.2 Energy Flow and Excitation Transfer

appear to be a miracle worker; if he can leave you walking on air after his rally, he becomes addictive, standing apart from other political rivals. Pumping up a follower's dopamine and testosterone therefore offers a brilliant conduit to the transmutation of a rallygoer from bystander to follower. It allows the charismatic populist leader to appear to 'work in miracles, if he wants to be a prophet' (Weber, 1978, p. 1114), and it requires him to rely on the help of the emotional contagion of the crowd to convert the individual; the process known as excitation-transfer.

Energy Flow and Excitation-Transfer

> Your dopamine system plays off my dopamine system. You buy, I buy, I worry about you, our systems become entrained. You sell, I sell.
>
> – *Montague, 2007, p. 3*

Excitation-transfer theory explains how the body's excitatory response (i.e. how we become 'excited') is amplified via exposure to others' emotions and powerful outside stimuli. During a populist political rally, the dangers of experiencing sentiment-led political activity, as opposed to engaging in reason-based analysis of the veracity of a leader's claims and manifesto, are high. The excitatory-transfer of emotions such as anger, fear or euphoria becomes commonplace (Bryant & Miron, 2003; Zillmann, 1998). Picciolino's formation of the Final Solution skinhead rock group capitalized perfectly on this phenomenon, combining the charisma of musical performance with bombastic, emotive lyrics to spread propaganda and recruit enthusiastic, pumped-up new members.

It pays to excite a crowd, which is why politicians and performers often employ warm-up acts or employ the help of celebrity endorsers: 'Residual excitation from essentially any excited emotional reaction is capable of intensifying any other excited emotional reaction. The degree of intensification depends, of course, on the magnitude of residues prevailing at the time' (Zillmann, 2006, p. 223).

Excitation-transfer and the evolutionary instinct to herd (see Chapter 6, 'Political Behaviours: A Taxonomy of Irrational Voting Behaviours' for more depth) seem to bear a close relation: for example, it has been said that:

> It is always easiest to run with the herd; at times, it can take a deep reservoir of courage and conviction to stand apart from it. Yet distancing yourself from the crowd is an essential component of long-term investment success.
>
> *(Seth Klarman, CEO of hedge fund Baupost, quoted in Cymbalista, 2003, p. 32)*

One reason for this might be because when we are in the company of others, emotions are literally contagious.

It has been said that 'The mass psychological aspect of trend formation is related to herding impulses involved in the limbic system, the part of the brain that

involves emotions and motivation' (Cymbalista, 2003, p. 32), so we can immediately see the value of emotional, utopia-inspiring rhetoric in motivating political
action. It is an instinct propelled by powerful emotional incentives to conform:

> when people did buck the consensus, brain scans found intense firing in the
> amygdala. Neuroscientist Gregory Berns, who led the study, calls this flare up
> a sign of 'the emotional lead associated with standing up for one's belief'…
> In short, you go along with the herd not because you want to, but because it
> hurts not to.
>
> *(Zweig, 2007a, n.p.)*

It is therefore not just the quest for homeostasis that keeps us in check in the
short term; if we commit to a longer-term membership of a group and rise in
stature, we benefit from the experience of drug-like changes in human biochemistry after changes in status (Mazur & Booth, 1998). To some, experiencing
the sensation of those drug-like effects and avoiding the pain of non-con-
formance are simply too powerful as motivators to allow an individual to question, or adequately question, a movement or political vision.

The Physiological Rollercoaster

Studies of the financial markets show us that the excitation-transfer experienced by
traders during violent market up- and downswings can cause vast swathes of the
markets to trade emotionally and irrationally (see Figure 2.2; also Bryant & Miron,
2003; Zillmann, 1998). The political rally is a valuable weapon in a politician's
arsenal in facilitating the upswing from voter indifference, to optimism, excitement
and a kind of irrational exuberance, particularly when propaganda and wildly emotional rally-based activities are formally planned into the process. US President
Donald Trump's practice of scheduling regular post-election rallies reflects his need
to perpetually situate followers in the optimism/exuberance portion of the cycle.

It has also been said that 'Watching one's heroes win or lose has physiological
consequences that extend beyond changes in mood and self-esteem' (Bernhardt,
Dabbs, Fielden & Lutter, 1998, p. 59) which explains Trump's tendency to use
the terms 'winners' and 'losers' (usually via Twitter) with frequency. There is
certainly a case to argue that the biological mechanisms that underlie emotional
trading are also of relevance to emotional voting (see Chapter 6 for more depth).

We know that 'Success in competition leads to an increase in status and an
increase in testosterone' (Bernhardt et al., 1998, p. 61) and that 'This combination
of direct and vicarious involvement for voters makes democratic political elections
unique dominance contests' (Stanton, Beehner, Saini, Kuhn & LaBar, 2009, p. 1).
In this sense, modern-era political elections also offer great analogies for sports
contests with the similarities between a political rally and spectatorship at a sport
event also relatively easy to argue.

The experience of vicariously-boosted testosterone levels as a result of seeing heroes win or lose seems clear: 'vicarious victory and defeat via democratic elections has similar physiological consequences for male voters as do interpersonal dominance contests' (Stanton et al., 2009, p. 4). This may be why former President Barack Obama spoke of his 2008 victory as belonging to his voters, with his followers probably feeling as if they, not just Obama, 'had personally fought' (Stanton et. al., 2009, p. 5). What we are seeing here is an extension of 'hormonal analysis of vicarious victory and defeat to the socio-political domain' (p. 5). It has even been reported that 'the stress of having one's political party lose control of executive policy decisions could plausibly lead to continued testosterone suppression in males' (p. 5).

Constructing a political rally around the communication of a divisive, right-wing populist discourse 'carries moral arrogance and high social costs' (Klapp, 1991, p. 189), yet rallies can also be used to invoke hope, change and the ubiquitous ability to rally around a common fight. Jon Stewart and Stephen Colbert's 'Rally to Restore Sanity and/or Fear' offers one such example.

Rally to Restore Sanity and/or Fear

In 2010, the Jon Stewart and Stephen Colbert-led 'Rally to Restore Sanity and/or Fear' – a name that poked fun at populist sentiment-driven politics – attracted an impressive 215,000 rallygoers. During the rally, Mark Zuckerberg was awarded (in his absence) a 'Medal of Fear' for what Stewart viewed as Facebook's role in encouraging polarizing, populist rhetoric.

Stewart's closing speech at the rally constituted a powerful emotional call to arms, criticizing 'the country's 24-hour politico–pundit perpetual panic "conflictinator" [which] — only amplifies problems and no longer makes a distinction between "hav[ing] animus" and "be[ing] enemies"'. Stewart used the event as a platform to unite, offering a welcome vision for change and unity that stood in stark opposition to the crisis rhetoric so favoured by the right-wing populist:

> This was not a rally to ridicule people of faith, or people of activism, or look down our noses at the heartland, or passionate argument, or to suggest that times are not difficult and that we have nothing to fear.
>
> (Ziegbe, 2010, para. 4)

An Age of Reason

If it is true that 'With the right psychological ingredients in place, narratives can make bad ideas appear attractive and good ideas wholly unappealing' (Decety, Pape & Workman, 2017, p. 8), then a great question to ask is exactly what role age might play, given the relative immaturity of the prefrontal cortex (an area that governs self-control) in the juvenile brain. Chris King, Chairman of the UK-based Headmasters' and Headmistresses' Conference (HMC) recently commented that 'Today's teenagers are increasingly overwhelmed by the pressures they feel to succeed in life', and that 'There is no doubt that we – parents, teachers, friends – must come to their assistance' (King, 2016, n.p.). It might be that the assistance King references includes a greater ability to recognize their susceptibility to dangerous radicalizing influences.

If we look at mass shooting occurrences in the United States, we can see a pattern emerge; four of the five mass shooting events with the most fatalities in US history were perpetrated by young white American males.[6] The murder of Heather Heyer in Charlottesville at a 'Unite the Right' rally by James Fields, Jr, 20, was also committed by a young, white, racist male, whilst 21-year-old William Atchison who shot and killed two students in Aztec, New Mexico, was also a known racist, prolific user of alt-right online sources and a fan of the neo-Nazi publication *The Daily Stormer*. The 'apocalyptic confrontation' that characterizes alt-right, racist discourse may have played a role in radicalization, particularly in a juvenile mind. Professor Laurence Steinberg points to a need to revisit the way that we approach criminal activity amongst adolescents; only 10% of adolescents who break the law in their teens perpetuate law-breaking as adults, for example, and MRI scans show that a teen's neural activity associated with risk-taking doubles as soon as they know their friends are watching:

> The reward seeking system is becoming more easily aroused, particularly during early adolescence, which makes kids seek and go after rewards. The braking system is still developing very, very slowly and it's not fully mature until people are well into their 20s.
>
> *(Kaiser, 2012, n.p.)*

Endocrinology and Entitlement

A 2013 University of Washington study reflects feelings of entitlement and the need for homicidal revenge against a specific demographic as motivators for a largely white, male demographic to commit mass shootings (Madfis, 2014). Professor of Psychology James Garbarino of Loyola University, a specialist in teen violence, speculated that 'School shooters typically do this out of a profound adolescent crisis' (cited by Koerth-Baker, 2018, n.p.), adding further weight to the idea that adolescents are still neurologically immature when it comes to an ability to self-regulate stress and anxiety.

General acts of aggression directed at minorities might also be driven by positive neurological feedback; watching rivals, against whom we feel aggressive, fail, produces feelings of pleasure (Cikara, Botvinick & Fiske, 2011) whilst the social bonding neuropeptide oxytocin greatly influences the humanization and favouring of in-group members. Out-group members are excluded during this neural process and become at far greater risk of dehumanization and less empathy-driven responses (e.g. Smith, Porges, Norman, Connelly & Decety, 2014). One is able to imagine how repeated immersion in an online world of radicalized, populist race-hate crisis rhetoric can induce this kind of neural process, offering a layer of dehumanization facilitated by the screen of a computer.

Political Rallies, Radicalization and Oxytocin

When we look at general patterns of radicalization, 'There is no typical social and economic profile of the radicalized' (Decety et al., 2017, p. 1). Terrorists are not particularly likely to have a psychiatric diagnosis for a pre-existing condition (Horgan, 2014), but 'people who are otherwise psychologically typical may develop values and strong emotional ties to narratives and causes and become radicalized' (Decety et al.,, 2017, p. 1). Some genetic variables, such as grey matter density in the insula and cingulate cortex, can predict empathy responses (Eres, Decety, Louis & Molenberghs, 2015), whilst conflict-related activity in the ACC (anterior cingulate cortex) appears negatively related with conservatism (Amodio et al., 2007) – yet the universality of appeal of rousing music, imagery and the camaraderie of fellow rallygoers holds.

A political rally will remain the mainstay of right-wing populists simply because it offers the ability to invoke root metaphors so powerfully, to benefit from evolutionary herding instincts and excitation-transfer, and to construct crisis rhetoric that communicates the kind of environmental threats that most effectively stoke fear, anger and loyalty; 'political attitudes emerge from general psychological processes, particularly those involved in motivation and self-regulation, and are deeply connected to basic biological mechanisms that serve to defend against environmental challenges' (Decety et al., 2017, p. 4). Invoking disgust towards specific out-groups and perpetuating a discourse of dehumanization offers a particularly effective strategy; studies show that viewing dehumanized group members triggered amygdala and insula responses in subjects consistent with disgust and blunted prefrontal cortex activation (Harris & Fiske, 2006), reducing analytic thinking and increasing dogma (Friedman & Jack, 2017).

Us and Them

We, as a species seem naturally designed to differentiate between 'us and 'them' from an early age (Diesendruck,, 2013), to be more helpful to those whom they feel are most similar to themselves (Hare, 2017), to dehumanize 'out-group' members more readily (Kteily, Hodson & Bruneau, 2016), and to target non-conformers and out-group members (Boehm et al., 1993). It has been said, as a result, that 'humans are the most ultra-social species on earth but also the most ruthless' (Decety et al., 2017, p. 5). Our practice of seeking out 'fictive kin' – and a need to display great loyalty within that group (e.g. Spruill, Coleman, Powell-Young, Williams & Magwood, 2014) – feed directly into desires to engage in the mass demonstrations of loyalty that participation at a rally can offer. Right-wing populist rallies, imbued as they are with charisma and with the stimulating sensory

effects of music, imagery and camaraderie, play directly into the process of excitation-transfer, androgenic priming and radicalization. Perhaps these universal
neurological and evolutionary factors contribute to a reality where 'almost anyone
can be led to perpetrate acts of violence or abuse under the right circumstances
and social pressures' (Decety et al., 2017, p. 6).

Summary

It has been said that 'Political science is often derided for being a "soft" science,
one unable to generate hard predictions about political behavior' (Friend &
Thayer, 2011, p. 231). Such criticism seems unfair. We can see, just from observations of political rallies, that emotions drive our political decisions, with the
ability of populists to reframe politics as entertainment causing the kinds of
endocrinological reactions that predispose us to unpredictable decisions. Some
things are simply unpredictable – including emotions.

One might instead turn for greater insight to evolutionary psychology, which
proposes that human behavior can be understood, in part, 'as the product of evolved
psychological mechanisms that depend on internal and environmental input for their
development, activation, and expression in manifest behavior' (Confer et al., 2010, p.
110, cited in Friend & Thayer, 2011, pp. 232–233). Political rallies create powerful
internal and external stimuli for the manifestation of political behaviours that more
orthodox theories of political behaviour can simply not measure, adding weight to
the argument that evolutionary theory and physiology offer greatly additive insights
into the minds and behaviours of a political animal.

Notes

1 Bentz, B. and Seavy-Nesper, M. (18 January 2018). 'A Former Neo-Nazi Explains Why
   Hate Drew Him In — And How He Got Out'. *Fresh Air*. Retrieved from: www.npr.org/
   2018/01/18/578745514/a-former-neo-nazi-explains-why-hate-drew-him-in-and-how-he
   -got-out
2 Taken from 'Boris Johnson's Top 50 Quotes', *The Telegraph* online. Retrieved from:
   www.telegraph.co.uk/news/politics/london-mayor-election/mayor-of-london/
   10909094/Boris-Johnsons-top-50-quotes.html
3 Three rhetorical strategies, or pillars of persuasion – see Chapter 5 and Chapter 6 for
   more depth.
4 Social instability resulting from a breakdown of standards and values.
5 'Hazing is any action or situation, with or without the consent of the participants,
   which recklessly, intentionally, or unintentionally endangers the mental, physical, or
   academic health or safety of a student'. Source: the Student Life: Dean of Students
   webpage at the University of Michigan (https://deanofstudents.umich.edu/article/wha
   t-hazing).
6 Adam Lanza, Sandy Hook Elementary School – 28 fatalities; Nikolas Jacob Cruz,
   Marjory Stoneman Douglas High School – 17 fatalities; Eric Harris and Dylan Klebold,
   Columbine High School –15 fatalities; James Holmes, Aurora movie theatre shootings –
   12 fatalities.

3

NATURE VERSUS THE ELECTION CYCLE

[S]omething as simple as rainy weather in some of the Florida counties may have played a critical role in determining the outcome of a presidential election.
                                    – Gomez, Hansford & Krause, 2007, p. 660[1]

Why was Donald Trump so focused on maximizing the reported crowd size at his inaugural ceremony? We know that herding represents a survival instinct (Baddeley, 2010), where our brains reward us for 'following the crowd' and cause us to feel pain when we choose not to (Baddeley, 2010). By pretending to be the most popular, Trump was encouraging people, at a primal level, to respond to their evolutionary instinct to join the strongest group and thus ensure survival. Herding is a powerful instinct amongst our species – the 80% of Americans who demonstrate partisanship tendencies are, after all, displaying powerfully motivating tribalistic tendencies (Westen, 2007), so clearly Trump's intuition may well have proven prescient.

We share nearly 99% of our DNA with chimpanzees who 'wage murderous warfare against neighbouring troops, are cannibalistic as well as meat-eating ... their highly structured society is characterized by an incessant and often bloody struggle among the males for dominance and status' (Westen, 2007, p. 5). To continue the chimpanzee analogy, political scientist Drew Westen wrote, as early as 2007: 'In chimpanzees, dominance or status hierarchies tend to be established by males, with female status depending substantially on connection to powerful males. (The analogy of Donald Trump comes to mind)' (p. 293).

Westen's words reflect the powerful interaction of evolution and *nature* in directing election cycles. It is a powerful and compelling interaction that forms the basis of this chapter, and one that pays testament to the extent to which we are still governed by the *reptilian* area of our brains (MacLean, 1990).

Stressful Encounters

If a political advertising campaign is stressful and frightening enough (e.g. Nigerian President Goodluck Jonathan's 2015 re-election campaign, a quintessentially populist endeavour), we might choose not to vote at all. If we feel confused by 'fake news' and cannot ascertain who, exactly, is telling the truth, we might opt out entirely. When it comes down to it, 'Politics and political participation is an inherently stressful activity … It would logically follow that those individuals with low thresholds for stress might avoid engaging in that activity and our study confirmed that hypothesis'.[2] Voters are usually not legally required to vote, so when work, weather, a movie or concert conflict with voting cycles, or if we simply cannot be bothered, we do not turn out to vote. Snow and bad weather can also prevent hundreds of thousands of voters from getting out to vote and 'validates the old adage that "Republicans should pray for rain' (Gomez et al., 2007, p. 658), with the power of nature exerting a truly almighty effect on the democratic process.

The Power of Nature

Nature, it turns out, wields an extraordinary influence on our emotions, strongly influencing our voting behaviours. Researchers (Gomez et al., 2007) studying the weather in 3,115 counties over the course of 14 US Presidential Elections found that a high rainfall could affect voter turnout by as much as 3.8% – and that Democrats were most likely not to go out and vote when the weather was particularly bad. An analysis of voting and weather patterns across 54 US states informed political scientists Larry Bartels and Christopher Achen that '2.8 million people voted against Al Gore in 2000 because their states were too dry or too wet' (cited by Menand, 2004, n.p.). Republicans appeared to perform better when it rains, a finding that the researchers attributed to a more 'peripheral' Democratic appeal (possibly reflective of a lower emotional connection with the party), and the fact that voters studied were more likely to report lower incomes, so they may not have had the access to adequate transportation that they would have needed to navigate poor weather conditions.

Geomagnetic and Political Storms

In a study of four stock markets (NASDAQ, S&P500, Amex, NYSE), geomagnetic storms were found to exert a profound effect on human behaviour to the point that a statistically significant – and negative – relationship was discovered to exist between stock returns and geomagnetic storm activity: 'Intense geomagnetic storms not only appear to affect people's mood during their recovery phase but also seem to affect US stock returns within a week from hitting the atmosphere' (Krivelyova & Robotti, 2003, p. 19). Voting could be considered an economic activity in the sense that who we vote for will dictate economic policy for (perhaps) generations. It is one of the most important economic decisions that we might ever make, so the findings hold relevance for political, as well as economic, disturbances.

Geomagnetic storms are also correlated with enhanced anxiety, sleep disturbances, altered moods, and greater incidences of psychiatric admissions (Persinger, 1987, p. 92, cited in Krivelyova & Robotti, 2003, p. 6) and can be divided into three phases: the initial phase (2–8 hours), main phase (12–24 hours) and recovery phase (tens of hours to days afterwards). They generally last 2–4 days, with a higher concentration of storm periods during March–April and September–October, a finding that suggests potential implications for political elections timed around those periods. It has been cautioned, given that 'the response of human beings to a singular intense geomagnetic storm may continue several days after the perturbation [deviation] has ceased' (Krivelyova & Robotti, 2003, p. 8) and the fact that 'the effects of unusually high levels of geomagnetic activity are more pronounced during the recovery phase of the storms' (Krivelyova & Robotti, 2003, p. 9; see also Belisheva et al., 1995; Halberg et al., 2000; Zakharov & Tyrnov, 2001), one can reasonably deduce a relationship between irrational voting activity and geomagnetic activity.

As far back as the late 19th century, Dexter (1899) wrote that bad weather contributed to negative emotional states and higher death rates, whilst Lawrence Smith (1939) discovered that 'Conditions which cause equal deviations in rainfall at New York tend to create equivalent changes in mass psychology, and consequently to the level of stock prices' (p. 102). If rainfall can sway mass psychology so powerfully as to affect patterns in stock returns, it is certainly possible that it could affect voting patterns, too. These geomagnetic effects are potentially compounded by geographic variables; if a polling station is located in, or near, a school or church, we are more likely to vote for an ideologically conservative party (LaBouff, Rowatt, Shen & Finkle, 2012).

Full Moons and Sun Spots

Can a full moon influence politics? It is an interesting – if not vaguely crazy-sounding – idea, particularly if one observes economic data describing a relationship between stock returns and lunar cycles. Lunar cycles produce

> effects in stock returns. Specifically, returns in the 15 days around new moon dates are about double the returns in the 15 days around full moon dates. This pattern of returns is pervasive; we find it for all major U.S. stock indexes over the last 100 years and for nearly all major stock indexes of 24 other countries over the last 30 years.
>
> *(Dichev & Janes, 2001, n.p.)*

Amazingly, the effect of the sun exerts a powerful effect on behaviour (Hirshleifer & Shumway, 2003). As long ago as 1934, MIT researcher Harlan Stetson concluded that:

> Variation in radiation, particularly in the ultra violet, is known to be capable of profound biological and physiological changes … Buying and selling waves with corresponding fluctuations in commodity prices will, in the long-run, reflect confidence or anxiety on the part of the buying public.
>
> *(cited in Lawrence Smith, 1939, p. 107)*

One way these physiological changes are manifested are via the effects of temperature change. The hotter it is, the more likely you are to turn out and vote (and prefer the incumbent):

> Hot weather can affect human behavior and has been linked to political rebellions and riots. A new study, the first to examine the influence of changes in temperature on peaceful and democratic political behavior, finds that voter behavior can change with increases in state-level temperature. For every 10C rise in temperature, voter turnout increased by 1.4 percent. In addition, when the weather was warmer, citizens chose to vote for the incumbent party.[3]

A voter's risk-tolerance, and, subsequently, voting preference, might shift with the weather, too: one study reported that 'after controlling for policy preferences, partisanship, and other background variables, bad weather depresses individual mood and risk tolerance' (Bassi, 2013, p. 1); in other words, voters were more likely to vote for the candidates who were perceived to be less risky.

The Sport of Politics

American readers might find the next fact interesting if they support a local college football or NCAA college basketball team. It turns out that there is

> clear evidence that the successes and failures of the local college football team before Election Day significantly influence the electoral prospects of the incumbent party, suggesting that voters reward and punish incumbents for changes in their well-being unrelated to government performance.
>
> *(Healy, Malhotra & Hyunjung Mo, 2010, p. 12805)*

The effect also held for basketball games (Healy et al., 2010), and reflected a 44-year period where voting preferences were seen to be commonly affected by sports results up to 10 days before an election (Healy et al., 2010).

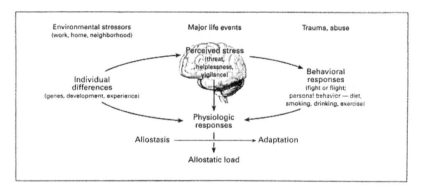

FIGURE 3.1 Allostasis and Allostatic Load
Source: McEwen, B.S. (2000), 'Allostasis and Allostatic Load: Implications for Neuropsychopharmacology', Neuropsychopharmacology, 22, 2, 108–124, Figure 2. Permission granted via Rightslink.

Whilst the idea of sports results as a politically influential variable might at first seem counter-intuitive, it makes sense in terms of what we know about politics as a form of dominance contest (see Chapter 1 and Chapter 5 for further depth). Sport is a highly-charged arena for displays of dominance, where the vicariously-experienced effects of a win or loss on the spectators' testosterone levels are clear; a spectator's testosterone can be raised for days after a great win, making them feel more confident, more able to take risks and primed for new competition. These endocrinological effects can exert a notable influence on subsequent behaviours, like voting. These findings suddenly become very relevant when we consider that 10% of voters in the 2008 US Presidential Elections made their decision on whom to vote for in the 2-week period before election day, with a further 4% deciding on the day. Timing, it turns out, is key, so sports results very close to an election might exert a really meaningful effect on the outcome, particularly noticeable amongst the 'swing' or 'floating' non-partisan voters who often decide the outcomes of elections amidst a relatively low-participation electoral group: 'As witnessed by recent voter turnout in primary elections, participation in U.S. national elections is low, relative to other western democracies. In fact, voter turnout in biennial national elections ranges includes only 40 to 60 percent of eligible voters.'.[4]

Witnessing a beloved sports team losing can lead to an increase in cortisol, a stress hormone, which can influence motivation to participate in political elections (the reader might recall the role of stress in allostasis, detailed in Chapter 1, 'Homeostasis'): for example, it has been noted that

> In explaining why elevated cortisol could be linked with lower rates of participation in elections, French cited previous experiments in which high levels of afternoon cortisol are linked to major depressive disorder, social withdrawal, separation anxiety and enhanced memory for fearful stimuli.[5]

'Ballot fatigue' reflects the stress associated with too many choices in a voting scenario, which can also promote disengagement.

Right-wing populist campaigns effectively articulate the presence of a perceived stressor, via the use of crisis rhetoric and a polarizing discourse (Figure 3.1). Micro-targeting technologies enable appeals to be micro-targeted based on individual differences, leading to physiological responses (allostasis and allostatic load) alleviated only by interaction with the reassuring charismatic dialogue of the populist leader, utopian promises and scapegoating of minorities towards which frustrations can be directed.

Politics and the Entertainment Effect

The 'entertainment effect' (Dorn & Sengmueller, 2009, p. 592) of trading has created a whole new legion of day traders who trade primarily for fun, not profit (e.g. Anderson, 2008; Dorn & Sengmueller, 2009), leading researchers to the conclusion that 'many private investors may simply enjoy trading and focus more on the thrill and less on the profit' (Markiewicz & Weber, 2013, p. 76). It remains to be seen if researchers conclude the same of politics, although a brief foray into the world of *Fox & Friends, The O'Reilly Factor, The Daily Show*, or *The Colbert Report* on any given day provides ample anecdotal evidence. What has been studied is the effect of the polar opposite of entertainment – a morbid fear of death – on voting behaviours (Cohen et al., 2005). A study by Cohen, Solomon, Maxfield, Pyszczynski and Greenberg (2004), for example, found that subjects who had been primed with a story of death prior to voting were more likely to vote for Republican candidate George W. Bush over Democrat John Kerry. Evangelical and black protestants who believe in an interventionist God are also less likely to vote than, say, Jewish voters, because of their deterministic belief that God would place the right person in charge (Bryner, 2008).

Food for Thought

If we are addicted to one kind of drug, it makes us more vulnerable to sensation-seeking behaviours that will enable re-stimulation of depressed dopamine levels. If our diet is very high in high-fructose corn sugar, for example, it can actually inhibit the ability of anti-depressants to stimulate dopamine-release. This causes the medication to be less effective, as found by a recent study which concluded that 'At the neural level, HFCS [high fructose corn sugar] exposure decreased oxycodone-induced release of dopamine, which is a desire-promoting neurotransmitter active in the brain's reward circuits' (Leri, 2017, n.p.). The study went on to say that not only did sugar compromise our brain's ability to produce dopamine, but it also removed the stimulating effects of other drugs, such as alcohol, or opioids, that can make us more sociable and extroverted:

> at low doses, sedative drugs like opioids and alcohol normally interfere with inhibition and stimulate a variety of "psychomotor" behaviors — such as sociability, extroversion, talkativeness, sensation seeking and interest in

novelty. Our study in rats found that exposure to the high fructose corn syrup reduced this psychomotor stimulation induced by oxycodone.

(Leri, 2017, n.p.)

Euromonitor statistics show that the United States consumes twice the average sugar intake of all 54 countries that they surveyed – twice the level recommended by the World Health Organization (Ferdman, 2015).

A salient question at this juncture might be: what do rats, corn sugar and oxycodone have to do with elections?

As it turns out – a lot.

If we look at the 10 US states most blighted by obesity, we can see that they are all 'Red' (i.e. Republican) states. Conversely, the 10 US states least blighted by obesity (except for Utah and Montana) are 'Blue' (i.e. Democrat). The analogous nature of junk food and junk news is an interesting one.

From Junk Food to Junk News

Sugar is a staple in junk food, but it seems as if an altogether different kind of junk – junk news – was being consumed before the 2016 Presidential Election – particularly in swing states. A recent report by the University of Oxford's Internet Institute (Howard, Kollanyi, Bradshaw & Neudert, 2017) which analysed 7 million Tweets in the period preceding the 2016 Presidential Election reported that consumption of junk news with a high polarizing content (e.g. conspiracy theories, inflammatory material or misinformation created by Wikileaks or Russian sources) was highest in battleground states, with 11 of the 16 swing states recording higher than average junk news consumption.

Arizona, Missouri and Nevada, states with large numbers of votes in the Electoral College, recorded a particularly highly concentrated exposure to hyperpartisan, propagandist, populist junk news, with senior researcher Professor Philip Howard stating that:

> We were surprised to find that the ratio of professionally produced news to junk news on Twitter was around one to one. Adding in content from Russia Today and unverified WikiLeaks rumours means that a really large portion of the political news and information being shared over social media was misleading.
>
> (Howard et al., 2017, n.p.)

The researchers referred to this systematic approach as a kind of computational propaganda designed specifically to manipulate public opinion. The World Health Organization recently cited this kind of 'junk news' (also termed false news, and misinformation) as one of the top ten threats to society that exist today; the obesity crisis, partly precipitated by the over-ingestion of junk food, constitutes another.[6]

Sensation-Seeking and Swing States

In the 2016 US Presidential Election, the Republican Party won 77 of the 82 counties that exhibited exceptionally high opioid death rates (CDC, 2017). It is a situation that has led historian Kathleen Frydl (2016) to create the term 'oxy electorate', offering an interesting observation on the phenomenon of raised overdose rates in swing states:

> In 9 of the Ohio counties that Trump successfully turned from Democrat to Republican, six log overdose rates well above the national norm. All of the Pennsylvania counties that chose Obama in 2012 and Trump in 2016 have exceptionally high overdose rates, averaging 25 people per 100,000; in none of these counties did vote totals fall.
>
> *(Frydl, 2016, para. 3)*

Taking a closer look, two-thirds of the nine Ohio counties that flipped from Democrat to Republican in 2016 also exhibit drug overdose death rates that far exceed the national average (Jacobs, 2016). Furthermore, almost every county in Ohio that exhibited a drug overdose-related death rate that rose above 20 per 100,000 also recorded a 10%+ swing to Trump (as compared to Romney), and/or a slump of 10%+ for Hillary Clinton (as compared to votes for President Barack Obama in 2012). The same pattern emerged for 29 of the 33 Pennsylvania counties, with many swinging entirely to Red (Kranz & Gould, 2017). Why might this be? The answer might partly be attributable to the deleterious effect of opioid use on empathy and moral processing which mediates increased vulnerability to right-wing, racist and denigrating rhetoric, an idea explored in depth in Chapter 4.

Addicted to the Internet

A recent study (Uhls et al., 2014) reported that after only 5 days of cessation of tech use, preteens improved their recognition of non-verbal and emotional cues considerably. The research led to concerns that Internet use might be stunting children's emotional development (Uhls et al., 2014). It is a concern shared in Silicon Valley. Two major shareholders of Apple, for example (Jana and CalSTRS, whose combined Apple stock is worth around $2 billion) recently referred to 'kids and smartphones as a toxic mix', pointing to a 'growing public-health crisis of youth phone addiction' (Benoit, 2018, n.p.). Pop star Selena Gomez cancelled her 2016 world tour because she needed to seek therapy for depression and low self-esteem, an issue she attributed partly to an addiction to social media and Instagram (Dilts, 2017). A study by the University of Glasgow (2015) reported that many teenagers were so addicted to their devices that they experienced anxiety and depression from a fear of missing important posts and online activity. Unsurprisingly, some prominent tech innovators and leaders have now publicized their imposition of strict screen-time limits on their own children (Bilton, 2014).

Tune In, Can't Tune Out

Facebook was designed to be addictive (Sloane, 2017). Sean Parker, founder of Napster, subsequently vocalized his fear that: 'God only knows what it's doing to our children's brains' (Sloane, 2017, para. 5). An early investor in Facebook, Parker discussed the role of 'shares' and 'likes' as ways of consuming as much of a user's time and attention as possible, exploiting the human need for social validation and pleasure via a range of imagery and interactivity, and engineering peak compulsivity of a Facebook user's engagement. He conceptualized it as a 'social-validation feedback loop … exactly the kind of thing that a hacker like myself would come up with, because you're exploiting a vulnerability in human psychology' (Sloane, 2017, para. 9). Parker explained that Facebook founders were fully aware of these vulnerabilities and exploited them consciously, which is why recent studies show that SNS (Social Network Service) use can now mimic the effects of suffering an addiction to drugs: 'The perceived need to be online may result in compulsive use of SNSs, which in extreme cases may result in symptoms and consequences traditionally associated with substance-related addictions' (Kuss & Griffiths, 2017, p. 1). Professor Mauricio Delgado of Rutgers University referred to it as a 'daisy chain of dopamine' (Soat, 2015, para. 6).

Professor Adam Alter (Yates, 2017) equates social media use directly with alcohol, drug and nicotine use:

> When someone likes an Instagram post, or any content that you share, it's a little bit like taking a drug. As far as your brain is concerned, it's a very similar experience. Now the reason why is because it's not guaranteed that you're going to get likes on your posts. And it's the unpredictability of that process that makes it so addictive. If you knew that every time you posted something you'd get 100 likes, it would become boring really fast.
>
> *(Alter, cited in Yates, 2017, n.p.)*

Napster CEO Sean Parker similarly referred to Facebook's 'like' and 'comment' facility as providing 'a little dopamine hit' (quoted in Parkin, 2018, para. 1). *The Guardian* newspaper opined of Facebook that it is 'an empire of empires … built upon a molecule' (Parkin, 2018, para. 1).

What does all of this have to do with political election cycles? The problem arises when we consider the dependence of recent right-wing, populist strategies on the use of Internet technologies. These strategies, designed to manipulate voters' emotions, are played out against a backdrop of escalating social media and smartphone addiction. When viewed in this context, voting suddenly becomes an intensely irrational affair.

Interestingly, the 8.4 million voters who voted for Obama in 2012, and then Trump in 2016, also demonstrated a disapproval rating of Trump, post-election, that was twice as high as other Trump voters (Griffin, 2017). There were more first-time voters (15% of the electorate – Reuters Staff, 2016) and more last-minute deciders in the 2016 US Presidential Election than ever before. Thirteen percent of voters reported that they didn't decide who to vote for until the week preceding the election. Taken together, these statistics suggest a sensation-seeking engagement with politics, and a knee-jerk regret that one might experience after feeling hungry and speed-eating a box of doughnuts (Drutman, 2018).

Eat the Doughnut

But maybe, in the context of politics, you did really want those doughnuts. Tristan Harris, one of Silicon Valley's most prominent and influential critics likens Facebook's offering up of clickbait, algorithmic suggestion and video content to offering a box of doughnuts to a gym goer:

> People in tech will say, "You told me, when I asked you what you wanted, that you wanted to go to the gym. That's what you said. But then I handed you a box of doughnuts and you went for the doughnuts, so that must be what you really wanted."
>
> *(Harris, cited in Klein, 2018, n.p.)*

The problem, says Harris, relates to profit motives; addictions are monetizable because they guarantee an engagement level that drives up advertising revenues. Harris believes that Facebook algorithms push users towards outrage-based content that pushes our primal buttons, including extreme political content, commenting that, 'All of our minds can be hijacked. Our choices are not as free as we think they are … Outrage just spreads faster than something that's not outrage' (Klein, 2018, n.p.). Harris explains the process whereby logging on to Facebook activates algorithms that try to figure out exactly what content to show you that will engage you best. It does not engage in intelligent analyses, but simply figures out what gets the most clicks – and that translates to the wider dissemination of clickbait over high-quality content.

Vicarious Trauma (PTSD)

A recent study found that 22% of participants exposed to violent images and coverage of news events on social media scored high on clinical measures for Post-Traumatic Stress Disorder (PTSD), leading researcher Dr Pam Ramsden to subsequently comment that 'Social media has enabled violent stories and graphic images to be watched by the public in unedited horrific detail. Watching these events and feeling the anguish of those directly experiencing them may impact on our daily lives' (British Psychological Society, 2015, n.p.). Political news coverage, including the dissemination of clickbait by Facebook algorithms and the re-tweeting of outrage-inducing populist videos, contributed volubly to levels of what Ramsden refers to as vicarious traumatization, commenting that 'People who are affected may engage in obsessive consumption, such as watching and re-watching a traumatic video long after its message has been absorbed' (Willingham, 2016, para. 8). Dr Margot Jacquot, founder of The Juniper Center, a counselling and therapy organization, similarly refers to concerns that the 'bombardment of graphic images of disasters, terror attacks or events over which we have no control can impact our mental health', and can harm us psychologically (The Juniper Center, 2017, n.p.).

This kind of obsessive repeat consumption is amplified in the presence of tech addiction and invokes a fear-based response via the primal region of our brain which can precipitate isolationist practices:

> While prescriptions of resilience often dominate a post-trauma narrative, those who are especially affected may isolate themselves, change their routines, make decisions based out of fear – essentially all of the things we are taught not to do when dealing with terrorism and other threats.
>
> *(Willingham, 2016, para. 8)*

Isolation can, in turn, further exacerbate PTSD and increase vulnerability to radicalization.

These statistics become even more alarming in the context of user statistics; approximately 90% of US young adults use social media (Lin et al., 2016). Studies of social media now reflect a 'strong and significant association between social media use and depression' among users of Twitter, Google+, Instagram, Tumblr, Snapchat, and Vine (Lin et al., 2016, p. 323. Calls for the recognition of 'Internet addiction' as a distinct psychiatric condition closely associated with depression are now on the rise, and consultant psychiatrist Louise Theodosiou reflects the concerns of many in highlighting Internet-based abuse: 'Teenagers who dare to express alternative views, particularly about "diverse sexuality", open themselves up to the risk of a torrent of abuse on platforms such as Twitter' (cited in Wakefield, 2018, n.p.). The situation is made even more worrying in the context of the immaturity of an adolescent's brain which inhibits self-control and the moderation of risk, but enables the expression of emotionally rash expressions and acts.

The Truth about Tech

Following concerns about Internet addiction, anxiety and depression, Silicon Valley heavyweights formed a campaign known as the 'Truth About Tech'. The campaign aims to uncover the explicit ways in which social media technologies were designed to elicit addictive behaviours. Targeting up to 55,000 US public schools, this team of former Google, Apple and Facebook employees (including Justin Rosenstein, the former Facebook employee who created the 'Like' button) now actively educates young people in the dangers of tech addiction. Funded by the non-profit media watchdog group Common Sense Media, the $7 million campaign constitutes the first campaign of its kind for the newly-formed Center for Humane Technology and will benefit from an additional $50 million in donated media and airtime from a range of partners, including Comcast (Weller, 2018). Campaigners cite tech addiction as a 'huge public health problem' that has contributed to higher levels of depression, anxiety and suicide (Weller, 2018, n.p.).

Ripping Holes in the Fabric of Society

Venture capitalist and former Vice President of Facebook, Chamath Palihapitiya, recently accused Facebook of 'ripping apart the social fabric of how society works' (Vincent, 2017, para. 1). Palihapitiya professed guilt at what he had helped to build, specifically referencing the role of dopamine-targeting in building addiction when he said that, 'The short-term, dopamine-driven feedback loops that we have created are destroying how society works' (Vincent, 2017, para. 2). Palihapitiya's concerns necessarily acknowledged the role of Facebook in driving divisive, right-wing populist rhetoric, characterizing the ensuing deconstruction of societies' fabric via the dissemination of mistruths as a distinctly global one: 'No civil discourse, no cooperation, misinformation, mistruth. And it's not an American problem – this is not about Russians ads. This is a global problem' (Vincent, 2017, para. 2).

Lizard Brains

> Facebook appeals to your lizard brain — primarily fear and anger. And with smartphones, they've got you for every waking moment.
>   – *Roger MacNamee, early Facebook investor (cited in Bowles, 2018, n.p.)*

Former Facebook senior executive Chamath Palihapitiya was not the only Silicon Valley titan to acknowledge the role of social media as a threat to democracy. In a recent *USA Today* Op-Ed, for example, Roger McNamee, an early investor in Facebook and Google, warned that social media constitutes 'a menace to public health and democracy' (McNamee, 2017a, n.p.) where the dangers of addiction and destabilizing political propaganda result in powerful destabilizing forces based on 'persuasive techniques developed by propagandists and the gambling industry' (McNamee, 2017b, n.p.).

Populism: Unregulated Advertising

> Who knew that all it would take to make progress was vision, chutzpah and some testosterone?[7]

The now defunct political consulting firm Cambridge Analytica recently stated that it had been 'vilified for activities that are not only legal, but also widely accepted as a standard component of online advertising in both the political and commercial arenas' (Solon & Laughland, 2018, n.p.). Cambridge Analytica essentially reduces right-wing populist discourse to nothing more than a necessary component of an advertising strategy, which seems to be a fair characterization, given its relatively ubiquitous and formulaic modern-day expression across continents and borders. However, difficulties arise when we acknowledge the fact that political advertising remains largely unregulated. Voters are subsequently left in the curious position of consuming political advertising, unsure of the truth of political statements upon which they must execute meaningful voting decisions. When one considers the continuingly outlandish nature of rhetoric and propaganda-based campaigns (Carly Fiorina's assertion that a foetus, legs kicking, heart beating, would be kept alive so that its brain could be harvested, for example: PBS, 2016), the need for regulation of political advertising campaigns seems more and more crucial.

A Unique Amateurism

Cas Mudde, a political historian based at the University of Georgia commented in an article in *The Atlantic* that 'The amateurism of Trump is absolutely unique. I honestly have never seen anything like that in an established democracy' (cited in Friedman, 2017, n.p.). Italians might beg to differ, given the success of Silvio Berlusconi and Beppe Grillo. Nevertheless, Mudde's words may reflect a wider trend: the desire for an anti-elite, 'non-politician' whose incompetence might be interpreted as endearing, given the departure that it represents from the regular 'elite' status quo of political leaders, and the continued frustration of voting in a boundedly rational two-party state. Whilst the anti-elite focus of populism is often disregarded as simplistic hyperbole, it nevertheless reflects a genuine failure of democracies to adequately represent their people.

Great Britain offers one example of inadequate representation of the populace in the context of race, and concomitant concerns of elitism within society, in this instance based on school and university attendance; 27 British Prime Ministers were educated at the same university – Oxford – with a further 14 attending Cambridge University. Recent concerns about a 'social apartheid' at both institutions underline concerns that only the upper classes are in a position to govern:

> Nearly one in three Oxford colleges failed to admit a single black British A-level student in 2015 … Oriel College only offered one place to a black British A-level student in six years … Similar data released by Cambridge revealed that six colleges there failed to admit any black British A-level students in the same year.
>
> *(Adams & Bengtsson, 2017, n.p.)*

Without doubt, the increasingly polarized nature of partisan politics has empowered our evolutionary tendencies to herd, and to become increasingly more receptive to a political strategy that at the very least articulates an interest in fairer representation.

A Golden Age of Ignorance

One way in which populism has met, and catered to, the frustrations directed at a mainstream, exclusionary political landscape is via the reframing of politics as entertainment. Although we touched on this idea earlier in the chapter, there is value in revisiting the concept under the auspices of what Stanford University historian, Professor Robert Proctor, refers to as a 'golden age of ignorance' (cited in Harford, 2017, n. p.). Proctor coined the term 'agnotology' to explain the deliberate production of ignorance by society (the stylized ignorance of Kardashian-era reality TV stars, for example), packaged as attractiveness or cuteness ('is this chicken that I have, or fish?', as Jessica Simpson asked of a can of 'Chicken of the Sea' tuna in an episode of *Newlyweds*, a moment that perhaps opened the floodgates in the reification of stupidity as a form of social entertainment).

Proctor's insights corral well with the phrase 'post-truth' becoming the Oxford Dictionaries' 'word of 2016' and shed light on one (perhaps overlooked) contributor to the historically aggressive spiking of populism in the 1930s pre-World War II period and in the present era (2015 onwards) (e.g. see Chapter 2, Figure 2.1; Bridgewater's Developed World Populism Index [Dalio et al., 2017, p. 1]); that a culture which praises wilful ignorance is less interested in facts, and more open to the thrall of entertaining appeals, including those packaged as charisma-imbued populist appeals. Figure 3.2 reflects a notable upward drive in populism over the previous decades.

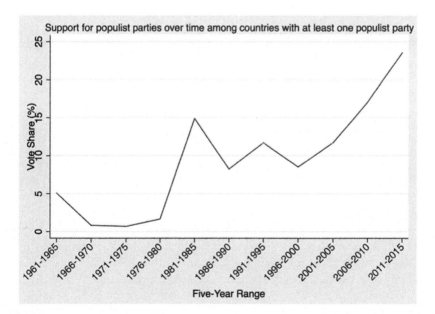

FIGURE 3.2 The Global Rise of Populism
Source: Rodrik, D. (2017a), 'Economics of the Populist Backlash', VOX CEPR Policy Portal. Permission granted directly by the author of the image.

Celebrity, Charisma and Catastrophes

In 1938, 9/10 November represented a historically ruinous date in German history. It will be remembered always as Kristallnacht, or the 'Night of Broken Glass'. Whilst Dachau, the first Nazi concentration camp, had opened 6 years before, Hitler had, until that point, presented a more sanitized political agenda to the world. On that night, synagogues were torched, Jewish homes and schools were vandalized. Many Jews lost their lives, including an estimated 30,000 Jews who were taken from their homes and sent to Nazi concentration camps.

Nine months later, *The New York Times* magazine ran an upbeat, 'at home'-style editorial on Hitler's life in his mountain chalet retreat. A similar piece appeared in the British *House and Gardens* magazine, good humouredly chronicling Hitler's interest in gardening and choice of colour schemes. Why would mainstream publications choose to do this?

Despina Stratigakos, an architectural historian at the University at Buffalo believes that the wilful profiteering from people's newly-discovered interest in celebrity culture had a lot to do with it: 'People developed a strong desire to know what the private person was like behind the public facade. Hitler's propagandists took advantage of the new celebrity culture and even helped to shape it' (cited in Hsu, 2015, n.p.). It came at a time when advances in the printing press and television revolutionized the way in which people consumed entertainment and news; Hitler used the 1938 Berlin Olympic Games as a platform to legitimize the Third Reich, becoming the first Games to be broadcast on TV. As Reich Minister of Propaganda for Nazi Germany, Joseph Goebbels engaged extensively with the use of escapist, glamorous and entertaining movies as a tool of propaganda, nationalizing the film industry and recognizing the value of entertainment- and celebrity-focused propaganda alongside carefully-produced recordings of the Nuremberg Rallies and other political events.

As stated by journalist David McNair in a piece for The Rutherford Institute (a leading non-profit civil liberties organization based in Charlottesville, Virginia):

> It's no accident, I think, that celebrity worship took hold in America during the Depression. While the economy and spirit of America floundered in the 1930s, the illusion called Hollywood and our media culture filled the void and flourished. Eighty million people a week went to the "picture shows" and bought up celebrity paraphernalia. The music recording industry showed a 600% increase in sales between 1933 and 1938, and radio brought entertainers such as Rudy Vallee, Jack Benny, and Burns and Allen into millions of living rooms, where they began to make themselves at home in the minds and imaginations of the public. During that bleak time, the illusion of celebrity manufactured on the screen, in magazines and photos, and on the radio offered a seductive, larger-than-life presentation of reality.
>
> *(McNair, 2003, n.p.)*

Enjoying a movie or concert as a means of escapism is understandable and healthy. Reframing politics so that it is situated in an entertainment-driven, celebrity-culture-filled space, however, creates ethical difficulties, in that it alters the original purpose of politics from one that 'enable[s] the members of society to collectively achieve important human goals they cannot otherwise achieve individually'.[8] Nevertheless, it has proven an incredibly successful strategy, appealing to our emotionally-driven primal instincts, hopes and fears, and allowing us to uncritically endow our vote on a candidate who might, on the surface, be the funniest, most entertaining, or the most physically attractive (e.g. Milazzo & Mattes, 2016). In evolutionary terms, 'people's preferences for good-looking politicians may be linked to ancient adaptations for avoiding disease' (White & Kenrick, 2013), again alerting us to the prominence of the lust–disgust axis mentioned earlier, and to the powerful draw of our hedonic instincts. But it also reflects a triumph of emotion over rationality that plays into the hands of a populist agenda.

Summary

It has been said that, 'Like the moth, we are only aware of the more proximal reasons for our behaviour' (Dabbs, 2000, p. 27). This chapter tells us that nothing could be truer of the political animal, for whom lunar cycles, temperature, storms, rain, sugar addictions, the sexual attractiveness of candidates and even our local college teams' ability to bring home a trophy all dictate how we eventually choose to vote. We know that the brain's resources are finite and can be depleted relatively easily, so the brain's ability to engage in constructive, and highly precise, evaluation and decision-making behaviour is relatively unsustainable at the best of times (Muraven & Baumeister, 2000). Throw too many mental demands at us, and we become overwhelmed and irrational. Factor in the aggressive, heavily micro-targeted and relentless nature of right-wing populist advertising campaigns, Russian bot interference, Facebook algorithms, social media addictions, the threat of PTSD from chronic Facebook and Twitter usage, the confusion surrounding 'fake news' and rampant propaganda, and we emerge wholly unable to engage in politics in a rational way.

Emotion remains the first responder in every one of our decisions – whether we like it or not (Zajonc, 1984), and if those emotions are powerful enough, they can 'short circuit rational deliberation altogether' (Lo, 2005, p. 28). In a political scenario, then, we need to remain critically aware of these emotional influencers if we are to safeguard democratic checks-and-balances and counter the damaging, yet powerfully seductive, draw of entertaining, primally-rousing populist campaigns. In other words, 'While its importance in political science has frequently been either dismissed or ignored in favor of theories that privilege rational reasoning, emotion can provide an alternate basis for explaining and predicting political choice and action' (McDermott, 2004, p. 691).

Notes

1 Gomez, B.T., Hansford, T.G., and Krause, G.A. (2007), 'The Republicans Should Pray for Rain: Weather, Turnout, and Voting in U.S. Presidential Elections', *The Journal of Politics, 69, 3*, 649–663.
2 Professor Jeff French, Varner Professor of Psychology and Biology and Director of the University of Nebraska, Omaha, neuroscience programme, as quoted in 'Hormones Affect Voting Behavior, Researchers Find'. Science Daily. Retrieved from: www.scien cedaily.com/releases/2014/06/140624172157.htm
3 As noted in 'Voter Behavior Influenced by Hot Weather', Science Daily, 16 August 2017. In discussion of the journal article: Van Assche, J., Van Hiel, A., Stadeus, J., Bushman, B.J., De Cremer, D. and Roets, A., 'When the Heat Is On: The Effect of Temperature on Voter Behavior in Presidential Elections', *Frontiers in Psychology*, 8 June 2017. Retrieved from: www.sciencedaily.com/releases/2017/08/170816100216.htm
4 'Hormones Affect Voting Behavior, Research Finds', Science Daily, 24 June 2014. Discussion of journal article 'Cortisol and Politics' (French et al., 2014). Retrieved from: www.sciencedaily.com/releases/2014/06/140624172157.htm
5 See Note 4.
6 Excess body weight causes an estimated 3.4 million deaths worldwide each year according to comprehensive new analyses; e.g. as summarized in the Mercola article 'Obesity Epidemic Goes Global: One-in-Three Is Now Overweight or Obese'. Retrieved from: https://articles.mercola.com/sites/articles/archive/2014/06/11/globa l-obesity-epidemic.aspx#_edn4
7 Steven Sanabria, in a letter written to *The New York Times*, published in the Op-Ed piece, 18 January 2018: www.nytimes.com/2018/01/17/opinion/trump-voters-supp orters.html
8 E.g. as defined on the Q&A 'Reference' website: www.reference.com/government-p olitics/purpose-politics-2f742bd7c0fff5c9

4

THE PHYSIOLOGY OF POLARIZATION

Dehumanization is a way of overcoming our inhibitions against performing acts of violence for our own advantage. Conceiving of other people as rats, snakes, lice, dangerous predators, or beasts of burden, makes it much easier to treat them inhumanely … Racism is often a precursor to dehumanization.

– Benz, 2017, n.p.

You wouldn't believe how bad these people are. These aren't people, these are animals, and we're taking them out of the country at a level and at a rate that's never happened before.

– US President Donald Trump, cited in Hirschfeld Davis, 2018, n.p.

What's past is prologue

– Norman Ohler, author of Blitzed: Drugs in Nazi Germany

Whilst we like to believe that we are the most intellectually developed, sophisticated species on the planet, in reality our barbarism remains completely unmatched by any other animal (Engelhaupt, 2016). Biological anthropologist Richard Wrangham notes that when it comes to murderous tendencies, 'humans really are exceptional' (Engelhaupt, 2016, n.p.); it would be difficult not to be floored by the stunning reality that as many as 1 billion humans have perished in war (Hedges, 2003) – at the hands of each other – over the course of history. It remains a truth of human nature that we are capable of incredible empathy, yet we have also been the perpetrators of the greatest evils. Evolutionary psychology tells us a fascinating explanatory story; that we are hardwired for war,[1] but also built for great kindness, with an imagination unique to our species (Brown & Muotri, 2018) that makes us extremely vulnerable to environmental cues (such as Russian reflexive control techniques; see Chapter 5 for more depth) that seek to shape our realities.

The previous chapter detailed the effect of technology in vastly accelerating and heightening our endocrinological exposure to populist appeals. This chapter extends that conversation by exploring the highly monetizable value of the right-wing populist phenomena, explaining how profiteering opportunities and the emergence of clientelism (i.e. patronage for profit) have significantly enabled and amplified the reach and voice of right-wing political parties. It is a relationship that underlines the emergence of modern right-wing populism as a profitable strategy, rather than an ideology, and a rationale for why we see clientelism emerge with such frequency during the tenure of right-wing populist political leaders. Jared Kushner, US President Donald Trump's son-in-law and White House Senior Adviser, for example, allegedly earned $500 million in loans after two White House business meetings (Tau & Orden, 2018). The firm of Michael Cohen (Essential Consultants), President Donald Trump's lawyer, was paid $50,000 per month by AT&T for 'insights' into how to best navigate the new Administration – a contract that AT&T later referred to as a 'mistake' (McLaughlin & Moritz, 2018). *The Guardian* reported that online US political spending was likely to surpass $1 billion in 2016 (Davis & Yadron, 2016), whilst the Facebook-hosted 'Trump TV' enabled the Trump campaign to garner $9 million in donations in 120 minutes (Funk, 2016). Fox News, for example, saw a 26% increase in advertising revenue in 2016, reaching $621 million (Atkinson, 2017). The highly polarized, racially-charged backdrop for the 2016 Presidential campaign and the reframing of politics as entertainment drove engagement to historic levels; CNN increased advertising revenue by 58%, Time Warner increased viewing figures by 77% and MSNBC increased advertising revenue by 48%.

Elixirs of War

Bridgewater's Developed World Populism Index (Dalio et al., 2017), as featured in Chapter 2 (see Figure 2.1) clearly highlights the fact that we are currently living through a spike in populism never seen since the pre-World War II era. Populist appeal rests, in large part, on the construction of crisis rhetoric. In a recent *Wall Street Journal* interview, Steve Bannon, Former White House Chief Strategist for the Trump Administration, was quoted as saying that 'Politics is war' (Strasel, 2016, n.p.) which innervates us as noble fighters for a cause. It also feeds powerfully into an 'us-and-them' discourse, allowing us to excuse ignoble acts as necessary casualties of (an often imagined) conflict. As stated by the renowned War Correspondent for *The New York Times* Chris Hedges, 'War is an enticing elixir. It gives us resolve, a cause. It allows us to be noble' (Hedges, 2002, p. 3). William James, seminal psychologist and author of *The Moral Equivalent of War* (James, 1910/2015), similarly spoke of the way that war made civilians and soldiers feel more alive. Man is so naturally attuned to the idea of war that our species has managed to create a 'theatre of war' that is globally accessible, enjoyable, relatively safe yet extremely entertaining, providing an outlet for expressions of tribalism, dominance and combat (usually) without a drop of blood being shed; sport (Taylor, 2014). The evolution of sport has, in fact, been directly linked to a decline in conflicts over recent years – a fact that is elaborated upon later in this chapter (Taylor, 2014).

Ultimately, a question that this chapter seeks to answer is how, amongst a species also so capable of compassion (Keltner, 2004), have we been able to repeatedly engage in such acts of barbarism? The answer lies in another unique ability of our species; the ability to dehumanize.

Dehumanization and Imagination: An Explosive Evolutionary Mix

Dehumanization relates to our ability to see other humans as animals, insects, or inferior to ourselves in some way, as evidenced in a (truly shocking) guide to producing an 'ideal slave', printed in 1850 (Christian & Bennet, 1850/1998): slave owners were advised to maintain strict discipline and unconditional submission, to create a sense of personal inferiority so that the slaves would 'know their place', to instil fear, to teach them to take an interest in their 'master's' affairs, and to deprive them of access to education and recreation so that they remained uneducated, helpless and dependent.

As stated by evolutionary psychologist Professor David Livingstone Smith,

> Dehumanization isn't a way of talking. It's a way of thinking—a way of thinking that, sadly, comes all too easily to us. Dehumanization is a scourge, and has been so for millennia. It acts as a psychological lubricant, dissolving our inhibitions and inflaming our destructive passions. As such, it empowers us to perform acts that would, under other circumstances, be unthinkable.
>
> *(Livingstone Smith, 2011, p. 13)*

The psychological lubricant of dehumanization is alive and well in the right-wing media; US TV host Laura Ingraham responded to the audio of immigrant children crying out for their parents disparagingly, likening detention centres to summer camps; right-wing commentator Ann Coulter accused the same crying children of being child actors.

A bizarre defence of the Trump Administration's policy of automatically separating immigrant children from their parents at the US-Mexican border came from US Attorney General Jeff Sessions who said that, 'In Nazi Germany they were keeping the Jews from leaving the country' (*Times of Israel* Staff & Agencies, 2018, n.p.). High-profile media figures have subsequently spoken out against this practice. For example, leading American TV Producer Judd Apatow voiced his feelings in a tweet on 18 June 2018, acknowledging the vital role of right-wing media in creating the propaganda that fuels this kind of dehumanizing discourse ('The MURDOCH family is part of this torturing of children').

Our ability to dehumanize seems empowered by another unique quality of ours – our incredible imagination. Imagination is 'Arguably ... what distinguishes us most profoundly from other animals', according to Dr Christian Jarrett, Editor of the British Psychological Society's Research Digest blog (Jarrett, 2018, n.p.). We can imagine the greatest glories, or the most disgusting threats. So, when dehumanizing rhetoric, imagery, metaphors, jokes and propagandist videos threatening apocalypse (or utopia) reach us with adequate frequency, our imaginations are capable of taking those concepts to a logical frightening – or euphoric – conclusion.

One of the common ways in which we can see dehumanization emerge in populist discourse is via the framing of 'out-group' members as animals: 'Almost without exception, the people who are transformed into subhuman creatures— specifically, pigs, apes, and rats—are Jews' (Livingstone Smith, 2011, p. 43) (see Trump's 19 July 2018 tweet about immigrants, for example, as people who 'pour into and infest our country').

The Art of Self-Deception

Self-deception, it has been said, is an indispensable element of war (Livingstone Smith, 2011), with one notable strategy being the simplistic labelling of other humans into 'races' so that we might more easily discount, categorize and stereotype them. The United States, for example, has 3,205 million citizens, who are extremely phenotypically diverse. Whilst phenotypic diversity is a fact, race is 'a theory. It's what we call a folk-theory. It's a way of trying to explain human diversity by positing that there are a small number of "pure" types (races) of human beings—black, white, etc.' (Benz, 2017, n.p.). Basic racial categorizations sit well in a populist 'us-and-them' discourse; phenotypic diversity does not. Author David Livingstone Smith further opines that 'race is a destructive and oppressive delusion—a nightmare. The idea of race has facilitated war, genocide, chattel slavery, and oppression for thousands of years' (Benz, 2017, n.p.). In the context of the suitability, and extreme utilization, of race in right-wing hate-based campaigns, his words reflect a sad reality.

Voter Suppression by Race

Voter suppression of African Americans in the United States emerges as a historically traceable pattern (US District Court N.D. of Alabama, 2017); in the early 20th century, the Ku Klux Klan (KKK) openly endorsed political candidates, threatening black Americans with violence during polling periods. The KKK endorsed candidate Donald Trump during the 2016 Presidential Election, an endorsement rejected by the Trump Campaign. In 2011, US District Judge Myron Thompson concluded during a corruption trial that former Alabama State Senator Scott Beason, and former Representative for Dothan, Alabama, Benjamin Lewis, had tried 'to maintain and strengthen white control of the political system', concluding that 'It is intolerable in our society for lawmakers to use public office as a tool for racial exclusion and polarization'. He spoke of 'a deep-seated racial animus' and a desire to suppress black voter turnout in the actions of the two senators (Douglas, 2017, n.p.). In July 2016, a North Carolina court rejected North Carolina's strict voting laws, with a judge ruling that the provisions contained within the law 'target African Americans with almost surgical precision' and reflected not the goal of preventing voter fraud, but of disenfranchising voter minorities (Ingraham, 2016, n.p.).

The US Democratic Party is, at the time of writing, suing Donald Trump for alleged voter intimidation in four US states (Sullivan, 2016). Trump weaves racist rhetoric into a powerful populist discourse (referring to Mexicans as rapists and gang members, for example), with the practice commonly invoked by populist charismatic politicians who favour right-wing rhetoric (e.g. British Foreign Secretary Boris Johnson's 'piccaninnies with watermelon smiles' and the assertion of journalists that black people have lower IQs and Caribbeans were multiplying like flies, as printed in *The Spectator* magazine whilst under his Editorship [e.g. Evening Standard, 2008, n.p.]).

The Torturers' Lobby

One way in which a right-wing discourse is amplified is via its monetizable quality, which can be discussed principally in the context of political consulting. Paul Manafort is probably best known publicly for his recent role as President Donald Trump's former Campaign Manager. But long before his brief tenure in the White House, Manafort successfully co-founded a very successful political consulting firm named Black, Manafort, Stone and Kelly (later acquired by international PR firm Burson-Marsteller). The firm, which once themed an annual event 'Excess Is Best', gained a reputation for working with a swathe of authoritarian regimes across the globe (including the Philippines, Nigeria, Kenya, Somalia, Angola, Zaire and Equatorial Guinea), profiting substantially from their work. Black, Manafort, Stone and Kelly received a reported $3.3 million for work undertaken for the so-called 'torturers' lobby' (Brogan, 1992). Powerful UK-based PR consulting firm Bell Pottinger also engaged with many authoritarian regimes – the Pinochet Foundation, for example. Founder Lord Timothy Bell, formerly an adviser to South African Prime Minister F. W. de Klerk, saw his company face accusations of incitement of racial tension, including charges of the operating of fake social media accounts as a strategic means of inflaming racial tension.

The campaign in question was funded by Oakbay Investments Pty Ltd, owned by the South African Gupta brothers – and it was lucrative; it would have generated a reported £100,000 per month for the firm (Cave, 2017). Bell Pottinger constructed a campaign based around the racially divisive theme of 'white monopoly capital' and 'economic emancipation'. A damning report written by a South African prosecutor subsequently accused the PR firm of creating a hateful and divisive campaign bent on dividing South Africa along the lines of race.

Bell Pottinger's role in the divisive campaign led to the PRCA (Public Relations and Communications Association) ejecting Bell Pottinger from its membership. The PRCA (2018, n.p.) commented that it had never 'passed down such a damning indictment of an agency's behaviour' in its history.

Political Clientelism

One major reason why right-wing hate-rhetoric continues to be monetizable, and therefore impactful, is because it lends itself so easily to political clientelism. Political clientelism can be defined as 'giving material goods in return for electoral support, where the criterion of distribution that the patron uses is simply: did you/will you support me?' (Stokes, 2011, n.p.). It also explains the escalation in a trend for private individuals to exert a profound influence on modern elections: the wealthy Gupta brothers played a defining role in their Oakbay Investment-driven bankrolling of the £100,000-per-month Bell Pottinger 'white monopoly capital' campaign that divided South Africa. Davide Casaleggio's powerful role as the CEO of the Rousseau Association that governs Italy's Five Star Movement's operations, or Arron Banks's extensive involvement in directing the discourse of the British Leave.EU and Project Leave campaigns, for which he earned a reported £12.7 million, offer further powerful and current examples.

Political Renaissance

Strategic Communication Laboratories (SCL), parent company of SCL Elections and Cambridge Analytica, reportedly played a key role,[2] via establishment of a lucrative clientelist relationship with political parties and candidates, in furthering a right-wing, populist agenda. The company is so specialized in psychological warfare that the British Ministry of Defence recently praised them for their work with the 15 Psychological Operations Group (a British Territorial Army support group for the British Army, specializing in psychological operations). Parent company of Cambridge Analytica, which at one time included Breitbart Editor Steve Bannon as a member of its Board of Directors, SCL is reported to have subsequently played a major role in shaping election cycles and regime changes across the world (Channel 4, 2018; see also Note 2). A former anonymous employee of Cambridge Analytica alleged that the company's key approach was one that clearly rested on psychological warfare (psy-ops) techniques:

> Psyops. Psychological operations – the same methods the military use to effect mass sentiment change. It's what they mean by winning 'hearts and minds'. We were just doing it to win elections in the kind of developing countries that don't have many rules.
>
> (Cadwalladr, 2017a, n.p.)

Robert Mercer constitutes another high-profile figure in the recent explosion of right-wing populist strategies in Western political campaigns. Former Renaissance Technologies hedge fund CEO and billionaire Robert Mercer has played a notable role in the recent rise of right-wing populist politics, donating £15 million to Donald Trump's Presidential Campaign at a time when Trump's popularity was floundering. Mercer's donation was reportedly contingent on Trump's hiring of Steve Bannon as Chief Strategist, catapulting Bannon, a fervent far-right ideologue and, until then, an extremist figure, into the US political mainstream. Bannon's and Mercer's voices and shared far-right ideologies have subsequently driven political discourse in a major way in recent years (Channel 4, 2018; Devine, O'Sullivan & Griffin, 2018; OpenSecrets, 2017).[3] An extremely talented computer scientist (the Association for Computational Linguistics referred to Mercer's work at IBM as 'revolutionary' whilst awarding him the ACL Lifetime Achievement Award [see Association for Computational Linguistics, 2014]), Mercer has subsequently played a key role in the emergence of technology in the micro-targeted, online juggernaut of alt-right and right-wing political content that has swamped political dialogue in recent years. According to British newspaper *The Observer* (Cadwalladr, 2017b), Mercer has donated $45 million to Republican campaigns and $50 million to ultra-right-wing non-profit organizations in recent years alongside a $10 million investment in the alt-right monolith Breitbart.com (a site that logs around 2 billion page views per year).[4]

Propaganda and other standard psy-ops techniques clearly enabled the right-wing populist voice to spread with far more veracity, relying completely on pathos to spin emotions and mobilize voters. Propaganda specialist Emma Briant[5] clearly noted that SCL, experts in military and defence consulting[6], have been 'making money out of the propaganda side of the war on terrorism over a long period of time' (Cadwalladr, 2017b, n.p.). Briant referenced the use of different arms of SCL to reach audiences and shape discourse, noting a subsequent sharp ideologic turn to the right in modern campaigning: 'They are trying to amplify particular political narratives. And they are selective in who they go for: they are not doing this for the left' (Cadwalladr, 2017b, n.p.). With reference to the role of clientelism and the monetizable nature of propaganda, Briant went on to comment that, 'It seems significant that a company involved in engineering a political outcome profits from what follows. Particularly if it's the manipulation, and then resolution, of fear' (Cadwalladr, 2017b, n.p.).

Despite Briant's concerns, it must be made clear that the SCL Group should not be targeted unnecessarily by allegations of wrong doing simply because of their successful history in the field of military and defence consulting (such targeting is certainly not an aim of this book). Instead, it is the intersection of a purported use of psy-ops and propagandist techniques, in a wider sense, and by a wide network of individuals, that remains most interesting within the pages of this chapter with regard to their applications in recent political elections and cycles.

Diffusion of Political Clientelism and Monetization

In the United States, lobbying is subject to federal disclosure rules whereas Public Relations work is not, which makes PR a very attractive prospect for political parties seeking to reach a large base (Quinn & Young, 2015). This diffuses opportunities for clientelism and monetization across a wider spectrum to include the work of PR agencies. Trump lawyer Michael Cohen's Essential Consultants, for example, allowed AT&T to gain insights into the best ways to navigate the Trump Administration for a purported $10,000 per-month fee (McLaughlin & Moritz, 2018) without officially engaging in lobbying activities.

This diffusion of monetizable, clientelism-focused activity extends volubly to the media sector. In 2016, for example, political advertising spending reached a record $9.8 billion, with TV spending significantly down, but digital revenues way up. Donald Trump spent in excess of $8 million in the month of July 2016 alone on digital spending, according to marketing firm Giles-Parscale's figures (Stewart, 2017). Placing those figures into perspective, the figure for political PR, advertising and marketing spending from 2008 to 2012 was a comparatively small $1.2 billion (Quinn & Young, 2015). The market is providing a gold rush of opportunity where the best opportunities seem to reside in divisive campaigns (negative affect content reflects the highest engagement and resharing activity). Micro-targeting offers an amazingly monetizable means of constructing the social realities of voters and most effectively selling the repeat purchase of, and gaining loyalty to, a product – the candidate. Chris Wylie, former Cambridge Analytica employee and whistleblower, has described the way that Cambridge Analytica reportedly:

> create[d] a mediated reality for someone … you target someone because you know they are more susceptible to believe conspiracy theories because you have profiled them, and you send them a spiral of fake news. It's different to knocking on a door and identifying yourself as part of a campaign.
>
> *(Guimón, 2018, n.p.)*

The Producers

Boris Johnson's speech immediately following the announcement of the Brexit Leave vote seemed remarkably awkward, almost reminiscent of a scene from *The Producers* (a film based on the premise that the lead character did everything he could to *avoid* having a hit on his hands!). Having won what was referred to as a 'pyrrhic victory' by *The Guardian* newspaper, he did not, it seems, enjoy having a hit on his hands at all (Hinsliff, 2016). Speculations subsequently surfaced of Johnson's strategic use of the Referendum as a means of challenging Prime Minister David Cameron for the leadership of the Conservative Party, not expecting to secure a win.

Cambridge Analytica whistleblower Chris Wylie recently said that:

> There could have been a different outcome of the referendum had there not been, in my view, cheating … What a shame it would be if we found out that there had been pervasive cheating in the referendum and Brexit has already happened and you can't go back.
>
> *(quoted in Guimón, 2018, n.p.)*

Chris Wylie, as the quote reflects, believed that Brexit would not have happened without Cambridge Analytica, whose involvement he regarded as a form of 'cheating'.

Anti-Immigration Rhetoric and Other Gateway Drugs

The Conservative Party's strategic adoption of populist, anti-immigrant discourse characterized the spirit of Brexit, and also proved a success in appealing to UKIP (United Kingdom Independence Party) voters who subsequently migrated in significant numbers. In the May 2018 elections, for example, UKIP lost 145 seats, winning only one, whereas the Conservative Party gained an unexpectedly high 550 seats. UKIP leader Paul Nuttall subsequently attributed his party's devastating losses to the Conservative Party's adoption of UKIP principles. This led political analysts subsequently to refer to the UKIP–Conservative Party relationship as analogous to a 'gateway drug' for voters, providing a 'halfway house' for voters to migrate across the political spectrum (Curtis, 2017).

Integration, Not Demonization

A recent British All-Party Parliamentary Group on Social Integration offered a damning indictment of the demonizing rhetoric surrounding the Brexit Vote Leave campaign. The report *Integration Not Demonisation* (Bell, Plumb & Marangozov, 2018) cited increases in racist abuse occurring around the Referendum as a shame on the UK: 'The demonization of immigrants, exacerbated by the poisonous tone of the debate during the EU referendum campaign and after, shames us all and is a huge obstacle to creating a socially integrated nation' (Bell et al., 2018, n.p.). The report identified a critical need to safeguard communities from 'the peddlers of hatred and division while addressing valid concerns about the impact of immigration on public services, some of which can contribute to local tensions' (Bell et al., 2018, n.p.).

Commissioner of the UK's Metropolitan Police Sir Bernard Hogan-Howe noted that he: 'saw this horrible spike after Brexit. We couldn't say it was absolutely down to Brexit, although there was obviously a spike after it' (Weaver, 2016, n.p.). NCPP True Vision research (Civitas, 2016) points to a 31%+ increase in hate crimes in June–August 2016, the period surrounding the Referendum, when compared to 2015 figures from the same period (15,863, up from 10,883).

The Independent newspaper similarly noted historic spikes in hate crime with the headline 'Brexit vote sees highest spike in religious and racial hate crimes ever recorded' (Bulman, 2017). Maike Bohn, a founding member of the3million, an EU citizens' group, blamed anti-immigrant Vote Leave rhetoric directly for spikes in hate crimes, telling *The Independent* (Dearden, 2017) that

> what is clear to me that during the referendum and afterwards everything has been lumped together – refugees, Muslims, people who are 'not us' coming here ... Government rhetoric used very early led a lot of people to the conclusion it's absolutely fine to tell an EU nurse to 'go home'.
>
> *(Bohn, cited in Dearden, 2017, n.p.)*

The Vote Leave campaign benefited significantly from the work of the Leave.EU campaign, to which consultant Arron Banks, a UKIP supporter and far-right ideologue provided almost £13 million of services over a 2-year period (Pegg & Campbell, 2018).

In 2013, Government-funded vans emblazoned with the tagline 'Go Home or Face Arrest' were seen driving around London. The vans, brain child of then Home Secretary Theresa May as a part of official immigration policy, prompted ex-Civil Service Chief Sir Bob Kerslake to comment on the vans as being 'almost reminiscent of Nazi Germany' (Perkins & Quinn, 2018).

Methamphetamines and Opioids: Political Blitzkrieg

When Hitler invaded Western Europe, the world was stunned, unable to believe the sheer brute strength, force, speed and power of a *Blitzkrieg* that wiped out entire battalions and claimed the lives of hundreds of thousands of soldiers and civilians. It turns out that methamphetamines had a lot to do with it (e.g. Ohler, 2016), with the methamphetamine Pervitin quite literally enabling them to run faster, jump higher and feel stronger than any other fighting force on earth. One can only guess at the role that Hitler's systematized prescription of methamphetamines played in the Berlin 1936 Olympic Games – a charismatic display designed to embolden the power of his Aryan Race philosophy and legitimize his regime on a global stage.

It seems that drug use, compellingly, played a key role in the sharp rise in populism that ended in the onset of World War II. But what emerges in a similarly fascinating way is the equally powerful role of opiate use in shaping and forming our reactions to, and consumption of, right-wing populist rhetoric that focuses aggressively on the communication of dehumanizing, degrading and combative racial content.

The Fifty-Two Million

Under Hitler, public consumption of Pervitin, a methamphetamine, was so strongly encouraged that Pervitin-laced chocolates became a regular favourite of German housewives. As stated by Snelders and Pieters (2011),

> the use of Pervitin in the Third Reich was not only 'pushed' on the population by the Nazi political and military authorities, but also became endemic in German society as it addressed the needs and problems of various users including employees, housewives, and soldiers. The drug was a cultural ambiguity of life in Nazi Germany, integrated in everyday life, notwithstanding its regulation by drug laws.
>
> *(Snelders & Pieters, 2011, p. 686)*

Methamphetamines' effect in promoting emotional dysregulation amongst the population at large would have carried obvious deleterious consequences (e.g. Miller, Bershad & de Wit, 2015).

The Blitzkrieg, it is thought,[7] would not have been possible without the German Army being dosed up on massive amounts of amphetamines. The chronic utilization of methamphetamine across Germany at the time of the Holocaust might also go some way to explaining a kind of mass psychosis, paranoia and general debilitation of rational thought that one might consider necessary for such a terrible transgression of human ethics and morality to occur. Certainly, drug use is well-known for creating psychoses (e.g. Thirthalli & Benegal, 2006).

Hitler's policy of doping amongst the German population may have also been required as a means of perpetuating the theory of a superior Aryan race alongside a programme of eugenics (via doping at the Berlin 1936 Summer Olympic Games, for example). Encouraging widespread public consumption, for example, may have amplified the fear responses of users when faced with anti-Semitic, sensationalist propaganda (e.g. Watt, 2005).

When one considers that even consuming painkillers regularly can cause a blunting of empathy and an inability to engage in moral processing (Mischkowski, Crocker & Way, 2016), the impact of heavy drug use on moral reasoning appears concerning.

Politics on Steroids

> Facebook and Twitter were the reason we won this thing
> – *Trump Campaign Manager Brad Parscale (cited in Stahl, 2018, n.p.)*

Gary Coby, Director of Advertising at the US Republican National Committee, reported that on any given day, the Trump campaign was running around 40,000 to

50,000 variants of its ads, with a record 175,000 running on the day of the third Presidential debate in October 2016 (Lapowsky, 2017). Coby referred to this approach as 'A/B testing on steroids' (Lapowsky, 2017, n.p.). Speaking in a CBS *60 Minutes* interview, Brad Parscale, Donald Trump's Digital Director credits Facebook and Twitter directly for Trump's winning the election, partly because they enabled 'fake news' and were able to generate $250 million in online fundraising, but also because of their vast micro-targeting[8] potential.

Your medical data are currently for sale, representing part of a far wider and highly lucrative marketplace (Tanner, 2016). As a result, these data may have mediated the way in which you, or your family, were micro-targeted during political campaigns.

A recent *Scientific American* article detailed the way in which data brokers have monetized the sale of medical data as a meaningful source of profit for political campaigners. IMS Health, for example, is currently valued at around $9 billion, making it the largest player in a multi-billion-dollar industry that buys and sells anonymized medical data. Pfizer was reported to spend around $12 million annually on the acquisition of anonymized private medical data, with recent advances in technology highlighting concerns about the potential for cross-referencing of – and thus de-anonymizing – much of that data: 'Straightforward data mining tools can rummage through multiple databases containing anonymized and non-anonymized data to re-identify the individuals from their ostensibly private medical records' (Tanner, 2016, n.p.). This represents an incredibly monetizable opportunity for political strategists who are cognizant of the effects of drug use in influencing behaviour.

Empathizing on Acetaminophen

The English seaside town of Blackpool gained the nickname 'crackpool' after winning the dubious title of the drugs death capital of England and Wales (UK Addiction Treatment Centres, 2016). It also reported the largest majority in the North West of England (67.5%) in favour of leaving the European Union in the context of the Brexit Referendum (and ironically, it also stands to lose the most from Brexit, in economic terms, according to Conservative Party research – Baynes & Mortimer, 2018). Correlation certainly does not infer causation here, but the relationship is still compelling enough to investigate further.

Seaside and coastal towns like Blackpool, as it happens, are leading the charge for Brexit. In fact, of the areas recording the largest Vote Leave votes, all three were seaside towns (Boston, 75.6%; South Holland, 73.6%; and Castle Point, 72.7%; Perraudin, 2018) that record the highest national death rates from heroin and morphine misuse. In fact, over half of heroin and morphine misuse deaths in England and Wales are occurring in seaside locations (Perraudin, 2018). One of the biggest concerns for drug support workers in Blackpool is the rise of a cannabinoid named 'Spice' which makes users aggressive and, in the words of drug support workers, is 'turning their empathy off' (Mortimer, 2015, n.p.).

Clear links have already been found between drug use and criminal activity (e. g. US Department of Justice, 1994), and research also tells us that the brain damage caused by regular cocaine and methamphetamine use prevents the user from recognizing right from wrong, hampers moral judgements, prevents the user from recognizing emotions, particularly fear, in others, prevents empathy and causes anti-social behaviour (Springer, 2016).

Hillbilly Heroin

Oxycodone is known colloquially as 'hillbilly heroin' – a semi-synthetic opioid which is loosely related to morphine, and which constitutes the key ingredient of the widely-prescribed OxyContin – a prescription that has 'become ground zero in an opioid crisis that has now engulfed the United States' (Walters, 2017, n.p.). Pills based on oxycodone and hydrocodone are now aggressively marketed as a solution for anything from accidents to non-specific lower back pain, reaching the medicine cabinet of millions of Americans. Recent fears – and lawsuits – pertaining to the addictive nature of over-prescription (e.g. Sullivan, 2018) – are now emerging with force, with the APHA (American Public Health Association) referring to the widespread prescription of opioid OxyContin as far back as 2009 as 'commercial triumph, public health tragedy' (Van Zee, 2009).

Elliott County, Kentucky, is 99.4% white, strongly Evangelical Christian, rooted in Confederate history and has an estimated 31% of residents living below the poverty line. Historically, it has been more loyal to the Democrats than any region in the United States, demonstrating a 144-year streak of voting Democrat. That is, until 2016, when Donald Trump shot to victory with an astonishing 70% of the vote. Why was the shift so aggressive?

No Monopoly on Pain

The complex causes of such a violent swing are undoubtedly multifarious. But if we look at opioid use, we might be able to add just a little extra colour to the picture. Local Sheriff, Ronnie Stephens, says that heroin and methamphetamine usage rose 'massively' in 2017 to the extent that the region has now been referred to as the 'ground zero of the US opioid crisis'.[9] Similarly, neighbouring West Virginia has been recognized as the most pro-Trump state in the United States, demonstrating the worst opioid crisis figures in the United States, with the highest rate of fatal drug overdoses of any state, and the highest reported rate of babies born on opioids (Joseph, 2016).

As stated by UK newspaper *The Guardian*, 'the US is the epicentre and the origin of the [opioid] crisis, consuming more than 80% of global opioid pills even though it has less than 5% of the world's population and no monopoly on pain' (Walters, 2017, n.p.). Opioid prescriptions in the United States have reportedly quadrupled in the last 20 years (CDC, 2017) and 40% of all opioid overdoses included prescription opioids. Most individuals who overdose using heroin or a synthetic opiate (e.g. Fentanyl) first became addicted to prescription opiates (Walters, 2017), reflecting the worrying role of legal prescriptions as gateway drugs. It also shines a light on the potential role of opioids and other drugs in the ongoing 'charismatization' of politics; massive swings towards maverick, charismatic right-wingers may well have been aided by a catastrophic level of engagement with drugs that increase risky, sensation-seeking behaviours, that blunt empathy, that push the user to perpetually seek out pleasure-inducing sources of dopamine, that diminish attention spans and generally impair cognition.

One example of this might be 'ground zero' West Virginia, which seems to have become a magnet for extreme populist, charisma-laden political pathos in recent years. Patrick Morrisey, West Virginia's Attorney General, for example, believes that 'We need to reinvent Washington. We need to blow it up, not just change it' (Khalid, 2018, n.p.). Don Blankenship, former CEO of Massey Energy, and campaigning for the Republican Primary, is also a big character – and a contentious one; positioning himself as an outsider to the mainstream political establishment, he recently spent a year in jail for a violation of safety law that led to an explosion at one of his mines which killed 29 men.

Vaping to Victory

It is not only methamphetamines and opioids that blunt empathy. Vaping, the phenomenon of e-cigarettes positioned as an alternative to smoking, or a means of stopping smoking, has also escalated since its introduction in 2008 and grown into a $4 billion industry. The CDC (US Centers for Disease Control and Prevention) states that nicotine, found in both e-cigarettes and regular cigarettes, is as addictive as cocaine, alcohol and heroin (Addiction Resource, n.d.), and that vaping acts as a potential gateway drug to harder addictive drugs amongst young people (Kandel & Kandel, 2014).

As stated by Dr Eric and Dr Denise Kandel, theorists who originated the widely-used 'gateway drug' theory of addiction, 'These results provide a biologic basis and a molecular mechanism for the sequence of drug use observed in people. One drug affects the circuitry of the brain in a manner that potentiates the effects of a subsequent drug' (Kandel & Kandel, 2014, p. 7). Earlier chapters have detailed the phenomenon of tech and social media addiction which has, no doubt, propelled the phenomenon of chronic exposure to populist political content (according to IPA Touchpoint 2017 statistics, 65% of people look at their smartphone within 5 minutes of waking up, and 60% look at their phone in the 5 minutes before going to sleep [IPA, 2017]). So we can immediately see how attractive dopamine- and endorphin-inducing political messages (i.e. the general reframing of politics as a source of pleasure and entertainment) can provide the pleasurable high absent to a mind compromised by opioid use.

Microsoft founder Bill Gates even noted that technology can play a direct role in drug addiction and death: 'Right now cryptocurrencies are used for buying fentanyl and other drugs, so it is a rare technology that has caused deaths in a fairly direct way' (Hern, 2018a, n.p.).

Dopamine Separates Us from the Animals

A study from the CDC recently reported a 350% increase in ADHD (Attention Deficit Hyperactivity Disorder) prescriptions for US privately-insured women aged 15–44 (between 2003 and 2015), with a 700% increase in the 25–29-year-old age group. Attention Deficit Hyperactivity Disorder is a neuropsychiatric illness (e.g. Leung & Lemay, 2003; Ricuarte et al., 2005) generally treated with psychomotor stimulant drugs, the most popular for adults' and children's treatment being amphetamine-based (e.g. Dodson, 2005; Fone & Nutt, 2005; Greenhill et al., 2002). The prevalence of ADHD and amphetamine-drug-based treatment has risen exponentially over the last 20 years, a worrying statistic as amphetamines have the potential to damage brain dopamine-containing neurons, including a risk of a decrease of striatal dopamine (Fone & Nutt, 2005; Gibb, Hanson & Johnson, 1994; Ricuarte et al., 2005). An epidemic of ADHD drug use in otherwise healthy young people, alongside other performance-enhancing drugs, is currently sweeping across Western European campuses; whilst there is currently little research into the impact of teen misuse of stimulants (Goldberg, 2016), we do know that ADHD and other amphetamine-based medications blunt empathy just as powerfully as opioids do.

The role of dopamine in our ability to practise empathy is enthralling. Drugs blunt empathy partly because they damage dopamine receptors in the brain (an outcome of the addictive process) – a key factor in our ability to empathize. Dopamine is, in fact, one element of the human species that seems to set us apart from the animal kingdom. A recent study led by Kent State University anthropologists (Raghanti et al., 2008) reported that dopamine (specifically increased striatal dopamine activity) constituted a major differentiator between humans and other primates (i.e. chimpanzees, baboons, gorillas and monkeys), and one that ultimately allowed our species to outcompete other apes and hominids. Alongside elevated striatal serotonin levels, dopamine facilitates empathy and elevated cognitive control. Lower levels of acetylcholine, which functions as a neurotransmitter, were also observed to facilitate lower levels of aggression.

As stated by Clifford Jolly, New York University anthropologist,

> The suggestion that differences in [neurochemical profiles] are correlated with particular ape–human differences in temperament and behavior remains a hypothesis, although a strongly-founded one. It's certainly probable that the described striatal reorganization played an important role in the evolution

of distinctive human behavior, especially the striking level of empathy with other humans that appears to be an innate characteristic of the species.

(cited in Stetka, 2018, n.p.).

We know that dopaminergic systems play a critical role in empathy and the regulation of social behaviour, where meso-corticolimbic dopamine, for example, remains central in our ability to create and maintain social bonds. It exerts a crucial effect on oxytocin which facilitates prosocial behaviours and inequity-averse behaviour (Sáez, Zhu, Set, Kayser & Hsu, 2015) and in doing so, raises an interesting metaphysical question about the nature of man; if increased striatal dopamine activity represents a central evolutionary development that sets us apart from chimpanzees, baboons, gorillas and monkeys, then has widespread opioid abuse facilitated a collective regression in our evolutionary progress?

Summary

The physiological impact of polarization relies on the manipulation of evolutionary survival instincts (herding, tribalism, pathogen-disgust), partly via an extensive and explicit use of charismatically-imbued pathos (charismatic populist rhetoric) and an aggressive dependence on pathogen-disgust-provoking themes (e.g. Trump's assertion that immigrants are 'infesting' America). Right-wing pathogen-focused appeals are, unintendedly, implicitly propelled by the empathy-blunting effects of an opioid epidemic and the litigiously inflammatory rates of over-prescription observable in Western nations (Sullivan, 2018). The right-wing juggernaut has been powered further by its powerfully monetizable status, opening the door to clientelism on a major scale and demoting human rights and ethical concerns to a litigious footnote. A senior manager at a child detention centre in Texas, for example, chose to speak out against Trump's 'zero tolerance' policy, citing it as a 'dumb, stupid decision ... All it did was harm children' (Tripp, 2018, n.p.). It is, however, a profitable one; in 2014, BCFS (Baptist Child & Family Services) was awarded almost $191 million in one grant alone (Altman & Dias, 2014), with the 2018 border separation policy also providing highly profitable opportunities in the form of government grants.[10]

Cognizant of recent removals of campaign limits (in the United States) and the relative weakness of the Electoral Commission (in the UK), social media giants have profited hugely from hosting lucrative pathogen-disgust-focused political campaigns. In short, pathos-imbued polarization sells; by weakening democracy, it has, in turn, strengthened the ideological and financial influence of those powerful individuals who seek to manipulate our highly malleable political landscape for their own personal and political gain.

Notes

1 As Lionel Beehner of the Modern War Institute says, 'Put simply, humans are hard-wired for violence'. As stated in 'Are We Hardwired for War?': https://mwi.usma.edu/are-we-hardwired-for-war/
2 See Channel 4's undercover investigations broadcast as a series entitled 'Data, Democracy and Dirty Tricks', available to view at www.channel4.com/news/data-democracy-and-dirty-tricks-cambridge-analytica-uncovered-investigation-expose
3 OpenSecrets.org lists over $15 million donated to the pro-Trump SuperPAC 'Make American No 1'. The fiercely anti-Clinton SuperPAC was founded by David Bossie (allegedly a close friend of Robert Mercer), who subsequently left the SuperPAC to join the Trump campaign as Deputy Campaign Manager.
4 For a fuller breakdown of alleged spending, *The Washington Post* has created this report: www.washingtonpost.com/news/politics/wp/2018/04/05/the-amount-robert-mercer-spent-on-politics-in-2016-likely-topped-30-million/?utm_term=.b96bb220ef3c
5 Emma Briant, from the University of Sheffield, wrote about the SCL Group in her 2015 book, *Propaganda and Counter-Terrorism: Strategies for Global Change*.
6 'SCL Group provides data, analytics and strategy to governments and military organizations worldwide. For over 25 years, we have conducted behavioural change programs in over 60 countries & have been formally recognized for our work in defense and social change' (see https://sclgroup.cc/home).
7 As theorized by Ohler (2016), and as reflected in research such as Snelders and Pieters (2011).
8 Micro-targeting refers to the practice of algorithmically-generated adaptations of political content, tailored for every individual social media user based on their social media history, likes, dislikes, posts, usage, mental and emotional profile, etc., to maximize their potential to engage with a political campaign.
9 As quoted in the Noted article, 'Elliott County: Revisiting the Democratic Stronghold that Embraced Trump'. Retrieved from: www.noted.co.nz/currently/world/elliott-county-revisiting-the-democratic-stronghold-that-embraced-trump/
10 No claims of immorality or otherwise are intended towards BCFS in the use of this example.

5

THE LIFE CYCLE OF CHARISMATIC POPULISM

> The insights generated by neuroscience permit the study of politics to be anchored on a scientific foundation for the first time. They also allow insights into the biological origins of political behavior.
>
> – *Friend & Thayer, 2013, p. 72*

> Twitter breeds dark, degrading, and dehumanizing discourse; it breeds vitriol and violence; in short, it breeds Donald Trump.
>
> – *Ott, 2017, p. 62*

The role of neurobiology in politics continues to emerge with great strength (Friend & Thayer, 2013), with the theoretical convergences of neurobiology and politics (McDermott, 2009) shedding great light on the role of biology and evolution in the ability of our species to engage in political reasoning. It is why 'political behaviour can be understood only in terms of tendencies, which are a legacy of our species' evolutionary past' (Blank & Hines, 2001, p. 80), and why drilling down to the minutiae of gamma-aminobutyric acid (GABA) levels, for example, or our continual pursuit of homeostasis, are all necessary in understanding our decisions as political animals. Evolutionary-shaped genetic tendencies are 'startling' when it comes to their influence on politics (Friend & Thayer, 2013, p. 75), where voters with 'high' MAOA[1] polymorphism and 'long' 5-HTT[2] polymorphism, for example (where a polymorphism of the MAOA gene is associated with emotional brain markers and personality traits on an antisocial index), are more likely to turn out for voting (Friend & Thayer, 2013, p. 81). Voters with the A2 allele of the dopamine receptor gene are also more likely to be partisan (Fowler & Dawes, 2008). The minutiae of physiology in influencing our political decisions – at every stage of a campaign cycle – is truly profound. It is an observation that subsequently forms the basis of this chapter.

The Power of Emotion

Populist appeals are driven by emotion. Emotion, we now know, reflects a deeply physiological foundation (McDermott, 2004), where the rational part of the brain remains subservient in terms of power and speed to its primal, survival-led processing centre.[3] It was the power of emotion that motivated *New York Magazine*'s Olivia Nuzzi in her in-the-moment decision to play a ProPublica (Thompson, 2018) audio recording of the cries of children of detained immigrants, separated from their parents, during a White House briefing. It was the power of emotion that motivated Democratic California Representative Ted Lieu to play the audio on the House floor, defending his right to play the audio against protestations from Representative Karen Handel, a Georgia Republican, who demanded that he stop (Giroux, 2018). Nuzzi and Lieu realized that the sounds of abandoned children crying out in fear and anguish would connect with the primal, animalistic instincts of most people in the room far more powerfully than any argument or press statement ever could do – and they were right. Their actions helped to build a firestorm of controversy that forced the White House to face one of the greatest scandals of the Trump Administration, thus far. Emotion, it has been said, 'is part of rationality itself' (McDermott, 2004, p. 693), and their decision, whilst emotionally motivated, appeared rational in the circumstances.

The Life Cycle of Charismatic Populism

Emotion drives the wave of charismatic euphoria and the endocrinological crash of populist appeal in a remarkably formulaic and cyclical way. This cycle is represented here by the 'Life Cycle of Charismatic Populism' (Figure 5.1). The Life Cycle draws inspiration from US economist Hyman Minsky's Credit Cycle, an elucidating theoretical commentary on the sentiment-driven, boom-and-bust nature of credit cycles, and sociologist Max Weber's theory of charismatic authority, which similarly details the sentiment-driven, and profit-taking nature, of a leader's ascension and swift fall from grace. Situating physiology theory at key points in the Life Cycle allows us to gain great explanatory power from the juxtaposition of these elucidating theories.

The role of Weberian theory in politics is well-established (e.g. Weber's essay 'Politics as a Vocation', 1919),[4] with ample justification for its explanatory power here. At first glance, the utilization of Minskyian theory might be less intuitive. However, it should be acknowledged that Minsky's economic theory carries great explanatory power in helping us to understand sentiment-driven, boom-and-bust cycles. Given that 'There is nothing that restricts the application of Minsky's insight to the pecuniary realm' (Galbraith & Sastre, 2009, cited in Papadimitriou & Wray,

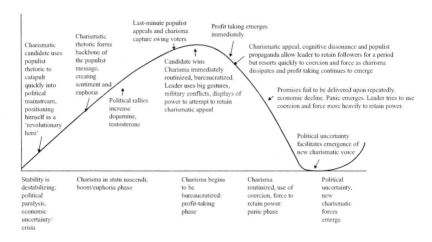

FIGURE 5.1 The Life Cycle of Charismatic Populism

2011, p. 263), it seems sensible to argue for a transference of Minsky's theorems to a political arena, specifically via engagement with a 'generalized Minsky moment' (Galbraith & Sastre, 2009; i.e. adoption of key principles of Minsky's Credit Cycle; Papadimitriou & Wray, 1999). This allows Minsky's innovative insights into the irrational sentiment- and hubris-driven investing that leads the markets to a boom-and-bust to be analogized in a populist political setting. The use of Minsky's theories in the context of this book to explain political behaviours subsequently supports the notion that 'It is ... astonishing how little has been done to extend the basic conceptual framework to other areas of social science' (Galbraith & Sastre, 2009, cited in Papadimitriou & Wray, 2011).

Stability Is Destabilizing: The Displacement

Minsky's Credit Cycle (1986), a theory that vastly informs the structure of the Life Cycle of Charismatic Populism, details five key stages: an initial displacement, boom and euphoria phases, profit taking, and a panic phase (as featured within this Model, juxtaposed alongside physiological and charismatic theory to offer amplified explanatory power). The first stage – displacement – reflected Minsky's supposition that 'there is an inherent and fundamental instability in our sort of economy that tends toward a speculative boom' (Levy Economics Institute of Bard College, 2008, para. 2). It is a supposition that rests, in part, on our inherently primal nature which predisposes us to emotion, and which also underlies our tendency to gravitate towards hubris, and sentiment-driven political and economic appeals. In economic terms, a displacement could refer to an event of some kind such as the failure of US investment bank Lehman Brothers in September 2008.

The phrase 'stability is destabilizing' originally referred to Minsky's analysis of the period of calm immediately preceding a financial markets bubble, or of a displacement event.[5] In the context of recent political events, this constituted advances in micro-targeting technologies that spawned an entirely new means of monetizing right-wing, populist online political content. Algorithmic analyses rapidly led to the creation of a multi-million-dollar marketplace in right-wing, negative affect populist clickbait. It was an innovation that represented a drive to create new opportunities for profit in an otherwise stagnant market.

Venture capitalist and former Wall Street analyst Mary Meeker recently commented that: 'At 3.6 billion, the number of Internet users has surpassed half the world's population. When markets reach mainstream, new growth gets harder to find — evinced by 0% new smartphone unit shipment growth in 2017' (Swartz, 2018, n.p.; see also Kleiner Perkins, 2017). Given that adults now spend almost 6 hours a day using digital media (Kleiner Perkins, 2017), the profit opportunities provided by these sophisticated, algorithmically-informed, populist-driven campaigns offered significant new growth.

A powerful recent example is that of Davide Caseleggio, the CEO of Casaleggio Associati, and President of the Rousseau Association, the media company that governs Italy's Five Star Movement's web presence. Five Star is a completely virtual political force, affording Caseleggio a potentially huge but unelected political influence over the Movement. The Movement itself represents a new technological innovation as it commodifies (left- and right-wing) populism as a powerful marketing tool to achieve both the aims of Caseleggio's online corporation, and the power-focused aims of the Movement. As stated by Nicola Biondo, former Communications Chief for the Five Star Movement in Italy's lower house, Five Star 'was conceived as a marketing product. Its only aim is to get power and consensus. Once it takes power it has no ideology, so it immediately becomes a tool for other structures, business, or even states' (Roberts, 2018, n.p.).

A quintessential recent example of the 'stability is destabilizing' phase resides in the case of Russian interference in the 2016 US Presidential Election. An ODNI (Office of the Director of National Intelligence) report alleged that the highest echelons of Russia's government had authorized political interference: 'We believe, based on the scope and sensitivity of these issues, that only Russia's senior-most officials could have authorized these activities' (Homeland Security, 2016, n.p.). An ODNI release of a report on 6 January 2017, entitled *Assessing Russian Activities and Intentions in Recent US Elections*, cites the St Petersburg-based IRA (Internet Research Agency), as the prime suspect. Multiple US state election databases were reported to have been accessed (but not compromised) by the IRA and a US FBI indictment[6] followed soon after, alleging that since 2014,

Defendants knowingly and intentionally conspired with each other (and with persons known and unknown to the Grand Jury) to defraud the United States by impairing, obstructing, and defeating the lawful functions of the government through fraud and deceit for the purpose of interfering with the US political and electoral processes, including the presidential election of 2016.

(United States of America vs. Internet Research Agency, 2018, pp. 2–3)

The IRA purportedly spent millions of dollars in waging 'information warfare against the USA' (United States of America vs. Internet Research Agency, 2018, p. 6), with the goal of undermining the US political system and the candidate Hillary Clinton. Activities were extensive and included posing as US citizens, infiltrating US political grassroots organizations, the creation of hundreds of social media accounts (many of which became leaders of public opinion), the use of day- and night-shift operatives to enable posting patterns to match local US time zones, the creation of fake email and Facebook accounts and pages such as a 'Blacktivist' Black Lives Matter-themed page, a 'United Muslims of America' page and a 'Heart of Texas' page, numerous fake Twitter accounts (e.g. the 100,000-follower @TEN_GOP account), the theft of US social security IDs, creation of popular hashtags and Twitter accounts such as 'March for Trump', '#Trump2016' and '#MAGA', involvement in rallies and direct support for the Trump Campaign.

The Boom and Euphoria Phases

The boom and euphoria phases represent what US economist John Kenneth Galbraith referred to as

a vested interest in euphoria [which] leads men and women, individuals and institutions, to believe that all will be better, that they are meant to be richer, and to dismiss as intellectually deficient what is in conflict with that conviction.

(Galbraith, 1954/1988, pp. xii–xiii)

In Minsky's model, they are phases where asset prices begin to move away from asset fundamentals because of a euphoric belief in the ever-rising nature of the value of the asset.

In populist terms, they represent the use of pathos and charisma to encourage a groundswell of emotion, invoking the idea of a charismatic revolutionary fighting for the rights of the people whom an uncaring elite have left behind. To incite the greatest emotion, religion, family, nationalism, tradition, pride, honour and respect are invoked, with invocations imbued with emotionally-appealing imagery, music, phrases and slogans to amplify their appeal. Erdoğan's 'We are the people. Who are you?', Trump's 'the only important thing is the unification of the people – because the other people don't mean anything', UKIP former leader and Brexit campaigner Nigel Farage's characterization of Brexit as 'a victory for real people', Austria's Freedom Party leader Norbert Hofer's 'I have the people with me' (all quoted in Müller, 2016) all exemplify this approach.

Technological innovation enables an aggressive emotional tsunami, where Twitter and Facebook, YouTube, click farms and fake bots are mobilized with devastating effect. Excitation-transfer-imbued charismatic rallies are videoed for posterity, shared thousands, if not millions of times. The reason that Cambridge Analytica and other populist campaigns invested so heavily in degrading, right-wing content is because algorithms identified them as the easiest motivators of re-tweets, shares and likes (a reflection of emotional engagement). In fact, political advertising firms have long appreciated the fact that affectively-charged tweets demonstrate a re-tweet rate that is far higher than for neutrally-toned ones (Stieglitz & Dang-Xuan, 2013, p. 217). Twitter, it has been observed, 'promotes public discourse that is simple, impetuous and frequently denigrating and dehumanizing ... Twitter ultimately trains us to devalue others, thereby, cultivating mean and malicious discourse' (Ott, 2017, p. 60). Thus, right-wing populist appeals explicitly target our powerful and primal pathogen-disgust/anger response simply because it is the most effective.

Trump refers to the free press as 'the enemy of the American people' (Donald J. Trump tweet dated 17 February 2017) and ramps up rhetoric by attacking and demonizing opponents:

> So funny to watch the Fake News especially NBC and CNN. They are fighting hard to downplay the deal with North Korea. 500 days ago they would have 'begged' for this deal – looked like war would break out. Our Country's biggest enemy is the Fake News so easily promulgated by fools!
>
> *(cited in Stelter, 2018, n.p.)*

His polarizing rhetoric stokes the fire of euphoria by ramping up crisis rhetoric ('right-wing populists refuse the give and take of political compromise and demand radical solutions'; Greven, 2016, p. 1), Right-wing populism 'rejects nuanced political arguments in favour of moral outrage' (Bonikowski, 2016, p. 22) simply because anger and negative affect drive a voter's loyalty and engagement so volubly.

Weaponizing Tweets

SCL Elections, the parent company of the UK-based Cambridge Analytica, claims to have worked on more than 100 elections in over 30 countries across five continents. SCL Elections offered a unique pitch:

> Unlike commercial PR agencies and communications firms, we use advanced scientific research and social analysis techniques, adapted for civilian use from military applications, to better understand behaviour within electorates. Our unique, measurable and effects-based methodology, developed by the Behavioural Dynamics Institute, enables us to understand how people

think and identify what it would take to change their mindsets and associated voting patterns.

(cited in Ghoshal, 2018, n.p.)

It is a pitch that revolves heavily around negative affect, encouraging simplicity, impulsivity and incivility (Ott, 2017), drives the emotional contagion of social media (Auflick, 2016; also see excitation-transfer in Chapter 2 and Chapter 6) and manufactures an image of popularity and dominance so inherent to the evolutionary appeal of 'herding' behaviours (e.g. 64–79% of the accounts that follow President Trump's Twitter account, @realDonaldTrump, are thought to be fake or inactive, according to research [e.g. Petersen, 2016]).

The CIA, Charisma and Psychological Warfare

One reason, perhaps, that SCL Election's subsidiary, Cambridge Analytica, was so successful in 2016 in influencing election outcomes was because its parent company excelled in its ability to provide consultancy to, and engage with, military and defence organisations, including national governments, in the area of behaviour change. These approaches appear similar to the psy-ops strategies more uniformly utilised in CIA and Russian Reflexive Control approaches where psychological techniques are used to complement or replace militarised action to achieve specific predetermined political objectives. The CIA *Manual for Psychological Operations in Guerrilla Warfare* (n.d.) sheds valuable light on why psychological operations, or 'psy-ops' are so fundamentally incendiary in the context of political advertising campaigns. One look at the CIA Manual immediately elucidates as to why: 'Once his mind has been reached, the "political animal" has been defeated … The target, then, is the minds of the population' (CIA, n.d., p. 7).

The CIA Manual details how 'social crusaders' must be recruited to create a front, or façade. Their aim is to create a mental attitude amongst a populace which – at a crucial moment – can be turned into anger and fury (p. 12) – something that works well online in the mobilization of aggressive, partisan discourse. Using a systematized approach of indoctrination and motivation, opponents must be framed as 'foreignizing', 'repressive', 'puppets', etc. (p. 15). These disparaging frames must be delivered in the simplest way (e.g. 'conclusions will be summarized in the form of slogans, wherever possible', p. 18). The frequent use of ridicule, humiliation, jeering, and denigrating slogans is encouraged, which again, we see demonstrated online almost continually in the context of US politics, or the British Brexit Referendum. The enemy is formulaically situated as 'enemies of the people', using a 'principle of psychology' (p. 34) that exploits the evolutionary tendency for man to construct 'us-and-them' categories. The Manual specifies the use of simple, concise rhetoric, realistic, lively examples and gestures, using tactics that are flexible and malleable enough to be differentiated where required (in the political advertising context, e.g. micro-targeting via

Facebook campaigns). In a powerful nod to charismatic, populist rhetoric, operatives are instructed to use techniques that appeal to different groups, in a way that is always pleasing, that masks ideological ambitions (at least in the early stages of a campaign) and in a way that allows the operative to remain in the shadows, thus giving an impression that a manipulated hostility towards the enemy simply occurred in an organic and spontaneous way.

God, Homeland and Democracy

The invocation of God, homeland and democracy is used as a cornerstone (CIA, n.d., p. 53) in the Life Cycle, particularly in the boom and euphoria phase. The political rally constitutes a vital part of this phase (as the reader will recall from Chapter 2): 'In a revolutionary movement of guerrilla warfare, the mass concentrations and protest demonstrations are the principle essential for the destruction of enemy structures' (CIA, n.d., p. 58).

In summary, military psychological warfare techniques such as those detailed here bear remarkable similarities to the political strategies that marked a major present-day shift towards populism. The invocation of democracy in populism is ironic given the often close relationship between populism and authoritarianism (authoritarianism constituting the advocacy of obedience to authority at the expense of one's personal freedom). As stated in the Timbro Authoritarian Populism Index 2017, 'The long-term trend is very clear. Authoritarian populism is growing faster than any other ideology' (Johansson, 2018, p. 25) (see Figure 5.2).

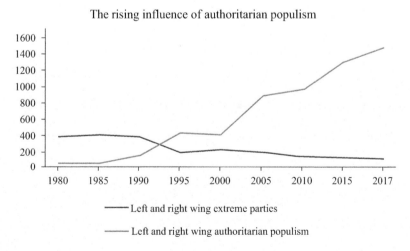

The rising influence of authoritarian populism

———— Left and right wing extreme parties

———— Left and right wing authoritarian populism

FIGURE 5.2 The Rising Influence of Authoritarian Populism
Source: originally printed in the Timbro Authoritarian Populism Index 2017 (Johansson, 2018); permission received from Timbro.

Soviet Reflexive Mind-Control

The CIA's approach, adopted by political advertisers, may have clearly influenced modern campaigns – but they were also undoubtedly influenced heavily by Russia's mastery of reflexive mind-control techniques, specifically in the context of Russia's interference in the 2016 US Presidential Elections. Reflexive control can be defined as a means of communicating carefully prepared information, at the right time, using the right medium, to the opposition, or target of the reflexive control techniques, to make the target respond in the way that you wish him (or her) to, but in a way that makes the target feel that he is the initiator of the thought and action himself. As the target feels his response is voluntary and organic, it becomes more powerful, and thus achieves the predetermined conclusion desired by the reflexive controller, whose involvement remains unseen. The target 'owns' and protects his response, often feeling defensive of it, and passionate about it, as he feels that he was the originator of it.

Reflexive control relies on a complex, long-term strategy that involves techniques such as misinformation and propaganda. Studies of reflexive control (e.g. Chotikul, 1986), for example, detail 5- to 10-year plans of disinformation, deception, *kompromat* (the use of compromising material to control a target – in other words, a form of blackmail), and a clear understanding of the role of physiology in making sense of one's social world (Chotikul, 1986, p. 44). There are also ways to create a 'siege mentality', articulate 'dark, sinister forces' (p. 50), encourage out-group hostility and cognitive dissonance, artificially create hypervigilance, engage with *maskirovka* (camouflage, concealment and deception), *dezinformatsiya* (disinformation), *vozhd* (idealizing the leader), *edinonachalniye* (one-man control), and *poslushanie* (obedience), and deploy strategies of *dvoemyslie* (doublethink) and *vranyo* (untruths with some grounding in reality) (Chotikul, 1986).

As far back as 1986, Chotikul's report, funded by the US Military, stated that 'reflexive control is more highly and scientifically developed than is realized and therefore deserves more serious national security attention than it presently receives' (p. 6), and that, as a result, 'technological subversion is being allowed to continue unabated' (p. 21). One might argue that the powerful collision of Western and Eastern psychological warfare techniques in the public political space from around 2014 onwards constitutes the greatest exposure to populist propaganda that voters have ever experienced or known.

Military defence specialist Lockheed Martin's 'Cyber Kill Chain®'[7] was recently adapted to create Trend Micro's 'The Public Opinion Cycle' (Gu, Kropotov & Yarochkin, 2017: see Figure 5.3) as a means of gaining insight into how easily these techniques can be transferred to politics. In The Public Opinion Cycle, which largely pertains to the creation of 'fake news' (i.e. propaganda, a central pillar of psychological warfare techniques in the East and West), we can clearly see a path from reconnaissance (micro-targeting), to weaponization,

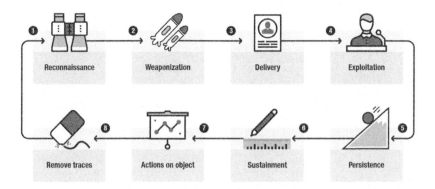

FIGURE 5.3 Trend Micro's The Public Opinion Cycle
Source: Gu, Kropotov & Yarochkin, 2017a, Figure 77, p. 64. Permission granted directly by Trend Micro.

delivery of the message (e.g. via Facebook, Twitter), exploitation of the electorate, persistence of delivery (e.g. engagement with click farms, fake accounts), sustainment, actions on object and then removal of traces, where required.

Trend Micro states that 'fake news is just one facet of public opinion manipulation and cyber propaganda' (Gu, Kropotov & Yarochkin, 2017b, n.p.), with propaganda strategically timed to reach the electorate at the most crucial time (e.g. to elicit the 'last minute swing effect' [Black Hat, 2017] that maximizes voter turnout and swing voter reach). Grey market services such as the 'Boryou Public Opinion Influencing System' can post manually and/or automatically at a rate of 100 posts per minute to around 30,000 websites, whilst many others offer real or bot followers and comments for small fees. Companies such as 118t Negative News or Weberaser offer quick removal of offending web content.

Click farms like Weibosu can flood online polls with thousands of votes, and many are able to run as many as 10,000 devices simultaneously. VTope, a Russian crowdsourcing company, leverages around 2 million memberships to offer real-life posts and activity for a client in exchange for credits and other incentives. Voter manipulation also exists as a service; Russian firm Siguldin offers a means of

> Manipulating votes, competition, and polls on social media and other online platforms [that] can be one of the most effective means to influence public opinion … Siguldin markets itself as being capable of manipulating almost any voting system on the Internet.
>
> *(Gu et al., 2017b, n.p.).*

In keeping with the requirements of The Public Opinion Cycle presented earlier (Figure 5.3), all of these services are relatively cheap and offer complete anonymization to clients. Trend Micro offers an excellent visual (see Figure 5.4) of the

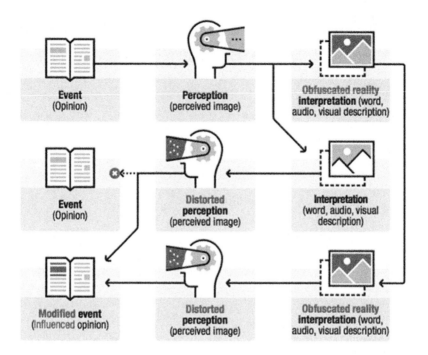

FIGURE 5.4 Trend Micro's fake news opinion formation
Source: Trend Micro. Permission granted directly by Trend Micro.

overall process of distortion, thought modification, obfuscation and opinion formation via the utilization of 'fake news' and other political campaigning tools.

Modern-Day Colonialism

The effects of this kind of campaigning can be devastating. Christopher Wylie, Cambridge Analytica whistleblower, referred to the extensive work conducted in India by his previous employers as 'modern-day colonialism' (Jaipragas, 2018, n.p.), whilst Sunil Abraham, Executive Director at the Centre for Internet and Society in Bangalore, India, expressed concern that Indians would be more effected by propaganda as much of its 1.3 billion population was being exposed to digital media for the first time:

> It's like the first time a movie was screened. The audience had never seen a cinematographic work, and when the image of a moving train came on the screen, the audience ran out of the hall. That is the impact.
>
> *(cited in Jaipragas, 2018, n.p.)*

Populism as a Strategy

The utilization of psychological warfare techniques and monetizable algorithmic data to drive political activity furthers an argument that populism is not an ideology, but a strategy. Academic Bart Bonikowski (2016, p. 10), for example, refers to populism as 'a discursive strategy selectively employed by political outsiders on both the left and right extremes of the political spectrum to challenge the political status quo'. It is a strategy of political outsiders (Bonikowski & Gidron, 2015), where 'larger-than-life charismatic leaders' (Bonikowski, 2016, p. 11) effectively mobilize support for their causes by framing the message in a way that will appeal most effectively to followers. These emotive frames are powerful: Leave.EU campaigner Andy Wigmore (a key figure in the UK's 2016 Brexit Referendum) asserted that 'referendums are not about facts, it's about emotions and you have got to tap into that' (Hern, 2018b, n.p.).

The role of propaganda, including misinformation, is vital in perpetuating a state of confusion, partisanship, loyalty and dogma amongst voters, particularly in terms of discrediting 'fake news' sources which might provide a valid source of contradictory data to one's own populist message. Loyalty in part derives from a voter's failure to know what isn't known and a subsequent *escalating commitment* (Bénabou, 2013, p. 450) to a charismatic, populist leader who targets the right emotions (heady dopamine surges at rallies, for example). This also reflects the 'exploitation' phase (phase 4) of The Public Opinion Cycle discussed earlier (Figure 5.3).

Profit Taking

The boom and euphoria stages reach a peak when the populist rises to power, which is followed immediately by a phasic stage where profit-taking activity usually takes place, emerging either immediately or shortly thereafter. Profit taking is, in essence, the act of informed insiders who extract profit, illegally, legally and/or malfeasantly, from their access to power and/or privileged knowledge (e.g. insider trading, fraud, clientelism), often at the expense of a wider populace. An example from the 2008 financial crisis, for example, involved the CEO of Lehman Brothers Dick Fuld's decision to continue to invest excessively in subprime debt, fatally over-leveraging Lehman Brothers. Fuld had privately acknowledged a year before the bank filed for bankruptcy that investing in subprime debt was a bad idea.

In the context of the recent Cambridge Analytica scandal, for example, an undercover investigative televised report named *Data, Democracy & Dirty Tricks* (Channel 4, 2018) led to the dissolving of the company. The scandal involving Bell Pottinger (see Chapter 4 for more depth) led to the winding down of the company, whilst Facebook CEO Mark Zuckerberg faced extensive US and

European governmental hearings relating to Facebook's role in enabling Russian political interference in the 2016 US Presidential Election.

The Brexit Referendum offers another example; in the context of £700,000 spending limits for Remain and Leave campaigns, it soon emerged that Leave.EU Group Limited paid over £12 million to UKIP supporter Arron Banks's company 'Better for the Country Ltd' in the year preceding the onset of the campaign cap. 'Better for the Country Ltd' were subsequently paid a total of £611, 184[8] during the official campaign year, a pattern of payment that eventually prompted an investigation by the UK Electoral Commission (The Electoral Commission, 2017). Regardless of the legality of the financial interaction between Leave.EU and Better for the Country Ltd, the deal seemed to promote a malfeasant approach that would have led to an unfair advantage for the Leave camp.

Lawsuits, Narcissists and Charismatics

Allegations of misconduct have swirled around Donald Trump long before, and throughout, his Presidency, and it would be consequently difficult not to focus on Trump as an archetypal example of post-euphoria profit taking in this phase of the Life Cycle. A populist authoritarian, Trump reported, for example, a $37 million income from his 'Winter White House', the Mar-a-Lago resort owned by the Trump Organization in Palm Beach, Florida, and a $20 million income from a Trump-owned golf club in Florida in 2017 (Ford, 2017). The state of Maryland is currently suing Donald Trump (both as an individual, and as President) for a violation of the Foreign Emoluments Clause; the New York Attorney General is suing Trump, Ivanka Trump, Donald Trump, Jr and Eric Trump for violations of charity law involving the Donald J. Trump charitable foundation over a 10-year period; and Jared Kushner, Donald Trump's son-in-law, is alleged to have secured $500 million in loans shortly after an official White House meeting with financial institutions Citigroup and Apollo Global Management.

Donald Trump has been involved in over 1,300 lawsuits and has, at the time of writing, been sued 137 times since the Presidential inauguration (Viser, 2017). More than a dozen women have accused him of sexual assault or sexual misconduct, and *The Washington Post*'s Fact Checker reports that Trump has told an average of 6.5 lies per day since becoming President of the United States (Kessler, Rizzo & Kelly, 2018). Trump- owned companies have gone bankrupt six times, according to Politifact (bankruptcies related to the Trump Taj Mahal, Trump Castle, Trump Plaza & Casino, Plaza Hotel, Trump Hotels and Casino Resorts, and Trump Entertainment Resorts).

According to Professor Howard Gardner, a Developmental Psychologist at Harvard Graduate School of Education, Donald Trump is 'remarkably narcissistic' (cited by Alford, 2015, para. 1), a pattern that fits with the emergence of profit taking in populist cycles. Narcissists and white-collar criminals are drawn to environments where a high value is placed on material success and wealth (Coleman, 1987) – politics offering an obvious example. Narcissists are prone to overconfidence (Chen, 2010), which is linked to fraud (Schrand & Zechman, 2012), and narcissists are most successful when they are charismatic (Maccoby, 2000; Rosenthal & Pittinsky, 2006; Sankowsky, 1995). These insights provide a theoretical link that aids us in an explanation of why charismatic populism is usually accompanied by a phase of profit taking following the leader's ascension to power.

Charisma: It's Personal

Charisma – specifically personalized charisma (Popper, 2002) – is related to narcissism (House & Howell, 1992), where the strength of the relationship between narcissism and fraud increases in cases where a leader is also charismatic (Rijsenbilt & Commandeur, 2012; Young & Pinsky, 2006). The 'Dark Triad' of personality traits – narcissism, Machiavellianism and psychopathy – is, interestingly, positively related to Twitter usage (Sumner, Byers, Boochever & Park, 2012, p. 386), where the heaviest Twitter users favour negative appeals over positive ones. A desperate compulsion to seek attention has been linked to this unpleasant behaviour with modern commentary including the earlier quoted sentiment that 'Twitter breeds dark, degrading, and dehumanizing discourse; it breeds vitriol and violence; in short, it breeds Donald Trump' (Ott, 2017, p. 62).

Trump is widely and variably referred to as a narcissist, psychopath, and/or sufferer of Narcissistic Personality Disorder (NPD) by a wide range of psychologists,[9] so he fits the characterization of a populist at each stage of the Life Cycle particularly well. Profit taking can be legal, simply representing the extraction of profit from a populist scenario; a 2-day event hosted by the SuperPAC America First Action at the Trump International Hotel in Washington, DC, in June 2018, for example, invited 150 supporters, half of whom paid between $100,000 and $250,000 to attend, and included an hour-long address by President Trump himself. This reflects the extensive role of clientelism in populism, particularly ideologically right-wing populism, that the reader will recall from Chapter 4.

Power and Prestige

Narcissists habitually exhibit personalized charismatic behaviours (House & Howell, 1992), particularly with regard to image building, deception (Bass & Steidlmeyer, 1999; Howell, 1988), and the acquisition of symbols of power and prestige. A clear link between charisma, narcissism and authoritarianism emerges in a characterization of the force and coercion used by a charismatic leader in a bid to sustain their leadership after the initial charm of their charisma fades (De

Vries, Roe & Taillieu, 1999; House & Howell, 1992; Howell, 1988; Howell & Shamir, 2005; McClelland, 1970; Rosenthal & Pittinsky, 2006). This can be considered a precursor to the Panic phase of the Life Cycle (see later in the chapter). 'The next step' in populism, as Professor Emeritus Richard Batley states, 'is outright authoritarianism' (Batley, 2017, n.p.). Trump's assertion in a rally in Iowa on 23 January 2016 that 'I could stand in the middle of 5th Avenue and shoot somebody and I wouldn't lose voters' reflects his belief in his own dominance and authority, whilst FBI indictments against Michael Flynn, formerly Trump's NSA (National Security Adviser), a number of indictments against former Trump Campaign Chairman Paul Manafort, Rick Gates, Konstantin Kilimnik, and George Papadopoulos, alongside the jailing of Dutch attorney Alex van der Zwaan and the raiding of the home of Trump's long-time lawyer Michael Cohen, indicate that profit taking has become a regular occurrence in the current White House Administration.

Developing Demagoguery

A leader whose power rests predominantly on charismatic authority remains under considerable pressure to continually demonstrate superhero status ('when success deserts the charismatic leader, so does his authority'; Turner, 2003, p. 14) – another precursor to the Panic phase of the Life Cycle, and a contributory factor to the emergence of profit taking, criminal and malfeasant activities. A charismatic leader must 'work in miracles, if he wants to be a prophet' (Weber, 1978, p. 1114) and that kind of charisma is unsustainable; it can lead to increasingly risky acts or require the use of force and coercion to sustain the leader's power when charisma fades (e.g. House & Howell, 1992), often signalling a shift to authoritarianism.

From Populism to Authoritarianism

Professor Roger Berkowitz has warned, in reference to President Donald Trump, for example, that 'one of the core elements of totalitarianism is that it's based in a movement … and Trump has explicitly called himself the mouthpiece of a movement. That's a very dangerous position for a politician' (Berkowitz, quoted by DW, 2016, n.p.). Trump provides a great example of 'intra-party populism' in this sense (Greven, 2016, p. 1), where he retains charismatic intra-party power by referring to the party-at-large as the establishment, with himself framed as the perpetual revolutionary. A reverence, and admiration for, dictators such as North Korean dictator Kim Jong-Un ('He speaks and his people sit up at attention. I want my people to do the same' [Pengelly, 2018, n.p.]) betray Trump's authoritarian ambitions, and reflect his own 'dictator envy' (Samuels, 2018), underscoring his ambitions as a populist authoritarian leader.

Charisma, Cults and Radicals

Populist campaigns share similarities to the 'relationship zero' (A. Stein, 2017, p. 2) phase of the formation of cults, where a group becomes 'self-sealing' as a result of the charismatic authority, propagandist influences and mind-control techniques of the leader and organization. We can see this phenomenon emerge in the context of the 2016 US Presidential Election, where Donald Trump achieved a political shock of epic proportion across a vast and often disparate swathe of the population, enabled hugely by the construction of echo-chamber-style alt-right and right-wing discourse (e.g. Breitbart.com, Info Wars, some Fox News content, selected click bait, Russian bots); 'there is no single or simple, demographic or psychological profile of those likely to be indoctrinated' (A. Stein, 2017, p. 22).

We can note that in a cult relationship,

> The leader sets in motion processes of brainwashing and coercive per-
> suasion designed to isolate and control followers. As a result, followers are
> able to be exploited, and potentially become deployable agents, demon-
> strating uncritical obedience to the group, regardless of their own survival
> needs.
>
> *(A. Stein, 2017, pp. 23–24)*

The psychological warfare techniques discussed earlier, now clearly a key component of modern political campaigns, seek to emulate exactly this nature of persuasion, to create the feeling that emotions have been roused organically, and to appeal to evolutionary survival needs to achieve maximum engagement.

Authoritarian Instincts

Harvard Professor Steven Levitsky remarks that 'Trump has been remarkably consistent as long as he's been on the public stage in exhibiting authoritarian instincts' (cited in Rucker, 2018, n.p.). A combination of charisma[10] and authoritarianism, love and fear, is important in the expression of authoritarianism and in the development of a cult of personality (A. Stein, 2017, p. 16). What is interesting is that an awareness of being manipulated (Lifton, 1961/1989) can offer a useful counter. Professor Phil Howard, Director of the Oxford University Computational Propaganda Project also noted that 'only one part of the political spectrum – the far right – is really the target for extremist, sensational and conspiratorial content. Over social media, moderates and centrists tend not to be as susceptible' (University of Oxford, 2018, n.p.). Chapter 1 explained in depth the reasons why this should be the case, which we will not revisit further here.

The Panic Phase

Weber clearly identifies the need for crisis in the powerful emergence of the charismatic leader – a supposition driven forward subsequently by generations of charisma scholars (e.g. 'Scholars since Weber have suggested that times of crisis may create an increased opportunity for charismatic leadership to emerge'; Bligh, Kohles & Meindl, 2004, p. 211). Whilst crisis and uncertainty can also play a role at the displacement stage of the Life Cycle, it is discussed here at length as the phase in the Life Cycle where the shortcomings of the charismatic leader are laid bare, and the utopian promises of the displacement, boom and euphoria phases have begun to disappear.

Charisma and Crisis

Klein and House (1995) state that *crises breed charisma* (p. 185). One way in which the Panic phase of the Life Cycle is exhibited is in the leader's panic relating to his loss of charismatic authority. A populist will often revisit the mechanisms that provided the most effective conduit for his charismatic, populist appeal, which explains, for example, the 15 rallies that President Trump had held (at the time of writing) since his inauguration, in Florida, Tennessee, Kentucky, Pennsylvania, Indiana, Ohio, West Virginia, Arizona, Alabama, Michigan and Minnesota. The rallies are incredibly effective in that they provide the 'red meat' (Miller, 2017) of anger and emotion so fundamental to his base. His cult of personality imbues the events with extraordinary charisma, cementing his superhero status and benefiting hugely from excitation-transfer. Crisis rhetoric can also emerge at this stage as a conduit for a leader's panic, particularly if fear of incarceration, or litigation deriving from activities undertaken during the profit-taking phase, emerges.

President Trump's late-night tweets often reflect a state of high cortisol, allostasis or allostatic load, and a state of androgenic priming (essentially the increasing of testosterone, which can create a combative state – see Chapter 6 for more depth) as a response to his consumption of inflammatory politically-themed TV shows or Internet content. Often, inflammatory tweets can also reflect a need to again return to the revolutionary hero image that invigorated his base at the displacement and early euphoria stages of the Life Cycle of Charismatic Populism. FBI agent Peter Strzok, for example, was referred to as a 'sick loser' (Trump, 2018), Barack Obama as a 'sick man' (Trump, 2017), Hillary Clinton as 'Crooked Hillary' (Trump, 2018) and Mexicans and immigrants are 'druggies, drug dealers, rapists and killers' (Trump, 2015).

Hitting the Panic Button

As charismatic authority is routinized, or profit-taking activity begins to cloud the popularity of the leader within his own party or base, his supporters might also begin to panic. Republican Governor Scott Walker was reported, for example, to have been 'hitting the panic button for his party' (Phillips, 2018, n.p.) after a Democratic candidate decisively won a seat previously taken by Trump by a landslide 17 percentage points. At the time of writing, the Democratic Party had flipped 43 seats since the 2016 US Presidential Elections.

A statement of the US Southern Baptist Convention, that 'We declare that any form of nativism, mistreatment, or exploitation is inconsistent with the gospel of Jesus Christ' (Goodstein, 2018, n.p.) was made in the context of a direct denouncement by the Convention of the Trump Administration's policy of forced family separation at the US–Mexico border. The rhetoric of the US Southern Baptist Convention encapsulated a moral panic experienced amongst Trump's religious supporters who had earlier supported, or tolerated, his right-wing populist statements in the early phase of his campaign, but for whom the rhetoric – and accompanying actions – had become too extreme.

From Rage to Risk

At this stage of the Life Cycle of Charismatic Populism, a populist needs to escalate pathos to remain appealing to his base, which often requires a more extreme escalation of rhetoric. Yet he risks alienating party members upon whose democratic foundations his rise to power was enabled. He therefore faces a difficult choice, which can lead to much tumult and criticisms from both sides ('Turn the movement's rage into a political program and you've already betrayed it' [Weisberg, 2010, p. 33]). At this stage, the charismatic populist might turn to other means of displaying his powerful status to further his cult of personality, so that he is able to 'continuously undertake actions that reinforce their self-image and maintain their ideal ego' (Aktas, de Bodt, Bollaert & Roll, 2011, p. 2). One means of doing so is by engagement in high-profile, risky, exciting deals. This again draws a common thread between charisma, populism and narcissism, where narcissism is positively associated with initiating deals and with negotiating those deals at a faster rate, over-paying for an acquired company, a propensity to take greater risk (Li & Tang, 2010), and a subsequent more extreme and volatile operating and market performance for that firm (Aktas et al., 2011).

Electoral Violence

A displacement event can cause panic in the profit-taking phase of the Life Cycle, particularly when a new election cycle occurs. In 2007, for example, political protests and ethnic violence occurring around the election cycle led to the tragic loss of life of more than 1,200 people and displaced a further half a million people in Kenya (Cockburn, 2017). In 2017, the murder of Kenyan Chris Msando, the Head of Information, Communication and Technology for the Independent Electoral and Boundaries Commission (IEBC), and brutal aftermath of President Uhuru Kenyatta's re-election (where at least 24 people, including a 9- year-old

child, were shot dead during riots) represented a sad return to election-era bru-
tality. In 2018, in Southern Turkey, four people died and eight were wounded in
the mainly Kurdish town of Suruç when populist incumbent President Recep
Tayyip Erdoğan was reported to have encouraged party officials to use lists of
voter details to identify and intimidate Kurds to win more votes. In 2017, President Nicolas Maduro's controversial decision to hold elections in Venezuela led
to multiple deaths and widespread protests, whilst around 70 student protesters
have died so far (at the time of writing) in uprisings against autocratic President
Daniel Ortega in Nicaragua. A one-time legendary Marxist freedom fighter and
revolutionary populist icon, Ortega had once used the John Lennon classic, 'Give
Peace a Chance', during a successful electoral campaign.

Brexit Means Brexit

The 'Panic' phase of the British Government's implementation of Brexit offers a
clear example of crisis rhetoric (Kiewe, 1994, p. 17) used as a means of seeking to
perpetuate the initial charisma of the Brexit concept in the face of economic data
that would indicate that carrying it through would represent a poor logical
decision.

Crisis rhetoric can be defined as: 'the discourse initiated by decision makers in
an attempt to communicate to various constituents that a certain development is
critical and to suggest a certain course of action to remedy the critical situation'
(Kiewe, 1994, p. 17). In the immediate aftermath of the Brexit Referendum, a
British newspaper headline referred to three judges who were named-and-
shamed for ruling that the UK Government would require the consent of Parliament to enable the dismantling of the UK's EU membership – i.e. Brexit – to
begin. The labelling of the judges as 'enemies of the people'[11] carried clearly
populist invocations. Prime Minister Theresa May's subsequent dedication to a
'Hard Brexit' played into an escalating pathos-driven rhetoric that her base
necessitated; yet her pathos stood at odds with a Conservative Party-commis-
sioned report on the deleterious economic impact of Brexit (Owen & Lloyd,
2018) which detailed that the North-East of England would experience a 16% fall
in economic growth, alongside a 20% increase in retail trading costs, a 16%
increase in the price of food and drink, and an £80 billion overall cost associated
with exiting the European Union blighting the rest of the country.

In the 48-hour period immediately following the announcement of Brexit
Referendum results, $2 trillion was wiped from the value of global financial
markets, with concomitant fears of a British recession voiced by economists
(Wearden & Fletcher, 2016). Many companies have subsequently migrated,
planned to migrate or redirected operations from the UK, including Goldman
Sachs, Deutsche Bank, Unilever, EasyJet, Lloyd's of London, the European
Banking Authority, the European Medicines Agency, UBS, AIG and JP Morgan.
Hedge fund titan George Soros referred to Brexit as 'a lose-lose proposition,

harmful both to Britain and the European Union' (Eckett, 2017, n.p.). A sub-sequent controversial statement by Prime Minister Theresa May, that the NHS (the UK National Health Service) would receive £600 million a week post-Brexit, represented a clear attempt at re-escalating pathos,[12] whilst London Mayor Sadiq Khan shifted into panic mode immediately the day that the Referendum result was released: 'I want to send a clear message to the British people and to businesses and investors around the world this morning – there is no need to panic' (cited in Hooton, 2016, n.p.).

Charisma

The prevalence of charisma within the Life Cycle of Charismatic Populism reflects the centrality of charisma to the appeal of a populist, and populist authoritarian. It is therefore necessary to provide the reader with a more in-depth view of this oft-misunderstood, powerful and intuitively appealing phenomenon.

Eatwell (2006, p. 271) argues that a charismatic personality appears to be a missionary, communicates an impassioned vision, establishes a symbiotic hierarchy (i.e. they appear to be both above, and of, the people); and vocalizes the presence of an enemy, or threat, from which they can heroically deliver, or save, their followers. As mentioned earlier, the real presence of, or artificially-constructed invocation of, a crisis, provides great conditions in which charisma can appear (Klein & House, 1995, p. 185). References to history and tradition, emphasis on a collective identity, reinforcement of a collective efficacy and the communica-tion of a vision are all considered to be classic discursive elements (Shamir et al., 1993; Shamir et al., 1994). US Attorney General Jeff Sessions' use of Romans 13 to defend his border immigration policy, for example, or Christian Evangelist leader Reverend Franklin Graham's 10 November 2016 statement that 'God's hand intervened' to allow Trump to win the Presidency, offer sound examples of the invocation of religion. The same Administration provides us with examples of the central use of national pride ('America First'), tradition and nostalgia ('Make America Great Again') in campaign rhetoric.

Charisma, Pathos and the Charismatization of Politics

A tendency to pathos in recent years has led to US political parties being criti-cized as 'empty vessels' (Katz & Kolodny, 1994), where *pathos* (appeals to emo-tion) have usurped *ethos* – appeals to credibility – and *logos* (appeals to logic) (Heracleous & Klaering, 2014).

The use of metaphor is commonly invoked in pathos-driven appeals, providing distal but intuitively appealing visions of hope, camaraderie and other positive emotions, to voters (Hartog & Verburg, 1997). Metaphors can be divisive and aggressive, too, as the common use of animal and insect metaphors geared nega-tively towards immigrants and ethnic groups can attest (see Chapter 4 for more depth). Successful US Presidents use metaphors almost twice as much as less successful Presidents (Mio et al., 2005) and the use of root metaphors (Trump's reference to 'America' in 'Make America Great Again') has proven particularly powerful, explaining their repeated use (Audebrand, 2010). The power of charismatic rhetoric has been shown to be particularly great in conditions where negative feelings such as fear of persecution are present (Burns, 1978; House, 1977; House, 1996; House et al., 1991; Weber, 1924/1947), explaining the formulaic use of ethnic groups as threats in right-wing populist campaigns, and the regular threats of military action, military displays and general warmongering so favoured by populist authoritarians. In summary, it can be said that

> Populism is a political style which is a source for change based on the systematic use of rhetorical appeal to the people. In its discursive form, it is characterized by a programmatic minimalism but with a great symbolic plasticity which makes it a vector conducive to forge multiple and even heterogen[e]ous indignations (ethno-cultural, anti-tax, anti-elitist, Eurosceptics, etc.)
> *(Durant et al., 2013, p. 9)*

Citizens United

One reason that pathos has emerged with such force in recent years is due to a 2014 US Supreme Court Ruling that removed caps on political campaign donations.[13] The 5–4 Ruling extended significantly the scope of the 2010 Citizens United v. Federal Election Commission landmark US constitutional law, campaign finance and corporate law case, raising fears as it did that it 'could potentially funnel massive amounts of money to a favoured candidate' (Levy, 2015, n.p.). The effects of the reforms were immediate; during the 2012 campaign cycle, 646 individual donors contributed in excess of $93 million to political parties. In 2012, US Presidential Election spending surpassed $6 billion. In 2016, that figure rose to $6.8 billion, although that figure did not include the investment of Russian operations that were thought to have significantly swayed the outcome of the Election. The concomitant emergence of big-donor SuperPACs[14] raised concerns about the influence of certain powerful donors such as hedge fund CEO Robert Mercer and casino magnate Sheldon Adelson, underscoring the way in which the removal of caps has further facilitated clientelism and potential profit taking activities.

Pathos remains an extremely popular political strategy, one that US Attorney General Jeff Sessions attempted to tap into when he turned to the Bible as a means of motivating law enforcement officers in Fort Wayne, Indiana, to submit to the rule of law without question when tackling the contentious issue of familial separations at the US–Mexican border. As stated by Sessions, 'I would cite you to the Apostle Paul and his clear and wise command in Romans 13, to obey the laws of the government because God has ordained the government for his purposes' (quoted in Mullen, 2018, para. 1).

American History Professor John Fea subsequently pointed out in an article in *The Washington Post* (Zauzmer & Macmillan, 2018) that the Biblical Romans 13 passage chosen by Sessions – an argument promoting a blind acceptance of authority devoid of moral concern (and a quintessential assumption of author-itarianism) – had also been used to defend slavery.

Bastards and Sons of Bitches

It has been said that, 'As a civic religion, football has married Max Weber's *protestantische Ethik*, American capitalism, the worship of great men, and the individual narratives of sacrifice and superhuman feats' (Newkirk, 2017, n.p.). As a result, football (used here in the American sense, otherwise referred to as 'American football' outside North America) has become, in the American psyche, one of the most powerful forms of charisma that society has to offer. As such, it represents a powerful political force, including a status as a site of meaningful political protest. Sport has always provided a valuable means of conveying charismatic authority, domination and power (e.g. the 1936 Berlin Olympic Games), and most recently offered a podium for the 'Take A Knee' movement.[15] President Trump's demonization of NFL players who participated in the peaceful protest against racism in the United States as 'bastards and sons of bitches' (NBC Sports Bay Area Staff, 2017, n.p.) reflects his desire to com-modify, dominate and claim the charismatic authority of football in his own ideological image.

Biological Charisma

Charismatic authority, as opposed to traditional, or legal-rational authority (Weber, 1904/1958), resides in the perceived or attributed image of the leader as a revolutionary superhero. Pathos, as it turns out, does not provide the only basis for our attributions. We are also (almost inexplicably) drawn to attractive narcis-sists, whose unique biological profiles may well account for a great deal of their charismatic appeal. The first way in which we can explore this phenomenon is with reference to the endogenous steroidal hormone *testosterone*.

Mastering Facial Metrics

Testosterone, its relation to facial metrics, and its relationship to charisma paints a fascinating picture. Facial metrics provide an indicator of testosterone levels (Lefevre, Lewis, Perrett & Penke, 2013), which can, by extension, predict finan-cial fraud (e.g. Wong, Ormiston & Haselhuhn, 2011). Almost unbelievably, financial misreporting has been found to be up to 98% higher for CEOs whose face demonstrates an above-average width-to-height ratio (a marker of high tes-tosterone)[16]:

> A CEO's facial masculinity predicts his firm's likelihood of being subject to an SEC enforcement action ... an executive's facial masculinity is associated with the likelihood of the SEC naming him as a perpetrator ... facial masculinity also predicts the incidence of insider trading and option backdating.
>
> *(Jia, Van Lent & Zeng, 2014, pp. 1195–1196)*

Narcissism, a personality characteristic related to charismatic leadership (House & Howell, 1992) – specifically, *personalized* charisma (Popper, 2002) – can be both attractive to us, and exploitative (Choic, 2006). The most maladaptive narcissistic characteristics, in fact, are also those that prove most attractive to others. Narcissists with a sense of *entitlement* who seek to *exploit* others are also most likely to emerge as the most popular (Back, Schmukle & Egloff, 2010), explaining the appeal of Italy's Silvio Berlusconi, for example, who was handed a 5-year sentence for fraud. It also explains (at least in part) our tendency to fail to impose adequate accountability structures on politicians whom we find so charming and appealing. This failure can easily lead to failures of moral leadership and inadequate means of countering unethical behaviours (Chandler, 2009).

Narcissists are generally regarded as more agreeable, conscientious, open, competent, entertaining and well-adjusted by peers (Paulhus, 1998, cited in Back et al.,, 2010).[17] We seem to love them, and the construction of social media (e.g. short tweets, click bait, editing software; in short, an easy construction and manipulation of reality) can lead to very real consequences in the form of euphoria, profit taking and an eventual slide into authoritarianism or economic and political decline.

Returning to facial metrics, men with an above-average width-to-height face ratio were cited as being more likely to 'experience a greater sense of power ... more likely to deceive or cheat when this would increase their financial gain ... [and] were more prone to exploit the trust of others'; they are less likely to exhibit 'poise and polish' (Lewis, Lefevre & Bates, 2012, p. 855), with the link between facial markers, testosterone and aggression thought to be a 'situationally-contingent manifestation of a broader motivation to achieve status' (Lewis et al., 2012, p. 857). According to Dr Oguz Ali Acar, Cass Business School, who recently conducted studies on leadership (Tuncdogan, Acar & Stam, 2017), Donald Trump

> has a masculine, older-looking face with high width-to-height ratio (fWHR) ... Those who have a higher ratio, like Trump, are more likely to be more aggressive, dominant and powerful ... Trump has a masculine looking face, which is often perceived as dominant and is preferred in competitive settings, such as wartime.
>
> *(Acar, cited in Ripley, 2017, n.p.)*

Dr Acar's statement reflects Trump's conflict-based rhetoric, alongside his desire to move away from bipartisanship, co-operation, or peace-based rhetoric, with Dr Acar surmising that 'masculine faces are perceived as less trustworthy and are not preferred in cooperative settings such as peacetime. The current increased global terror threat may have contributed to his election' (cited in Ripley, 2017, n.p.). In other words, it benefits Trump to perpetuate war-based rhetoric as it plays to his biological strengths.

Presidents who display 'fearless dominance' – a form of narcissistic display – also seem to appeal to US voters, and when associated with psychopathy, this 'is an important but heretofore neglected predictor of presidential performance' (Lillenfeld et al., 2012, p. 489). President Trump's demand for personal loyalty and will to dominate contribute notably to the high staff turnover on perpetual display in his Administration; for example the high-profile exits of, Rex Tillerson (Secretary of State), Gary Cohn (Chief Economic Adviser), Hope Hicks (Communications Director), Rob Porter (Staff Secretary), Richard Cordray (Director of the Consumer Financial Protection Bureau), Tom Price (Secretary of Health & Human Services), Steve Bannon (Chief Strategist), Michael Flynn (National Security Adviser), Sean Spicer (Press Secretary, Communications Director), Anthony Scaramucci (Communications Director), Mike Dubke (Communications Director), Sebastian Gorka (White House Adviser), K. T. McFarland (Deputy National Security Adviser), Omarosa Newman (Director of Communications for the White House Office of Public Liaison), Dina Powell (Deputy National Security Adviser), Reince Priebus (Chief of Staff), Keith Schiller (Director of Oval Office Operations), Katie Walsh (Deputy Chief of Staff), Walter Schaub (Head of US Office of Government Ethics), Michael Short (Assistant White House Press Secretary), Jeff Comey (FBI Director) and Sally Yates (Attorney General).

Charisma and Narcissism

Narcissism is defined as a pervasive pattern of grandiosity, self-focus and self-importance (American Psychiatric Association, 1994), and as 'a pervasive pattern of grandiosity (in fantasy, or behaviour), need for admiration and a lack of empathy' (*Diagnostic and Statistical Manual of Mental Disorders* (DSM IV, American Psychiatric Association, 1994, p. 658). At the time of writing, it seemed as if lack of empathy constituted the greatest threat from within the United States, with almost 2,000 children forcibly removed from their parents as part of the Trump Administration's 'zero tolerance' immigration policy, around 100 of whom were under 4 years old (Gallucci, 2018). It was a practice that former Republican First Lady Laura Bush publicly admonished. In a personal statement, she said that, 'It is immoral. And it breaks my heart' (Bush, 2018, n.p.).

A lack of empathy appeared prevalent in the Administration at that time, with former Campaign Manager Corey Lewandowski publicly mocking the anguish of a 10-year-old Down Syndrome girl who had recently been separated from her parents (Laignee, 2018). US Chief of Staff John Kelly did not appear overly concerned by familial separations, commenting that, 'The children will be taken care of – put into foster care or whatever' (Lavandera, Morris & Simon, 2018, n.p.). As detailed earlier, a number of psychologists had earmarked the relative ease of diagnosis-from-afar of Trump as a classic sufferer of NPD (Narcissistic Personality Disorder); a lack of empathy constitutes just one of the dangers of voting for such an individual.

Politics and Grandiose Narcissism

The relationship between narcissism and charisma is a compelling one (e.g. Humphreys, Zhao, Ingra, Gladstone & Basham, 2010, p. 126). A narcissist is also more likely to invest in a well-groomed, expensive appearance, which will heighten their desirability to us (Back et al., 2010; Vazire, Naumann, Rentfrow & Gosling, 2008), to engage in image building and deception (Bass & Steidlmeyer, 1999; Howell, 1988), and to pursue the acquisition of symbols of power, status and prestige. Politics clearly offers many attractions and opportunities for this kind of personality. We can see, for example, that narcissists are 'people with an inordinately well-developed self-image, in which they take great pride and on which they reflect frequently' (Maccoby, 2000, p. 69). The perpetual stage-managing of a politician's image reflects such a tendency extremely well.

A recent presidential study (Lillenfeld et al., 2012) found that US presidents exhibit elevated levels of grandiose narcissism compared with the general population, a behaviour that leads to an increased likelihood of congressional impeachment resolutions and unethical behaviour. Narcissism ultimately leads to a greater propensity for fraud (Rijsenbilt & Commandeur, 2012; Schrand & Zechman, 2012; Young & Pinsky, 2006); a study of 953 S&P 500 CEOs (Rijsenbilt & Commandeur, 2012) provides empirical confirmation of narcissism as a cause of fraud in organizations (p. 425). This again provides support for the emergence of profit taking at the peak of a populist's power.

Productive Narcissism

Narcissism is not necessarily a negative characteristic; Rosenthal and Pittinsky (2006), for example, believe that 'productive narcissists would be good candidates to be socialised charismatic leaders and vice versa' (p. 126), a view supported by comprehensive reviews of the leadership literature (Humphreys et al., 2010; Maccoby, 2000; Rosenthal & Pittinsky, 2006) – an idea that we will revisit at the end of the chapter in the context of socialized charisma and France's Emmanuel Macron.

Charisma of Office

In addition to charismatic rhetoric and biological charisma, we can turn to a 'charisma of office' (Parsons, 1965) for explanatory power as to how, for example, criminal figures can become well-regarded as charismatic national political figures

(Magno, 2010). This kind of charisma reflects a tendency for followers to imbue charisma onto an individual by virtue of their holding a legitimate position of authority. If the leader loses their source of legitimate power, so their charisma of office disappears. This 'charisma of office' (Weber, 1958/1965) explains how 'in a revolutionary and sovereign manner, charismatic domination transforms all values and breaks all traditional and rational norms' (Weber, 1978, p. 1115), the revolutionary hero emerges to challenge an established elite. If the revolutionary ascends to power, his charismatic power is routinized into a legitimate position of office (Weber, 1968, pp. 1139–1141), but he may still benefit from an uptick in charismatic power, because of the dominant position that his official status affords him.

Legitimate Charisma

A charismatic, narcissistic leader often relies on a coterie of acolytes, opportunists, authoritarians and bystanders to further and cement his power. Thoroughgood,

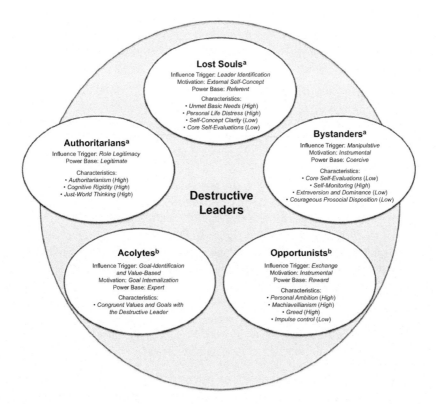

FIGURE 5.5 The Susceptible Circle
Source: Thoroughgood, Padilla, Hunter & Tate, 2012. Permission granted via Rightslink.

Padilla, Hunter & Tate's (2012) taxonomy of destructive followers (Figure 5.5) provides interesting insight into the process.

Parallels between destructive and charismatic leadership emerge clearly in the literature (e.g. Padilla, Hogan & Kaiser, 2007; Thoroughgood et al., 2012), for example, where *authoritarian* followers of the leader are motivated into conformity by a tendency to blindly accept legitimate power, imbuing the holder of that power with exceptional qualities. US Vice President Mike Pence, for example, expresses great deference to Trump, was recently referred to as 'the Kandinsky of kissing up' after comparing his boss to King David during an official trip to Israel (*The Week*, 2018, p. 16).

Opportunists are ambitious individuals whose relationship with a destructive leader is one mediated by the presence of *exchange-triggers* (i.e. what the leader can do for them if they remain complicit with the actions of the leader [Barbuto, 2000]). Trump's reliance on financially motivated opportunists reflects a lifetime as a real-estate dealer. Exchange-triggers are evident in his frequent practice of giving senior titles to vastly inexperienced individuals who subsequently owe their fortunes to him (e.g. Sarah Huckabee Sanders, Hope Hicks, Ivanka Trump, Jared Kushner, Kelly Anne Conway and Sean Spicer, all of whom possessed scant formal experience or qualifications to suit the seniority of their respective roles).

A Tinder Box of Populism

The fact that populism is non-ideological and instead highly opportunistic (Pappas, cited in Durant et al., 2013, p. 28) explains why it is 'transferable' or contagious (Durant et al., 2013, p. 30), widening the scope of a destructive leader's coterie-based appeal and reach; populism, it can be said, creates a kind of 'tinder box' that can be lit by any new candidate who picks up the populist baton, so the use of populist strategies as opportunistic (Greven, 2016, p. 1) increases. This might in part explain the hotbed of populist activity that emerged in 2013, which included the establishment of the German right-wing AfD (Alternative für Deutschland), British Prime Minister David Cameron's announcement of a Referendum on Britain's decision to leave the European Union, Greece's Syriza's evolution into a unitary party, and formation by SCL Elections of its political off-shoot, Cambridge Analytica. 2014 heralded the announcement of Donald Trump's Presidential campaign, the formation of Podemos in Spain, and Italy's Five Star Movement's coalition agreement with Britain's United Kingdom Independence Party (UKIP), as part of the EFDD (Europe of Freedom and Direct Democracy – a populist Eurosceptic political group that exists within the European Parliament).

Exchange-Triggers and Dominating Behaviours

Donald Trump's promotion of the vastly inexperienced Hope Hicks to Communications Director might reflect the tendency for destructive leaders to surround themselves with lesser known people who can be dominated (Winter, 1973). Hope Hicks may have been influenced by what Bénabou (2013, p. 451) identified as wilful blindness (either in the form of *ex ante* information avoidance, or *ex post* belief distortion) when she accepted her post; she may have felt qualified and able for the role, but the reality of her inexperience rendered her unable to appreciate the intricacies of her role sufficiently – including the expression of, and ability to exert, ethical and moral authority. A subsequent 9-hour testimony before the House Intelligence Committee pre-empted her resignation, with Hicks admitting that she had sometimes bent the truth as part of her job (Graham, 2018b). Trump himself reportedly[18] once commented that Hope Hicks reportedly possessed as much political experience as a coffee cup.

These kinds of opportunistic, exchange-trigger and authoritarian-focused relationships are reminiscent of the coterie charisma of Eatwell (2006) – a leader's magnetic power over an inner circle allows him to extend his power and develops a stronger network of *acolytes* using their loyalty as leverage. The potential dangers of groupthink[19] are obvious, the ability of acolytes to exercise intellectual, moral or autonomous power negligible.

Socialized Charisma

Charisma represents a powerful weapon for the populist, but it can be equally powerful in the hands of a morally and ideologically-driven leader. Charisma is amoral, meaning that it can be *personalized* or *socialized*. Socialized leaders possess ethical integrity and deploy their charismatic authority for the good of society (De Vries et al., , 1999; House & Howell, 1992; Howell, 1988; Howell & Shamir, 2005; Rosenthal & Pittinsky, 2006). It can be powerful enough to withstand the force of partisanship (for example, Austria's Independent Green Party candidate Alexander Van der Bellen defeated the far-right populist and favourite Norbert Hofer to win Austria's Presidential Election in 2016 with 53.3% of the vote). The win was viewed by European moderates as a victory against the spectre of populism, a moment that spurred then-French President François Hollande to comment that 'the Austrian people have chosen Europe and open-mindedness', and Greek Prime Minister Alexis Tsipras to describe Van der Bellen's success as 'a breath of fresh air in times when Europe is threatened by the rise of the far right'. European Parliament President Martin Schulz referred to Van der Bellen's victory as 'a heavy defeat of nationalism and anti-European, backward-looking populism' (Brady, 2016, n.p.).

Pro-Europe French President Emmanuel Macron's *En Marche!* Movement provides another example. Macron won the hearts and minds of a nation, crushing the National Front's Marine Le Pen. Hailed as France's 'boy wonder' (Walt, 2017), Macron is undoubtedly charismatic, but he is not a populist. His appeal resides instead in a form of socialized charisma built around the rejection of right-wing rhetoric, and in the embrace of *ethos* and *logos*, and the formulation of intellectually- and economically-founded strategies for reform. Macron now faces a difficult balancing act between enacting what he sees as often painful economic reforms – which can take time to bear fruit – and the need to retain some charismatic appeal that traditionally becomes routinized and bureaucratized (and thus weakened at this stage of his leadership; Weber, 1864–1920/1954). As stated by Macron himself, 'Some people are obsessed by [opinion polls], but what really counts is the work in depth you are doing for the country' (Chazan, 2018, n.p.).

The Courage to Change

One of the most quintessential recent examples of socialized charismatic appeal lies in the shock defeat of a 10-term Democratic incumbent by 28-year-old Democratic challenger Alexandria Ocasio-Cortez in the 14th District of New York. Ocasio-Cortez's campaign video, *The Courage to Change* (Ocasio-Cortez, 2018) was superbly constructed to appeal to passionate, liberal ideologues, embodying the ethos of a candidate whose background has been shaped by teaching (thus embodying *ethos*), a low-income upbringing, an intra-party appeal for change (thus challenging the status quo), a charisma borne of passion and rousing rhetoric (*pathos*), appeals to common sense concerning necessary legislative reform (*logos*), and an us-versus-them discourse that manages to remain measured in its message.

Ocasio-Cortez combines an articulate ability to invoke pathos, appeals to evolutionary instincts as a physically attractive individual, represents the optimism of youth, engages with root and personal metaphors, invokes the rhetoric of resistance, America and justice, displays a strong work ethic, and positions herself as a voice for the people. In this sense, she has captured the essence of each kind of charisma available to her, and even speaks to a tribalistic 'us-and-them' discourse.

Yet Ocasio-Cortez is not a populist; she clearly speaks for an under-represented group in an articulate and informed way, but promotes an ideal of ethically-underpinned unity. The weaponization of socialized charisma, in her case, demonstrates the powerful appeal of charisma as a potential source for good.

Summary

Some political observers believe that 'although populists can succeed in opposition, they inevitably fail once in power' (Mudde, 2016, p. 29). One reason for this is that charisma, emergent 'in statu nascendi' (Weber), is dependent, in a populist scenario, on the populist remaining a revolutionary hero. Once that image is bureaucratized, the charisma can no longer be channelled; hence a desire to return to rallies, pathos, intra-party populist appeals and risky deals, all of which provide a conduit for the re-invocation of the endocrinological, physiological effects – the charismatic authority, in other words – that appeal so powerfully to voters.

There remains no time when the schism between the promise of a utopian future and the stark reality of a life under a populist regime emerges more clearly than during the profit-taking phase of the Life Cycle of Charismatic Populism, during which the threat of authoritarianism looms large. It is a period during which the leader may seek to dismantle democratic checks and balances to pursue an authoritarian agenda as a means of personal profit taking, via the ongoing acquisition of power.

The inevitable fall from grace of the charismatic populist leader – whether characterized by a loss of democratic, legitimate authority, or in the form of political protests – accompanies a simultaneous moment or period of panic amongst a wider population (e.g. the $2 trillion that was wiped from the financial markets on the day that the Brexit Referendum results were announced), an uptick in litigation and the emergence of fraud and malfeasance, and, potentially, a rapid exit by many members of the leader's inner circle whose exchange-triggers and opportunities to profit may have evaporated. Charismatic populism is so formulaic because the crises caused by outgoing regimes can provide the economic, political and social displacement or period of 'stability as destabilizing' that allows the Life Cycle of Charismatic Populism to begin again.

Notes

1 Monoamine oxidase A (MAOA) is an enzyme that breaks down important neurotransmitters in the brain (including dopamine and serotonin). The MAOA gene has been colloquially referred to as 'the warrior gene'.
2 The serotonin transporter protein (5-HTT/SLC6A4) transports the neurotransmitter serotonin from synapses to presynaptic neurons. Interestingly, it also appears to play an important role in our physiological response to the ingestion of cocaine and amphetamines. See also Glossary.
3 In evolutionary terms, the older evolutionary pathway in terms of data processing required sensory information to go to the visual and auditory thalamus, then to the amygdala directly, where it would connect with the autonomic nervous system where somatic responses, like running from an angry bear, would immediately result. The newer pathway involves sensory data to be passed from eyes and ears to the visual and auditory cortices. From there, it goes to the neocortex, then to the hippocampus, where long-term memory and potentiation enable decisions to be reached. The first, older system is still much faster; thus we are still primed to respond quickest in survival-led terms.
4 See Weber, M. (1958/1965), 'Politics as a Vocation', in H. H. Gerth and C. Wright Mills (Eds.), *From Max Weber: Essays in Sociology*, New York, Oxford University Press.
5 In the context of the 2008 financial crisis, to which the Minsky Credit Cycle is often applied, this stage was characterized by the creation of subprime securitized vehicles – collateralized debt obligations (CDOs) that ultimately bankrupted Lehman Brothers and brought Wall Street to its knees. See Zehndorfer, E., *Charismatic Leadership: The Role of Charisma in the Global Financial Crisis* (Routledge, 2015) for more information.
6 United States of America vs. Internet Research Agency LLC A/K/A mediasintez LLC a/K/A Glavset LLC A/K/A Mixinfo LLC A/K/A Azimut LLC A/K/A Novinfo LLC,

Concord Management and Consulting LLC, Concord Catering, Yevgeniy Viktorovich Prigozhin, Mikhail Ivanovich Bystrov, Mikhail Leonidovich Burchik A/K/A Mikhail Abramov, Aleksandra Yuryevna Krylova, Anna Vladislavovna Bogacheva, Sergey Pavlovich Polozov, Maria Anatolyevna Belyaeva, Robert Sergeyevich Bovda, Dzheykhun Nasimi Ogly Aslanov A/K/A Jayhoon Aslanov A/K/A Jay Aslanov, Vadim Vladimirovich Podkopaev, Gleb Igorevich Vasilchenko, Irina Viktorovna Kaverzina, Vladimir Venkov. Case 1:18-cr-00032-DLF. Filed 02/16/18. Retrieved from: www.justice.gov/file/1035477/download

7 The Cyber Kill Chain® is widely used by the intelligence community, and can be accessed directly here if the reader would like to find out more about it: www.lockheedmartin.com/en-us/capabilities/cyber/cyber-kill-chain.html

8 Accounts available directly from Companies House records, figures taken directly from the company accounts, year end 31 May 2017, section 7 (p. 4).

9 While the view is widely taken that psychologists should not comment on the mental health of individuals whom they do not directly treat, it is nevertheless generally thought that the wide variety of videos, press calls, tweets, debates and other materials available for analysis, combined with the textbook nature of Trump's narcissistic symptoms, make classification of Trump as a sufferer of NPD relatively simple. There are many clinical psychologist/psychiatrist observations available in the public domain. /

10 One reason that charisma is so important is that without it, it makes the non-possessed an easy target. The European Union has long been a target of European populists, which is little wonder given that, amongst other details, voters feel heavily disenfranchised. In a June 2009 study, 62% of respondents did not know the dates of European elections and over half weren't interested in them! (Statistics taken from Durant, I., Cohn-Bendt, D., Hirsch, M., Schwan, G., De Waele, J., Hastings, M., … Pappas, T. (2013), *The Rise of Populism and Extremist Parties in Europe*, Brussels, European Parliament.

11 The judges were named, with large photographs, on the front page of the *Daily Mail* newspaper on 4 November 2016 . Supporting populist rhetoric is profitable; current outgoing Editor Paul Dacre warned the new editor that reversing the paper's direction of heavy support for Brexit would 'be editorial and commercial suicide' (see www.independent.co.uk/news/uk/home-news/brexit-daily-mail-paul-dacre-geordie-greig-editor-spectator-a8397401.html).

12 It subsequently emerged that this figure would have to be taxpayer-funded.

13 As long as limits on donating to individual candidates are still observed.

14 A SuperPAC is referred to officially as an 'independent-expenditure only committee' which is able to engage in unlimited spending independently of a campaign, i.e. via advertising, as long as it does not donate directly to the candidate's official campaign or political party.

15 'Take a Knee' refers to the act of protest that involves kneeling. The Movement in football began when NFP player Colin Kaepernick took a knee during the US national anthem, with his actions soon spreading across his, and other, teams.

16 Reactive testosterone (increase as a result of stimulation) as opposed to basal (base-level) testosterone, however, might be a more accurate indicator of behaviour.

17 With the exception of self-enhancing behaviour.

18 As recalled by Corey Lewandowski, reported by multiple sources, and also included in Lewandowski's memoirs.

19 Groupthink refers to a pattern of thought characterized by self-deception, forced manufacture of consent, and conformity to group values and ethics (*Merriam-Webster Dictionary*).

6

POLITICAL ANIMALS AND ANIMAL SPIRITS

Believe me: We're in a bubble right now. And the only thing that looks good is the stock market – but if you raise interest rates even a little bit, that's going to come crashing down. We are in a big, fat, ugly bubble. And we better be awfully careful.

– *Donald Trump, 1ˢᵗ US Presidential Election Debate, September 2016*

Orthodox political scientists and economists subscribe to the theory of rational expectations, where it is assumed that individuals use all information available to them in an efficient way when making political or economic decisions (e.g. Adolphs & Damasio, 2001; Baddeley, 2010, p. 281; McDermott, 2004). In this context, it seemed rational for (at-the-time) Presidential Candidate Donald Trump to heed the multitudinous warnings of high-level economic analysts and to issue a concomitant warning to the US electorate of 'a big, fat, ugly bubble'– as stated above. It was an efficient, rational warning to issue, mindful of the economic interests of the electorate.

Since winning the Presidential Election, President Trump has tweeted about the stock market more than 60 times, but none of these tweets have contained warnings. Instead, they are all remarkably ebullient and bombastic, referencing legendary and historic market gains (a classic feature of all bubbles), with no mention of a bubble. Take this January 2018 tweet, for example:

Dow goes from 18,589 on November 9, 2016, to 25,075 today, for a new all-time Record. Jumped 1000 points in last 5 weeks, Record fastest 1000-point move in history. This is all about the Make America Great Again agenda! Jobs, Jobs, Jobs. Six trillion dollars in value created![1]

This tweet was written only 4 weeks before a major market correction that saw a historic 1-day 1,000-point plunge in the Dow Jones – a correction that Fox News and other news outlets were reporting on as breaking news at the exact moment that President Trump was delivering a speech on the historic strength of the US economy. The dire warnings upon which Trump's 'big, ugly bubble' statement was based did not,[2] and have not, materially changed, but Trump's rhetoric did.

Trump's *volte face* in this example is not entirely rational and reflects instead what evolutionary science tells us so well; that higher cognition within the human brain can only take place under the guidance of a more primal, and more powerful, emotional processing system (Adolphs & Damasio, 2001) that prioritizes survival instincts completely and is 'hardwired to subserve emotion' (McDermott, 2004, p. 692). In other words, 'Whilst its importance in political science has frequently been either dismissed or ignored in favor of theories that privilege rational reasoning, emotion can provide an alternate basis for explaining and predicting political choice and actions' (McDermott, 2004, p. 691). It is an observation that has led to the emergence of the field of behavioural finance,[3] which influences heavily a taxonomy of irrational voting behaviours presented later in the chapter.

Behavioural finance tells us, for example, that when people feel happy, they are more likely to over-estimate the likelihood of positive outcomes. In this context, one can see the value in tying one's salience as a political leader to the euphoria phase of a financial market's bubble; in the immediate term, one's political success can be bolstered by tying one's political fortunes to an apparent economic boom that seems to reflect the economic brilliance of the political leader, when in fact, the ugly truth is that he has tied his fortunes to a boom-and-bust scenario that could wreak great economic ruin on a nation if left ignored and unchecked. In other words,

> Human behavior, in general, and presumably, therefore, also in the market place, is not under the constant and detailed guidance of careful and accurate hedonic calculations, but is the product of an unstable and irrational complex of reflex actions, impulses, instincts, habits, customs, fashions and mob hysteria.
>
> *(Viner, 1958, pp. 180–181)*

It is a kind of behaviour that has led to calls for references to *homo biologicus* (Zehndorfer, 2018) and *homo neurobiologicus* (Kenning & Plassmann, 2005) over the rational assumption of *homo economicus* in political and economic thought.

Reframing Politics; Reframing Rationality

What is also interesting, in the context of populist theory, is how consistent this reframing is with populist strategies. Post-election, Trump immediately reframed the threat of an epic stock market bubble as evidence of an historic and wildly successful gain – evidence of his superman status and fuel for his pathos-fuelled fire. This should not surprise anyone; politics is driven by physiology, at the end of the day, with economic rationality representing, in many ways, a balance of the hedonic concepts of pleasure and pain (Bernoulli, 1954; Hart, 1982) that direct our behaviours as political animals. The concept of issue framing and party frames is well-recognized in political science (e.g. Kinder, 2003; Slothuus & de Vreese, 2010), often discussed in the context of motivated reasoning (Mutz, 2007).

As stated by McDermott (2004), 'Emotion is intertwined with cognition in a way that requires the processes to be analyzed interdependently; emotion is, inescapably, an essential component of rationality' (p. 700). Or, in short, 'What fires together, wires together' (McDermott, 2004, p. 700). Building on Trump's earlier-quoted words, hedge fund Crescat Capital issued a stark warning of their own: 'The Trump bubble will likely prove to be the mother of all Republican presidential ebullience bubbles' (Crescat Capital, 2017, p. 1). Their research reflected a pattern of market history that is 'littered with downturns that followed new Republican presidents: Hoover (1929), Eisenhower (1953), Nixon (1969), Reagan (1981), and Bush (2001)' (Crescat Capital, 2017, p. 1).

At the time of writing (e.g. see Figure 6.1), the US stock market is displaying signals reminiscent of warnings that immediately preceded the 2008 global financial crisis. As stated by Paul Gambles, Managing Director of MBMG Group on CNBC's *Squawkbox* in Q2, 2018:

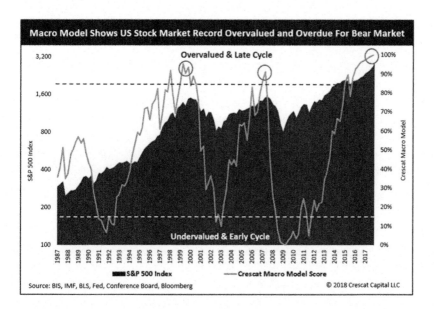

FIGURE 6.1 Macro Model Shows US Stock Market Record Overvalued and Overdue for Bear Market
Source: Crescat Capital, 2017. Permission granted by Crescat Capital.

This is quite a dangerous situation and it is creating a bubble, and that bubble has just got bigger and bigger and bigger … There isn't any doubt now (that) in valuation terms we're in epic bubble proportions, probably the biggest bubble of all time.

(quoted in Amaro, 2018, para. 3)

Gambles' words echo those of Trump's, pre-presidency, and reflect market indicators.

Rational Expectations and Charisma

Charisma scholars note that charisma is strongest during times of crisis and uncertainty (House, 1977; Rosenthal & Pittinsky, 2006; Shamir et al., 1993), meaning that the economy plays a valuable role in the rise – and fall – of a charismatic populist. The financial markets are, themselves, driven by sentiment and hubris, and as such, characterized by uncertainty (e.g. January 2018's historic 1,000-point rally, and February 2018's historic 1,000-point slump). The references to emotions in the markets – the VIX (Volatility Index, unofficially referred to as 'The Fear Index') and CNN's 'Fear and Greed Index'– reflect their emotionally-driven nature. Because money is so seductive to us (Zehndorfer, 2018) and appeals simultaneously to various lower- and higher-order needs (e.g. Maslow's Hierarchy of Needs, as discussed in Sanders, Munro & Bore, 1998), the fate of a politician can, in some circumstances, rest wholly in the hands of the markets. The greater the emotional disturbance, so charismatic theory goes, the greater will be the subsequent investment of some of this emotion in a charismatic hero (Bass, 1985; Pillai & Meindl, 1998). The same could be said of the way that we engage with our investments.

Trading these days requires the ability to navigate through the wild, heady swings of excitement and ominous warnings that accompany a market bubble, so we look for 'big men' to guide us (Zehndorfer, 2015). Turning to economic theory, Galbraith's theory of speculative bubbles requires a pervasive mood of confidence and optimism to emerge – one that leads to the building of 'a world of speculative make believe' (Galbraith, 1954/1988, p. 3, cited in Raines & Leathers, 2010, p. 541) and which necessitates 'reassurance from … the "big men" who are believed to know how to play the market' (Galbraith, 1954/1988, pp. 169–171).

The rise of populist leaders is often accompanied by specific economic indicators – relatively high levels of debt, high levels of central bank demonetization and interest rates that are near zero (e.g. Dalio et al., 2017); a weak overall economy and high income inequality. Economic gains and losses are routinely seized upon by populist leaders, although the relationship seems far more dualistic in the present era than it ever has been before. It is a duality that prompted hedge fund manager Ray Dalio to speculate that 'global populism will be an economic force more powerful than monetary and fiscal policies over the next year' (cited by Porzecanski, 2017, n.p.). These economic schisms provide the ideal conditions for populism to emerge:

> The Great Depression, beginning late in 1929 and not reaching its bottom until 1933, created extremely painful conditions that drove people to blame establishment politicians and seek answers from outside the political mainstream. Over the last 10 years, much of the developed world has seen the same dynamic – the end of the debt supercycle – play out again.
>
> *(Dalio et al., 2017, p. 6)*

Rational Expectations

The relatively recent emergence of the fields of behavioural finance and neuroscience have allowed scholars to successfully shine a light on the flaws in theories of rational expectations (e.g. Keynes, 1937; Kindleberger & Aliber, 2005; Minsky, 1975). As this book details, many other variables affect our ability to engage in economic or political decisions, which is why a varied landscape of academic fields – evolutionary theory, physiology, even meteorology – offers greatly additive and explanatory power to orthodox economic and political thought. Hedonistic theory, for example, posits that 'pleasure and pain are as much the province of logic as are harmony and discord' (Gassendi, 1972, p. 360) – and we have seen, from previous chapters, that pleasure and pain are key political drivers.

Neuroscientific advances have also enabled us to undertake 'a revision of our understanding of all human history, much – if not most – of political science, sociology, anthropology, and psychology as well as, perhaps, our understanding of what it means to be human' (Charney, 2008, p. 300, cited in Hibbing, 2013, p. 475). It is about time; economist Thorstein Veblen remarked over a century ago that 'biology should be considered a branch of economics' (Veblen, 1898).

Biology, as it turns out, might also be considered a branch of politics; just as John Maynard Keynes's 'animal spirits' (Keynes, 1936) and Aristotle's '*zoon politikon*' ('political animal' [Corning, 2017)] have a lot in common (see 'Behavioural Politics: A Taxonomy of Irrational Voting Behaviours', later in the chapter). Interestingly, the substantive implications of the rise of affective emotion in political and economic decision-making have led to a situation where 'political scientists and economists offer similar rationales' (Tingley, 2011, p. 189), noting that 'many decisions occur at an automatic level … which then have substantive different implications' for acts such as voting (Tingley, 2011, p. 189).

Primal Desires

One way in which we are guided in politics by automatic forces is via our evolutionary survival instincts. In the context of financial decisions, it is said that 'Investors are driven by two emotions – fear and greed' (CNN Money, n.d.), the primary drivers of CNN's Fear & Greed Index and the foundational philosophy of Wall Street anti-hero Gordon Gekko's worldview – that 'Greed, for want of a better word, is good'.[4]

Fear and greed reflect ancient primal instincts for survival; as noted by author Jason Zweig in his exploration of the seductive effect of money on the brain:

> Your brain developed to improve our species' odds of survival. You, like every other human, are wired to crave what looks rewarding and shun what seems risky. To counteract these impulses, your brain has only a thin veneer of modern, analytical circuits that are often no match for the power of the ancient parts of your mind.
>
> *(Zweig, 2007b, p. 104)*

It is exactly these impulses that govern our compulsive interest in narcissistic, charismatic showmen and the fast, heady culture of re-tweets and clickbait in which we now live. When it comes to political affairs, the thin veneer of modern, analytical circuits that Zweig refers to are simply no match for the primal instincts that modern populist campaigns so ably, and systematically, target.

Political Animals and Animal Spirits

The foundations of behavioural finance can be found in what former Chairman of the US Federal Reserve Bank Alan Greenspan termed 'irrational exuberance' (Greenspan, 1996, n.p.), and in what John Maynard Keynes referred to as 'animal spirits'.[5] First addressed by the Scot Charles Mackay (1841) in the seminal *Extraordinary Popular Delusions and the Madness of Crowds*, behavioural finance challenges economics orthodoxy to explain the biological foundations of irrationality. The run-up to the 2008 crisis was referred to as 'a classic delusion, a madness of crowds. We've lived through it over and over again' (Wharton University of Pennsylvania, 2008, n.p.). It is hard to hear those words and not to also feel that they hold great weight for the study of populism. As Alan Greenspan speculated, 'We will have more crises and none of them will look like this because no two crises have anything in common except human nature' (BBC News, 2009, n.p.). The same can certainly be said of politics.

Behavioural finance has been referred to as 'perhaps the most important conceptual innovation in economics over the last thirty years' (Schleifer, 2012, p. 1) and has emerged to offer scholars and investors a fascinating taxonomy of irrational behaviours (e.g. irrational exuberance, confirmation bias, euphoria, loss aversion). Behavioural finance – the study of what happens when agents fail to act rationally, fail to incorporate new information into their behaviour, and fail to make choices that are rationally consistent with maximizing expected utility (Barberis & Thaler, 2002, p. 2) – holds a great deal of transferable value to politics. This is particularly true in the context of populism (given its vastly exuberance- and emotion-led nature), and in relation to the tendency for political scientists to mirror the rational expectations of economists, and the failure of political polls to forecast what the hell is going on in any given recent election or campaign (e.g. 2016 UK Brexit Referendum, 2016 US Presidential Election, 2017 French elections, 2018 Italian elections).

Keynes warns of 'a spontaneous urge to action rather than inaction, and not as the outcome of a weighted average of quantitative benefits' (Keynes, 2007, p. 161). We saw in Chapter 5 that techniques of psychological warfare are now considered somewhat *de rigueur* in modern political campaigning, upending rational political thought to create exactly the mindset that Keynes warned against. If we turn to the CIA *Manual for Psychological Operations in Guerrilla Warfare*, we can see immediately how the invocation of animal spirits is explicitly targeted by modern campaigns:

> Guerrilla warfare is essentially a political war. Therefore, its area of operations exceeds the territorial limits of conventional warfare, to penetrate the political entity itself; the "political animal" that Aristotle defined … Once his mind has been reached, the political animal has been defeated … The target, then, is the minds of the population, all the population: our troops. The enemy troops and the civilian population.
>
> *(CIA, n.d., p. 7)*

Who knew, really, that the defeat of our minds represents the favoured goal of the modern political campaign?

Behavioural Politics: A Taxonomy of Irrational Voting Behaviours

Behavioural finance tells us that investors often deviate significantly from predicted norms (Schleifer, 2012, p. 2), a practice spurred on in no small part by the biologically seductive effect of money on an investor's brain (e.g. Zehndorfer, 2018) and via the effects of market hubris and sentiment on the primal instincts that drive us to invest. Voters, particularly in a populist context, also deviate significantly from predicted norms, a practice spurred on in no small part by the biologically seductive effect of populist political advertising campaigns on a voter's brain, and via the effects of political hubris and sentiment on the primal instincts that drive us to vote. As a result, the remainder of this chapter offers a fascinating and efficient means of categorizing political behaviours into a taxonomy of irrational, emotionally-driven behaviours. These behaviours constitute:

- Framing Effect
- Excitation-Transfer
- The Charisma/Gatekeeper Effect
- Herding
- The Winner Effect
- The Anticipatory/Challenge Effect
- Cognitive Dissonance
- Bias
- Availability Heuristic
- Churning and Overtrading.

These behaviours will now be elucidated upon separately.

The Framing Effect

The dominance of the amygdala in 'framing' ('a deviation from rational decision-making'; De Martino, Kumaran, Seymour & Dolan, 2009, p. 684) allows us to reframe data to suit our beliefs, either via wilful blindness (ignoring data that contradict our currently held position), or belief distortion (denying reality). It reflects the 'self-delusion' described by David Livingstone Smith earlier in the book: 'In evolutionary terms, this mechanism may confer a strong advantage … in modern society … such mechanisms may render human choices irrational' (De Martino et al., 2009, pp. 3–4). Framing is driven heavily by pathos, a rhetorical strategy designed to elicit emotion. Framing is likely to be far more efficient in modern campaigns given their micro-targetable nature.

A charismatic, populist politician can benefit significantly from the power of framing (also discussed in the context of The Charisma/Gatekeeper Effect [Zehndorfer, 2015; Zehndorfer, 2018] discussed later in the chapter) if he can communicate an image of dominant social status and wealth (both of which activate the brain's 'reward currency' – dopamine [Saxe & Haushofer, 2008]). Money can buy a more sophisticated social standing in the community – an alluring idea for some (Lea & Webley, 2006, p. 164), also offering 'an indicator of achievement, respect, and freedom or power' (section 4.4, in Lea & Webley, 2006, p. 179).

Excitation-Transfer

Research tells us that populist political rallies can pose a very real threat because they innervate testosterone and anger, and simultaneously direct that hostility towards an 'out-group'. The biological transfer of testosterone makes that anger and hostility potentially far stronger; 'the total group effects of testosterone may be more than the sum of the effects in all the individuals separately' (Dabbs, 2000, p. 84).

In the context of the economy, excitation-transfer (e.g. a euphoric upsurge in dopamine during a bullish market, or a mass downspike in cortisol in a bearish phase) has contributed significantly to market bubbles and crashes: 'Your dopamine system plays off my dopamine system. You buy, I buy, I worry about you, our systems become entrained' (Blakeslee, 2003, n.p.). This is the same reason why economist John Maynard Keynes reflected upon the fact that uninformed, inexperienced (mostly retail) traders could skew the markets, as their decisions would be based on sentiment – essentially excitation-transfer of emotions – rather than a rational analysis of data – and this would make the markets 'change violently as the result of a sudden fluctuation of opinion about factors that are of little importance to long-run yields' (Keynes, 1936, p. 154). The same can be said of populist-driven campaigns – the 'last-minute swing effect', for example, that can significantly impact voting decisions (e.g. Isaac & Ember, 2016), or political leaders' incitement of violence by supporters. In early 2017, for example, US federal judge David J. Hale allowed an incitement to riot, vicarious liability, and recklessness lawsuit against Donald Trump to proceed. The suit focused on the assault of two women and a teenage boy at a Trump rally in Kentucky, alleging that Trump had encouraged the assault from the podium.

The Charisma/Gatekeeper Effect

When we think about money, we experience a release of dopamine (Saxe & Haushofer, 2008). It is a response partly mediated by an 'anticipatory effect' (e.g. Zehndorfer, 2018) that we experience when we think about a desired future event, or experience. Subsequently, voting for a wealthy, socially powerful candidate can produce vicarious sensations of success or achievement for a voter (inducing testosterone release), and a seductive effect, as we daydream about wealth and luxury, and the utopian future that the populist has promised to us (releasing dopamine). Wealth and social standing can provide a valuable and – for some – irresistible indicator of achievement, respect, and freedom or power which, for many voters, represents a valuable set of traits in a political candidate. This is partly because money is our 'desire of desire' (Lea & Webley, 2006, p. 187), capable of seducing our prehistoric brain into feelings of admiration, envy or greed that may cloud subsequent judgements. These emotions can lead to our political decisions being made through a lens of a kind of 'money illusion' (Weber, Rangel, Wibral & Falk, 2009, p. 5026); if a candidate is rich, then presumably he is a better leader, or somehow worthier, than an opponent, and he becomes, in our minds, a gatekeeper to the acquisition of money, wealth and achievement for ourselves.

Herding

Evolutionary biology explains that the phenomenon of *herding* (i.e. following the crowd) reflects a survival instinct (Baddeley, 2010). Herding, or opting to run with a crowd, is something that we are hardwired to choose as a means of ensuring our own survival (the animal that gets separated from the crowd is, after all, the most vulnerable to predators). As legendary investor and CEO of the Baupost Group Seth Klarman noted, 'It is always easiest to run with the herd; at times, it can take a deep reservoir of courage and conviction to stand apart from it' (quoted in Cymbalista, 2003, p. 32).

Klarman's words ring true: when we herd, we can benefit from short-term endocrinological rewards (e.g. an uptick in oxytocin, serotonin, dopamine), but when we stand apart from the crowd, perhaps for ethical reasons, we experience a surge of stress hormones, such as cortisol: 'when people did buck the consensus, brain scans found intense firing in the amygdala. In short, you go along with the herd not because you want to, but because it hurts not to' (Zweig, 2007b, p. 109).

Klarman, alongside many other legendary investors, have made multi-billion-dollar fortunes by moving against market sentiment and basing their investing decisions on the rational analysis of data. Similarly, Michael Burry of Scion Capital, described by Forbes as an investor 'whose spellbinding all-in bet against the subprime mortgage market reaped a fortune' (Guru Focus.com, 2016, n.p.), earned his investors 489.34% in returns. Interestingly, he chose to close the firm soon after, as relentless questioning by investors, uncomfortable at moving against the crowd, even in the context of such historic returns, made him too miserable to continue.

The natural desire to herd is so strong that our limbic system rewards us when we see violators of social norms punished (de Quervain et al., 2004). This behaviour places the dominance of the emotional, primal part of our brains on full display and strengthens a populist authoritarian's grip on power as it exploits our natural tendency to follow the rules, and our fellow man; 'The mass psychological aspect of trend formation is related to herding impulses involved in the limbic system, the part of the brain that involves emotions and motivation' (Cymbalista, 2003, p. 32).

Another rationale for our deeply-evolved herding instinct is that we experience drug-like changes in human biochemistry after changes in status (Mazur & Booth, 1998) when we ascend to a new position within a social group. Conforming within that group, rather than speaking out against it, provides us with clear physiological benefits that are so pleasurable as to feel drug-like. As humans, we are designed to seek out pleasure and avoid pain, so it is unsurprising that we adhere to this behaviour as we do.

The Winner Effect

Emerging victorious from a debate or winning a campaign can lead to a 40% increase in testosterone (Carré & Putnam, 2010) for a politician *and* his base. Populists subsequently tend to frame themselves as a 'winner' (e.g. Trump's 27 November 2016 tweet that 'In addition to winning the Electoral College in a landslide, I won the popular vote if you deduct the millions of people who voted illegally'), align themselves with other 'winners' (e.g. Trump's tweet dated 27 September 2017 that read 'Spoke to Jerry Jones of the Dallas Cowboys yesterday. Jerry is a winner who knows how to get things done. Players will stand for Country!'), and label opponents as 'losers':

> The New York Times and a third-rate reporter named Maggie Haberman,[6] known as a Crooked H flunkie who I don't speak to and have nothing to do with, are going out of their way to destroy Michael Cohen and his relationship with me in the hope that he will "flip." They use ... non-existent "sources" and a drunk/drugged up loser who hates Michael, a fine person with a wonderful family.
>
> *(Trump's tweet dated 21 April 2018)*

The combative tone of Trump's tweets noted here are endocrinologically designed to fire up his base, a strategy he uses with ongoing and devastating effect.

A boost in testosterone experienced by a politician or his base reduces fear in the face of that conflict, partly as it downregulates our hypothalamic–pituitary–adrenal stress response (Hermans, Ramsey & van Honk, 2008). It offers an evolutionary benefit as it readies us quickly for a challenge ('Men who fought and hunted in dangerous primitive environments needed to focus on the task and move quickly with confidence and optimism' [Dabbs & Dabbs, 2000, pp. 42–43]) but it can be cognitively debilitating. It can, interestingly, be particularly amplifying and edifying for voters who possess high basal and reactive testosterone levels, partly because these individuals are more likely to feel drawn to symbols of power, social status and dominance (Eisenegger, Haushofer & Fehr, 2011). This brings a possible partial influence of genetics into politics in an interesting way.

The Anticipatory/Challenge Effect

This spiking of testosterone in anticipation of a challenge is also known as the 'Challenge Effect' (Eisenegger et al., 2011) or the 'challenge hypothesis' (Coates et al., 2010) – a powerful, edifying rush of steroidal hormones that makes us feel bullet-proof and ready to fight. It is the physiological basis for a decision by the Dallas Cowboys football team to employ an 'intimidation coach' (Bupp, 2016) who trains athletes in the art of intimidation. Perfecting this art pre-game can offer athletes – and politicians entering, say, an official debate – a meaningful competitive advantage.

Emmy-award winner Jane Bryant Quinn once coined the phrase 'financial porn' (Bryant Quinn, 1995) to describe a 24/7 financial news cycle, punctuated often with sensationalistic headlines and the rambunctious rhetoric of market makers. The same is now true of political news and entertainment, where the ability to intimidate, innervate, dominate, terrify, edify or encourage in a 24/7 cycle is alarmingly ever-present. When we factor in the prevalence of tech addictions, the reframing of politics as entertainment and the rousing identity of elections as almost a competitive sports event (the 'horse race coverage' of elections; Pyeongseon, 2016), we enter a scenario where the identity of a voter as a fervent cap-wearing, partisan-focused, tech-addicted, entertained individual replaces that of the objective political observer completely. To use a financial markets analogy, 'For people who trade because they like to do so, the monetary cost of trading is offset by non-pecuniary benefits from researching, executing, talking about, and anticipating the outcome of, or experiencing the outcome of a trade' (Black, 1986, p. 531). Just anticipating a win, or a hugely entertaining rally, can innervate us (e.g. Loewenstein, Weber, Hsee & Welch, 2001). Social media then allows us to disseminate our positive emotion widely, with click farms potentially replaying that emotive content to hundreds or thousands of others.

The 'neuropsychological mechanism that may underlie effective emotional appeals' (Knutson et al., 2008, p. 2) is reflected in the way in which media coverage of politics is packaged (bombastic, use of music, celebrity endorsements, stark or empowering imagery, attractive hosts, etc.), boosting our dopamine and testosterone (Apicella et al., 2008) when we engage with it.

Cognitive Dissonance

Belief perseverance, and the *sunken costs fallacy*, are associated with *loss aversion* – a desire to continue with a course of action simply because we have already invested so much in it, and because we do not want to feel as if we have wasted that investment. Both represent cognitively dissonant behaviours, with cognitive dissonance an explicitly targeted behaviour in right-wing populist campaigns. The Russian theory of reflexive control, including *dezinformatsiya* (disinformation), and the doctrinal tenets of *maskirovka*, for example (Chotikul, 1986, pp. 69–70), actively engages in facilitating cognitively dissonant behaviours (e.g. the ability to feel justified in immediately discrediting an opposing point of view or source of news as, say, 'liberal' or 'fake news' [US], or as that of a 'Remoaner' or 'Project Fear' supporter [UK]). The Soviet theory of reflexive control, particularly *maskirovka*, vigorously integrates the psychology of other disciplines, including physiology (Chotikul, 1986, p. 71).

Bias

There are many types of bias evident in politics, most clearly displayed in partisanship behaviours. Bias can be categorized into explicit sub-behaviours. *Confirmation bias*, for example, reflects a partisan voter's decision to only watch TV channels or engage with websites that support their preferred party. *Hindsight bias* leads us to over-estimate our ability to predict future events. *Self-attribution bias* reflects a common trait of narcissistic, charismatic leaders who tend to attribute all successes to themselves and all failures to others, often in the context of ignorance: 'we will consistently overrate our abilities, particularly in areas that are completely outside of our circle of competence' (Sinclair, 2013, p. 154). A *home bias* can be seen in political terms in the promotion of nationalistic sentiments.

Availability Heuristic

The tendency to make decisions based on the first piece of evidence that we come across is known as an *availability heuristic* – a clearly exploitable physiological peculiarity that can easily drive partisan voters – particularly those loyal to a particular TV station or newspaper – astray (Vis, 2017). In studies of investing, unknowledgeable, inexperienced traders are most likely to use an availability heuristic, which negatively contributes to sentiment-led investing practices: 'While calculating correct probabilities can be easy for those who know the appropriate rules of thumb and historical trends, traders who have not learned the valid shortcuts will naturally use the invalid ones' (Sinclair, 2013, p. 155). In political scenarios, a similar pattern emerges, where populist propaganda disempowers voters to lay themselves open to a less knowledgeable view of world affairs which heightens the populists' sway over their political choices (e.g. Brennan, 2016).

Churning and Overtrading

It has been said that the 'high trading volume on organized exchanges is perhaps the single most embarrassing fact to the standard finance paradigm' (De Bondt & Thaler, 1995, p. 392). Overtrading can be attributed to many competing and complementary factors, such as one's motivations to trade (e.g. trading as a form of gambling, or for the perceived social cachet of becoming a 'day trader'). It is certainly endocrinological – a successful streak of trades can lead to increased risk-taking and loss-making subsequent behaviours, for example. It can also be a part of the profit-taking phase of a market cycle (Minsky's Credit Cycle; see Chapter 5) where heavy churning represents an informed insider's motivation to extract optimal benefit from the dying embers of a bubble before an impending and inevitable crash. Without doubt, it contributes to market fragility. In political terms, we can apply this analogously and immediately to the Life Cycle of Charismatic Populism (Chapter 5) where 'churning' is immediately observable in the context of a high social media posting and re-sharing volume of propagandist and politically-oriented materials (by bots, click farms and humans).

Political Animals and Animal Spirits: From Boom to Bust

Mapping physiological and endocrinological variables onto a 'boom-and-bust' diagram allows us to draw direct analogies and comparisons between the earlier taxonomized behaviours in the context of political and financial scenarios (Figure 6.2). Political animals and animal spirits clearly engage with the same

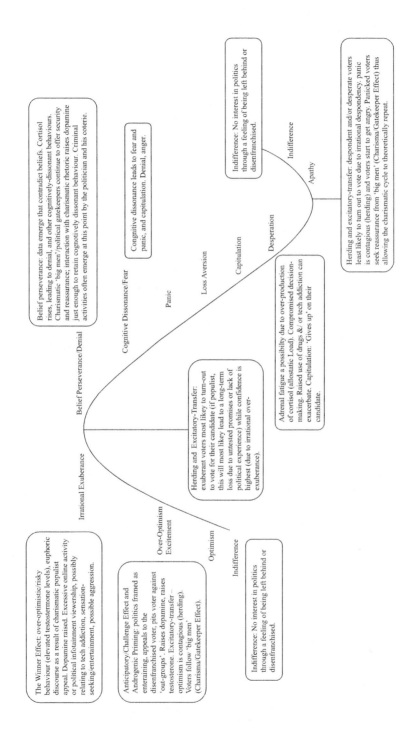

The Winner Effect: over-optimistic/risky behaviour (elevated testosterone levels), euphoric discourse as a result of charismatic populist appeal. Dopamine raised. Excessive online activity or political infotainment viewership, possibly relating to tech addiction, sensation-seeking/entertainment, possible aggression.

Anticipatory/Challenge Effect and Androgenic Priming: politics framed as entertaining, appeals to the disenfranchised voter, pits voter against 'out-groups'. Raises dopamine, raises testosterone. Excitatory-transfer – optimism is contagious (herding). Voters follow 'big men' (Charisma/Gatekeeper Effect).

Indifference: No interest in politics through a feeling of being left behind or disenfranchised.

Herding and Excitatory-Transfer: exuberant voters most likey to turn-out to vote for their candidate (if populist, this will most likely lead to a long-term loss due to untested promises or lack of political experience) while confidence is highest (due to irrational over-exuberance).

Adrenal fatigue a possibility due to over-production of cortisol (allostatic Load). Compromised decision making. Raised use of drugs &/ or tech addiction can exacerbate. Capitulation: 'Gives up' on their candidate.

Congnitive dissonance leads to fear and panic, and capitulation. Denial, anger.

Belief perseverance: data emerge that contradict beliefs. Cortisol rises, leading to denial, and other cognitively-dissonant behaviours. Charismatic 'big men'/political gatekeepers continue to offer security and reassurance; interaction with charismatic rhetoric raises dopamine just enough to retain cognitively dissonant behaviour. Criminal activities often emerge at this point by the politician and his coterie.

Indifference: No interest in politics through a feeling of being left behind or disenfranchised.

Herding and excitatory-transfer: despondent and/or desperate voters least likely to turn out to vote due to irrational despondency: panic is contagious (herding) and voters start to get angry. Panicked voters seek reassurance from 'big men' (Charisma/Gatekeeper Effect) thus allowing the charismatic cycle to theoretically repeat.

Indifference

Optimism

Over-Optimism
Excitement

Irrational Exuberance

Belief Perseverance/Denial

Cognitive Dissonance/Fear

Panic

Loss Aversion

Capitulation

Desperation

Apathy

Indifference

FIGURE 6.2 Political Animals and Animal Spirits

animus, simply because physiology and evolutionary factors remain such a defining and foundational driver of economic and political behaviour.

Riding the Wave ... Until the Crash

So where do the many theorizations and observations in this book leave us?

The powerful effects of biology and evolution on our ability to engage in modern politics cannot be ignored; that, we can state with certainty. Evolutionary science informs us that *homo sapiens* first appeared around 5 to 7 million years ago, and it might amaze some readers to discover that we may have developed the capacity for the sophisticated cognitive thought that we recognize as part of the human condition as little as 40,000 years ago (Wayman, 2012)[7] (in other words, for only 0.57% of our entire existence as a species).

Evolutionary science informs us that we were designed to live in small communities, where a mix of liberally-minded and conservatively pathogen-cautious individuals enjoyed a mutual bond – all informed by diverse genetic drivers, motivations and values – that strengthened the communities in which they lived. However, a sense of emotional amoral egoism – that is, the malleability of man's ethics and morals seen from a neuro-philosophical angle – shines a light on how easily manipulated our morals and ethics really can be (Al-Rodhan, 2015).

Populist authoritarian politics seeks to target these neuro-philosophical, physiological and evolutionary variables explicitly, systematically and relentlessly (e.g. Chotikul, 1986). An opioid epidemic and the over-prescription of drugs – including medications as seemingly innocuous as Calpol (e.g. Mischkowski et al., 2016) – disrupt our neural ability to empathize, rendering the right-wing populists' anti-immigrant, dehumanizing right-wing appeals more effective.

Politicians themselves can become more corrupt and extreme because of the power of dopamine in creating an addiction to power itself:

> Power, especially absolute and unchecked power, is intoxicating. Its effects occur at the cellular and neurochemical level. They are manifested behaviorally in a variety of ways, ranging from heightened cognitive functions to lack of inhibition, poor judgment, extreme narcissism, perverted behavior, and gruesome cruelty.
>
> *(Al-Rodhan, 2014, n.p.)*

Allowing heavily populist-driven, divisive campaigns, driven by sophisticated technological methods, to remain in the hands of such a leader represents an egregiously dangerous and ultimately reckless act.

Ultimately, the heavily monetizable and clientelism-enabling qualities of a right-wing, populist agenda make it a financial force to be reckoned with. In evolutionary terms, it is designed to sophisticatedly target evolutionary survival instincts in a way that standard democratic appeals have yet to match.

In 2016, a collision of Russian and Western psychological warfare techniques, sophisticated micro-targeting and social media sites with a multi-billion reach exposed voters to the kind of populist propaganda that the world has, until now, never seen, or experienced. Considering these factors alongside the evolutionary and physiological variables detailed in this book, it is clear to see that the populist wave currently sweeping across Europe, Africa and North America is just getting started.

Taming the Political Animal

A final question to answer is 'What can be done to tame the political animal?'. This book concludes with approaches that we can take to empower ourselves in the fight against the dangers of populism, whilst seeking simultaneously (from a physiological and evolutionary perspective) to strengthen and safeguard the appeal and power of democracy.

- *Recognize that Populism Is a Strategy, Not an Ideology:* Cambridge Analytica whistleblower and former Head of Research for the firm, Chris Wylie, claims that Cambridge Analytica had devised the slogans 'drain the swamp' and 'deep state' as early as 2014, boasting that they had crafted every part of the Trump campaign (CNN, 2018). These slogans betray the use of right-wing populism as a strategy, not an ideology, yet the campaigns still benefit from the romantic, emotive identity of an ideology that lets people fight for a cause, join a revolution, or emotionally connect with a charismatic personality.

Evolutionary science tells us that negative affect clickbait drives online revenues fastest. Bathed in pathos and propaganda, a failure by successive governments to subsume political advertising under the auspices of advertising regulatory bodies has allowed this kind of populist-focused strategy to flourish unchecked. Subsequently, one way that populism can be countered is via campaigning for legislation that would require political advertising to fall under the jurisdiction of regulatory bodies such as the UK's Advertising Standards Authority (ASA). The passing of legislation that would fine technology firms which fail to remove propagandist political materials as quickly as possible (such as the €50 million fine proposed by German politician Heiko Maas) would offer further protection.

- *Education: A Powerful Weapon Against Populism:* Manipulation is least powerful when we are aware that we are aware of it (e.g. Doyen, Klein, Pichon & Cleeremans, 2012). Establishing public or privately-funded educational programmes for school- and college-aged children, and adults, would subsequently enable an electorate to become far more informed about the political process and undermine the power of the populist voice.

The power of populist campaigns would be considerably weakened if its standard, formulaic approaches (pathos, charisma, 'us-versus-them' rhetoric, and so on) are made explicit, as illustrated in Chapter 5. Knowledge of how modern-era politicians rely on psychological warfare techniques to target us at an evolutionary and endocrinological level is likely, for example, to surprise a large swathe of voters. The dangers associated with heightened levels of PTSD (Post-Traumatic Stress Disorder), radicalization and tech addiction that appear to contribute to, or accompany, the execution of aggressive right-wing populist campaigns, are cause for considerable concern that should be addressed. Evolutionary science alone offers fascinating insights; our hunter-gatherer ancestors were designed to live in small communities of around 150 people, for example, where a mix of conservatively- and democratically-oriented minds would have greatly strengthened their collective chances for survival. Modern right-wing populism has essentially bastardized this genetic differential to divide and weaken. Education surrounding the predictable nature of profit taking in populist cycles is illuminating; presenting these facts offers a non-partisan reflection on what makes us human, and a realization that evolutionarily, we really are designed to be stronger together.

Finally, parents need to be conscious of the role of an immature prefrontal cortex in the juvenile brain in making their children potentially far more vulnerable to radicalizing, anxiety-inducing and addictive content.

- *Charisma Is Not Demagoguery:* Traditionally, US Democrats have viewed charisma as a form of demagoguery; evolutionary science tells us, however, that it simply represents a necessity of our biological design. Our primal brains process data emotionally, so charisma offers a valuable, perhaps necessary, conduit, for the communication of more complex political data that might otherwise feel like a chore to engage with. Charisma is amoral, so can be used to achieve hugely socially transformative outcomes; it benefits greatly from *ethos* and *logos* as well as *pathos*, and emanates hugely from a passionate, honest voice.

Twenty-eight-year-old Latina Democratic Socialist Alexandria Ocasio-Cortez offers a great recent example, storming to victory in New York's 14th Congressional District in June 2018, ousting a 10-term incumbent Democrat. Her victory was not only a victory for change, but for a need for passionate ethos-driven politics, a voice of charismatic, passionate resistance, and a voice for the frustrations of many disillusioned by a kind of perceived ideological inertia. It is this inertia that hands the populist easy power, reinforcing the idea of democracy as a system for entrenched elites.

Political scientist Cas Mudde points to anxiety around terrorism and immigration as factors that contributed to the 'perfect storm' of populism that we are now experiencing – a situation that 'favor[s] populists more than at any time since the end of World War II' (Mudde, 2016, p. 25) and which profits from weaknesses in democratic governance; 'The success of extremists often points to weaknesses and oversights by the political majority culture' (Backes, 2010, p. 192).We can see these weaknesses and oversights arising in Prime Minister Theresa May's insistence on a 'Hard Brexit', for example; by June 2018, 2 years after the original populist-driven Referendum, a majority of UK voters (53%) wished to remain in the European Union (Nell & Lees, 2018), with an estimated 100,000 people marching in the anti-Brexit 'People's March' demonstration in London on 23 June 2018, a number that had swollen to over 700,000 in a subsequent November 2018 demonstration. Neither appeared to affect the Prime Minister's strategy, bolstering the image of a democratic state as elitist and non-representative. This reflects a common pattern where a populist appeal, initially spiking in support, wanes as emotions fade and the impracticable nature of the proposition begins to emerge.

- *Recognize Politics as a Form of Hedonism:* In former times, economics theory freely acknowledged the role of hedonic theory – the centrality of pleasure and pain – as key influencers of utility analysis (Hart, 1982). To discard the role of pleasure and pain and other emotions – and, by extension, the fundamental role of the endocrinological, evolutionary and biological factors in current models of expected utility theory (and wider economic and political thought) – is to 'betray their intellectual foundations' (McDermott, 2004, p. 699).

There remains much evidence to support the notion that our compulsive wish to satisfy our short-term hedonic needs dictates much of our daily lives and choices (including our political behaviours), reflecting Keynes's conceptualization of 'animal spirits' as a recognition of man's irrationality (Keynes, 1936). The pages of this book have detailed a shift in political behaviour from politics-as-rational-engagement to politics-as-entertainment, where the charisma-imbued, pathos-fuelled, sports-framed horse race of the modern election cycle renders previous arguments of rationality redundant. If voters are made aware of the centrality of hedonism in political appeals, they can also be made aware that there is a responsibility that comes with engaging with it. From a physiological perspective, for example, the right-wing histrionics that ultimately led to a policy of forced removal of babies and toddlers from their parents into government-run 'tender age' facilities carried very real, and devastating, consequences. As detailed in a report by Dr Colleen Kraft, President of the American Academy of Pediatrics (Keneally, 2018), a forced removal of a baby or toddler from its parent at a critical developmental age can cause a potentially dangerous and damaging spike in stress hormones, resulting in negative consequences including possible brain damage.

Embracing this shift seems critical in tipping the scales from 'entertaining populist versus sober democratism' to a more fluid style of political interactions that enable voters to engage positively in democratic debates in a way that carries meaning, and intuitive appeal, to them. A failure to do so allows right-wing populists to continue to pick the lowest-hanging fruit, targeting evolutionary, primal instincts to divide and conquer.

- *Fighting Populism Requires a Contrarian View:* Bestselling finance author Michael Lewis noted of the 2008 financial crisis that

    It is ludicrous to believe that asset bubbles can only be recognised in hindsight. There are specific identifiers that are entirely recognisable during the bubble's inflation. One hallmark of mania is the rapid rise in the incidence and complexity of fraud ... The FBI reports mortgage-related fraud is up fivefold since 2000.

    (Lewis, 2011, p. 55)

    The same can be said of populism (including the mania, and rapid rise in the incidence and complexity of fraud).

The most successful investors – President and Founder of Kynikos Associates Jim Chanos, legendary investor and founder of Open Society Foundations George Soros, and Scion Capital CEO Michael Burry – are those who remain immune to the emotional contagion and irrationality so characteristic of the speculative investor (Zehndorfer, 2015). Similarly, for a voter, remaining immune to the emotional contagion and irrationality so characteristic of populism is tough, but can be done; disengaging from social media, for example, reduces one's exposure to distressing content and therefore to the anxiety, stress and depression that might prevent a voter from engaging in subsequent acts of resistance (Tenhouten, 2016). To paraphrase South African activist and father of Black Consciousness Steve Biko, the most potent weapon in the hands of the oppressor is the mind of the oppressed – and the fearless dominance and rejection of human rights so characteristic of the populist authoritarian regime seek to develop exactly that state of helpless oppression. To remain optimistic, to continue to engage in social and political activism and to always cast one's vote consequently constitute meaningful ongoing acts of rejection and resistance.

Disengaging from market sentiment carries many benefits. If the US mainstream media had not focused so heavily on sensationalistic, hubris-driven election coverage in 2016, the outcome of the Trump–Clinton contest might have been different. President Trump benefited from an estimated $2 billion in free media coverage during his 2016 Presidential Campaign, as multiple media outlets carried story after story of his (strategically) outlandish statements and actions (Confessore & Yourish, 2016) – undoubtedly a powerful driver in his ascension to the White House.

Whilst the free press now carries a responsibility to challenge propagandist content, regular voters can also fight populist strategies in several ways. By refusing to engage in online vitriol and remaining calm, by remaining polite and respectful in online exchanges, and by disengaging with social media altogether, individuals can gently counter a populist discourse that encourages hate, further polarizes, and stunts interactions. Achieving a modicum of respect, congeniality and conversation between ideologues offers a powerful means of fighting the stereotypes that facilitate and normalize abusive behaviours and the dehumanization of ethnic groups (e.g. the normalization of separating immigrant parents from children). Consensus is the best weapon against populism in that it brings people together and makes it much harder to subsequently believe divisive rhetoric.

Summary

We live in a hyper-competitive age, where the need to compete has transcended every area of life. Instagram filters offer a means of reframing our realities to appear richer, more popular, happier or more attractive than we really are. Brokers and financial advertisements offer great riches via the trading of FOREX (foreign exchange) and ETFs (exchange-traded funds) that in most cases are far removed from the truth.

The diet industry has exploded in recent years, and is now worth over $586.3 billion globally (Markets & Markets, 2009), yet we are all getting fatter (recent figures estimate a 40% obesity rate in the United States) (Lenihann, 2018). Students face greater exam and testing pressures than ever before, with the added pressure of graduating in excessive debt (American students currently owe around $1.48 trillion in debt, according to Student Loan Hero [2018]). The ETF industry is worth almost $5 trillion (Trefis Team, Great Speculations, 2018), with ETFs offering low transaction costs to retail investors and potentially significant cost-benefits, yet ETF-inclusive portfolios under-perform the markets by 2.8% because of overtrading and other ineffective, largely uninformed trading strategies (Zehndorfer, 2015; Zehndorfer, 2018).

The self-help industry has also demonstrated an explosion in growth in recent years, and is now worth $11 billion in the United States alone (Marketdata Enterprises, 2017), yet we have never needed more help; perfectionism is on the rise, with levels of anxiety, stress and depression higher than ever recorded (Curran & Hill, 2018). It is not surprising that today's cultural norm breeds an unhealthy competitiveness within society that can lead to mental health issues (Hendrickse, Arpan, Clayton & Ridgway, 2017). Psychiatrist and high-performance expert Steven Eikelberg notes that 'We define the American dream as people pulling themselves up by their bootstraps, but how many people do we walk over to be successful? When is this kind of competition admirable, and when is it pathological?' (quoted in Szegedy-Maszak, 2005, n.p.). Politics *has* become pathological when it emerges in a right-wing populist form, and it is a process that has been enabled by the explicit targeting of the evolutionary, primal instincts that make us who we are.

Throughout the pages of this book, we have traversed the nature of pathos-fuelled, right-wing populist advertising campaigns that so brilliantly exploit our hedonistic instincts, and reframe politics into the profitable 24/7 infotainment juggernaut that it has now become. Fox News Network, LLC remains a quintessential engager of this brave new world, expertly blending entertainment and news; the network's highest-rated chat show host, Sean Hannity, freely describes his show as a talk show, not a news vehicle ('I'm not a journalist jackass I'm a talk show host': tweet on 25 October [Hannity, 2016]), and trusts viewers to know when a show is simply entertainment. Concerned observers do not share his confidence (Farhi, 2017).

The monetizable nature of politics-as-entertainment is profound and we have detailed the effect of a removal of caps on campaign spending;[8] political advertising TV spend alone exceeded $4 billion during the US 2016 Presidential Campaign (Kurtzleben, 2015). Similarly, we have profiled the nature of right-wing, negative-affect populist appeals as a uniquely profitable strategy executed principally by political consultants and Russian interferers, questioning whether populism itself, as used in the current era, can make any claims to ideology at all. The fact that MSNBC, CNN and Fox News all reported jumps in advertising revenue in 2016 of 62%, 32% and 17%, respectively, provides just a small window onto the intensely profit-driven nature of politics today. In a dystopian twist on modern political reality, it is to entertainment-driven politically-focused chat shows – *Fox & Friends*, for example – that the President of the most powerful nation in the Western world now turns regularly for advice (Borchers, 2018).

We have considered the natural elements that shape our political decisions, from lunar cycles to geomagnetic storms – and tracked the endocrinological rise and fall of charismatic populism, discovering along the way, why populism is always so formulaic and cyclical in nature. The alarming amplifying effects of opioid use and tech addiction have been extensively profiled, with the book concluding with a useful means of categorizing irrational voting behaviours into an instructive taxonomy, and in the identification of effective interventions that will help us to fight the dangers of populism as we see them. Theory comes alive when it is applicable and applied, directly, to the current political events of today, and when it provides great emancipatory potential for any reader who engages with it. The need for informative theory is great, as a result, in the context of the alarming spike in authoritarian populism within which we now find ourselves. As European Council President Donald Tusk warns, 'The stakes are very high. And time is short' (Tusk, 2018).

The *raison d'être* of this book, ultimately, was to shed a new and informed light on the role of the incredibly elucidating fields of neuroscience, evolutionary biology, physiology, behavioural finance, political science and even meteorology in shaping our understanding of the new populist-driven, political landscape in which we now find ourselves. As philosopher George Wilhelm Friedrich Hegel (1975) once opined, 'The only thing we learn from history is that we learn nothing from history'. But maybe, just maybe, we can buck that trend if we succeed –for the first time – in truly appreciating the evolutionary and primal instincts that have made us the political animals that we find ourselves to be today.

Notes

1 Comments made on Twitter in a tweet dated 5 January 2018 via the @realDonald-Trump account.
2 With the exception of a pro-cyclical tax reform which supported earnings in the short term at the end of an already extended business cycle.
3 *Behavioural finance* sheds light on cognitive and emotional drivers of financial decision-making that can lead us to be irrational, and often includes studies of neurological or physiological drivers, such as testosterone or cortisol levels.
4 As quoted in the film *Wall Street* (1997), directed by Oliver Stone, 20th Century Fox.
5 A term created by economist John Maynard Keynes in his seminal 1936 work *The General Theory of Employment, Interest and Money*. New York: Harcourt, Brace and Company.
6 Maggie Haberman is a White House correspondent who joined *The Times* in 2015 and was part of a team that won a Pulitzer Prize in 2018 for reporting on Donald Trump's advisers and their connections to Russia.
7 Richard Klein, a palaeoanthropologist at Stanford University, suggested that a genetic mutation occurred 40,000 years ago, which caused a sudden revolution in the way that people thought and behaved. As stated in Wayman, 2012.
8 According to a Frontline Report, 'The decision leaves in place the $2,600 cap that an individual can give to any single candidate for Congress or the presidency. Yet even with that cap, individuals will now be free to spend as much as $3.7 million per election cycle, according to an estimate from the Center for Responsive Politics, up from the previous limit of $123,200'. Retrieved from: www.pbs.org/wgbh/frontline/article/supreme-court-strikes-down-limits-on-campaign-spending/

BIBLIOGRAPHY

Achen, C.H., & Bartels, L.M. (2016). *Democracy for Realists: Why Elections Do Not Produce Responsible Government*. Princeton, NJ: Princeton University Press.

Adams, R., & Bengtsson, H. (2017, 19 October). Oxford Accused of 'Social Apartheid' as Colleges Admit No Black Students. *The Guardian*. Retrieved from: www.theguardian.com/education/2017/oct/19/oxford-accused-of-social-apartheid-as-colleges-admit-no-black-students

Addiction Resource. (n.d.). Is There a Vaping Addiction and What Are the Dangers of Vaping? Addiction Resource. Retrieved from: https://addictionresource.com/addiction/vaping-addiction/

Adolphs, R., & Damasio, A. (2001). The Interaction of Affect and Cognition: A Neurobiological Perspective. In ForgasJ.P. (Ed.), *Handbook of Affect and Social Cognition* (pp. 27–49). Mahwah, NJ: Lawrence Erlbaum Associates, Inc.

Ahn, W.Y., Kishida, K.T., Gu, X., Lohrenz, T., Harvey, A., Alford, J.R... Montague, P. R. (2014). Non-Political Images Evoke Neural Predictors of Political Ideology. *Current Biology*, 24, 22, 2693–2699.

Ainslie, G. (1975). Specious Reward: A Behavioral Theory of Impulsiveness and Impulse Control. *Psychological Bulletin*, 82, 4, 463–495.

Aktas, N., de Bodt, E., Bollaert, H., & Roll, R. (2011). CEO Narcissism and the Takeover Process: From Private Initiation to Deal Completion. Retrieved from http://efa2011.efa-online.org/fisher.osu.edu/blogs/efa2011/files/BEH_2_3.pdf

Alford, H. (2015, November). Is Donald Trump Actually a Narcissist? Therapists Weigh In! *Vanity Fair*. Accessed at: www.vanityfair.com/news/2015/11/donald-trump-narcissism-therapists

Alford, J.R., Funk, C.L., & Hibbing, J.R. (2005). The Source of Political Attitudes: Assessing Genetic and Environmental Contributions. Paper presented at the Annual Meeting of the American Political Science Association, Chicago, September 2015.

Alford, J.R., & Hibbing, J.R. (2004). The Origin of Politics: An Evolutionary Theory of Political Behavior. *Perspectives on Politics*, 2, 4, 707–723.

Al-Rodhan, N. (2015, 18 February). Who Are We: Neurochemical Man and Emotional Amoral Man. OXPOL, the Oxford University Politics Blog. Retrieved from: https://blog.politics.ox.ac.uk/neurochemical-man-emotional-amoral-egoism/

Al-Rodhan, N. (2014, 27 February). The Neurochemistry of Power: Implications for Political Change. OXPOL, the Oxford University Politics Blog. Retrieved from: https://blog.politics.ox.ac.uk/neurochemistry-power-implications-political-change/

Altman, A., & Dias, D. (2014). This Baptist Charity Is Being Paid Hundreds of Millions to Shelter Child Migrants. *Time*. Retrieved from: http://time.com/3066459/unaccompanied-minor-immigration-border/

Amaro, S. (2018, April). 'Epic' Market Bubble Is Ready to Burst and Stocks Could Plunge, Strategist Warns. CNBC. Retrieved from: www.cnbc.com/2018/04/05/market-bubble-ready-to-burst-and-stocks-could-plunge-strategist-warns.html

American Psychiatric Association 1994 *Diagnostic and Statistical Manual of Mental Disorders* (4th ed.). Washington, DC: APA.

Amodio, D.M., Jost, J.T., Master, S.L., & Yee, C.M. (2007). Neurocognitive Correlates of Liberalism and Conservatism. *Nature Neuroscience*, 10, 1246–1247.

Anderson, A. (2008). Is Online Trading Gambling with Peanuts? SIFR Research Report Series 62. Retrieved from: https://ideas.repec.org/p/hhs/sifrwp/0062.html

Annenberg Public Policy Center. (2014). Stephen Colbert's Civics Lesson: Or, How a TV Humorist Taught America about Campaign Finance. Retrieved from: www.annenbergpublicpolicycenter.org/stephen-colberts-civics-lesson-or-how-a-tv-humorist-taught-america-about-campaign-finance/

Antonakis, J., & Dalgas, O. (2009). Predicting Elections: Child's Play! *Science*, 323, 5918, 1183.

Apicella, C.L., Dreber, A., Campbell, B., Gray, P.B., Hoffman, M., & Little, A.C. (2008). Testosterone and Financial Risk Preferences. *Evolution and Human Behavior*, 29, 6, 384–390.

Archer, J. (2006). Testosterone and Human Aggression: An Evaluation of the Challenge Hypothesis. *Neuroscience and Behavioral Reviews*, 30, 319–345.

Aristotle. (1996). *The Politics*. S. Everson (Ed.). Cambridge Texts in the History of Political Thought. Cambridge: Cambridge University Press. (Originally published in the 4th century BC.)

Ashbee, E. (2011). Bewitched: The Tea Party Movement. Ideas, Interests, and Institutions. *Political Quarterly*, 82, 157–164.

Association for Computational Linguistics. (2014). Robert L. Mercer Receives the ACL Lifetime Achievement Award. Association for Computational Linguistics. Retrieved from: www.aclweb.org/portal/node/2502

Atkinson, E. (2017, 24 January). Trump Has Been Great for the Cable News Business. *New York Post*. Retrieved from: https://nypost.com/2017/01/24/trump-is-good-for-the-cable-news-business/

Audebrand, L.K. (2010). Sustainability in Strategic Management Education: The Quest for New Root Metaphors. *Academy of Management Learning & Education*, 9, 413–428.

Auflick, T. (2016, 4 April). How Trump's High Level of Emotion Attracts and Repels Followers Simultaneously. LinkedIn. Retrieved from: www.linkedin.com/pulse/how-trumps-high-level-emotion-attracts-repels-auflick-ma-lmhca/

Back, M.D., Schmukle, D., & Egloff, B. (2010). Why Are Narcissists So Charming at First Sight? Decoding the Narcissism-Popularity Link at Zero Acquaintance. *Journal of Personality and Social Psychology*, 98, 132–145.

Backes, U. (2010). *Political Extremes: A Conceptual History from Antiquity to the Present*. Abingdon, UK: Routledge.

Bacon, F. (2014). *Novum Organum, Or True Suggestions for the Interpretation of Nature.* Ed. Joseph Duvey. The Project Gutenberg E-book. Retrieved from: www.gutenberg.org/files/45988/45988-h/45988-h.htm

Baddeley, M. (2010, 27 January). Herding, Social Influence and Economic Decision-Making: Socio-Psychological and Neuroscientific Analyses. *Philosophical Transactions of the Royal Society B: Biological Sciences,* 365, 1538, 281–290.

Ballew, C.C., & Todorov, A. (2007). Predicting Political Elections from Rapid and Unreflective Face Judgements. *Proceedings of the National Academy of Sciences,* 104, 46, 17948–17953.

Ballmaier, M., Toga, A.W., Blanton, R.E., Sowell, E.R., Lavretsky, H., Peterson, J., … KumarA. (2004). Anterior Cingulate, Gyrus Rectus, and Orbitofrontal Abnormalities in Elderly Depressed Patients: An MRI-Based Parcellation of the Prefrontal Cortex. *American Journal of Psychiatry,* 161, 99–108.

Balzer, A., & Jacobs, C.M. (2011). Gender and Physiological Effects in Connecting Disgust to Political Preferences. *Social Science Quarterly,* 92, 5, 1297–1313.

Barberis, N., & Thaler, R. (2002). A Survey of Behavioral Finance. Working Paper No. 9222. National Bureau of Economic Research., Cambridge, MA.

Barbuto, J.E. (2000). Influence Triggers: A Framework for Understanding Follower Compliance. *The Leadership Quarterly,* 11, 365–387.

Bargh, J.A., & Chartrand, T.L. (1999). The Unbearable Automaticity of Being. *American Psychologist,* 54, 462–479.

Bass, B.M. (1985). *Leadership and Performance Beyond Expectations.* New York: Free Press.

Bass, B.M., & Steidlmeyer, P. (1999). Ethics, Character and Authentic Transformational Leadership Behavior. *The Leadership Quarterly,* 10, 181–217.

Bassi, A. (2013). Weather, Mood, and Voting: An Experimental Analysis of the Effect of Weather Beyond Turnout. Retrieved from: www.unc.edu/~abassi/Research/weather-mood-voting.pdf

Batley, R. (2017, 5 May). From Populism to Authoritarianism. *Financial Times.* Retrieved from: www.ft.com/content/2a774346-2f4e-11e7-9555-23ef563ecf9a

BaynesC., & Mortimer, C. (2018, February). Brexit: Huge Economic Cost of Leaving EU Outlined in Government Study as May Insists She Has 'No Doubts'. *The Independent.* Retrieved from: www.independent.co.uk/news/uk/politics/brexit-latest-leaked-impact-assessment-economy-gdp-north-east-west-midlands-a8199746.html

BBC News. (2009, 8 September). Market Crisis 'Will Happen Again'. Retrieved from: http://news.bbc.co.uk/2/hi/business/8244600.stm

Beck, J.W., Carr, A.E., & Walmsley, P.T. (2012). What Have You Done for Me Lately? Charisma Attenuates the Decline in US Presidential Approval Over Time. *The Leadership Quarterly,* 23, 934–942.

Belisheva, N.K., Popov, A.N., Petukhova, N.V., Pavlova, K.S., Osipov, K.S., Tkachenko, S.E., & Baranova, T.I. (1995). Qualitative and Quantitative Evaluation of the Effect of Geomagnetic Field Variations on the Functional State of the Human Brain. *Biophysics,* 40, 5, 1007–1014.

Bell, R., Plumb, N., & Marangozov, R. (2018). Integration Not Demonisation. All-Party Parliamentary Group on Social Integration. Accessible at: https://socialintegrationappg.org.uk/reports/

Bénabou, R. (2013). Groupthink: Collective Delusions in Organizations and Markets. *The Review of Economic Studies,* 80, 2, 429–462.

Benoit, J. (2018, 7 January). iPhones and Children Are a Toxic Pair, Say Two Big Apple Investors. *The Wall Street Journal*. Retrieved from: www.wsj.com/articles/iphones-a nd-children-are-a-toxic-pair-say-two-big-apple-investors-1515358834

Bentham, J. (1823). *An Introduction to the Principles of Morals and Legislation*, vol. 1. Oxford: Clarendon Press.

Bentz, B., & Seavy-Nesper, M. (2018, 18 January). A Former Neo-Nazi Explains Why Hate Drew Him In: And How He Got Out. *Fresh Air*. Retrieved from: www.npr.org/ 2018/01/18/578745514/a-former-neo-nazi-explains-why-hate-drew-him-in-a nd-how-he-got-out

Benz, R. J. (2017). Race Delusion: Lies that Divide Us. Huffington Post. Retrieved from: www.huffingtonpost.com/robert-j-benz/race-illusion-its-all-in-_b_10095430.html

Berenson, T. (2016). 15-Year-Old Girl Assaulted at Donald Trump Rally, Police Say. *Time* online. Retrieved from: http://time.com/4276221/donald-trump-wisconsin-p rotest-pepper-spray/

Berger, J., Meredith, M., & Wheeler, S.C. (2008). Contextual Priming: Where People Vote Affects How They Vote. *Proceedings of the National Academy of Sciences*, 105, 26, 8846–8849. Bernhardt, P.C., Dabbs, J.M., Jr., Fielden, J. A., & Lutter, C.D. (1998). Testosterone Changes During Vicarious Experiences of Winning and Losing Among Fans at Sporting Events. *Physiology & Behavior*, 65, 1, 59–62.

Bernoulli, D. (1954). Exposition of a New Theory on the Measurement of Risk. *Econometrica*, 22, 1, 23–36.

Bierce, A. (1911). *The Devil's Dictionary*. *The Collected Works of Ambrose Bierce*, vol. 7. Neale Publishing Company.

Bilton, N. (2014, 10 September). Steve Jobs Was a Low-Tech Parent. *The New York Times*. Retrieved from: www.nytimes.com/2014/09/11/fashion/steve-jobs-apple-was-a -low-tech-parent.html

Black, D.W. (1986). Compulsive Buying: A Review. *Journal of Clinical Psychiatry*, 57, 50–55.

Black Hat. (2017, 4–7 December). Enraptured Minds: Strategic Gaming of Cognitive Mindhacks. Black Hat Europe 2017 presentation, Excel Centre, London, UK.

Blakeslee, S. (2003, 17 June). Brain Experts Now Follow the Money. *The New York Times*. Retrieved from: www.nytimes.com/2003/06/17/science/brain-experts-now- follow-the-money.html

Blank, J.M., & Shaw, D. (2015). Does Partisanship Shape Attitudes toward Science and Public Policy? The Case for Ideology and Religion. *The Annals of the American Academy of Political and Social Science*, 658, 1, 18–35.

Blank, R. (2011). Brain Sciences and Politics: Some Linkages. In A. Somit& S.A. Peterson (Eds.), *Biology and Politics: The Cutting Edge*. Research in Biopolitics, 9, 205–229. Bingley, UK: Emerald Group Publishing Ltd.

Blank, R., & Hines, S. (2001). *Biology and Political Science*. London: Routledge.

Blank, R.H. (2014). *Politics and Life Sciences: The State of the Discipline*. Bingley, UK: Emerald Group Publishing.

Blasco, N., Corredor, P., & Ferreruela, S. (2012). Market Sentiment: A Key Factor of Investors' Imitative Behavior. *Accounting & Finance*, 52, 663–689.

Bligh, M.C., Kohles, J.C., & Meindl, J.R. (2004). Charisma under Crisis: Presidential Leadership, Rhetoric and Media Responses Before and After 9/11. *The Leadership Quarterly*, 15, 211–239.

Block, J., & Block, J.H. (2005). Nursery School Personality and Political Orientation: Two Decades Later. *Journal of Research in Personality*, 40, 734–749.

Bolsen, T., Druckman, J.L., & Cook, F.L. (2014). The Influence of Motivated Based Reasoning on Public Opinion. *Political Behavior*, 36, 2, 235–262.

Bonikowski, B. (2016). Three Lessons of Contemporary Populism in Europe and the United States. *Brown Journal of World Affairs*, XXIII, 1, 9–23.

Bonikowski, B., & Gidron, N. (2015). The Populist Style in American Politics: Presidential Campaign Discourse, 1952–1996. *Social Forces*, 94, 4, 1593–1621.

Borchers, C. (2018, 11 January). 'Fox & Friends' Is Shaping Trump's Views before Our Very Eyes. *The Washington Post*. Retrieved from: www.washingtonpost.com/news/the-fix/wp/2018/01/11/fox-friends-is-shaping-trumps-views-before-our-very-eyes/

Bowles, N. (2018). Early Facebook and Google Employees Form Coalition to Fight What They Built. *The New York Times*. Retrieved from: www.nytimes.com/2018/02/04/technology/early-facebook-google-employees-fight-tech.html

Brady, K. (2016, December). Austria's Green-Backed Van der Bellen Wins Presidential Election. DW. Retrieved from: www.dw.com/en/austrias-green-backed-van-der-bellen-wins-presidential-election/a-36635159

Brennan, J. (2016, 10 November). Trump Won the Election Because Voters Are Ignorant, Literally. Foreign Policy. Retrieved from: https://foreignpolicy.com/2016/11/10/the-dance-of-the-dunces-trump-clinton-election-republican-democrat/

British Psychological Society. (2015, 6 May). Viewing Violent News on Social Media Can Cause Trauma. Science Daily. Retrieved from: www.sciencedaily.com/releases/2015/05/150506164240.htm

Brogan, P. (1992). The Torturers' Lobby. How Human-Rights Abusers Are Represented in Washington. The Center for Public Integrity. Retrieved from: https://cloudfront-files-1.publicintegrity.org/legacy_projects/pdf_reports/THETORTURERSLOBBY.pdf

Brown, S., & Muotri, A. (2018). Imagination and Human Origins. Center for Academic Research and Training in Anthropogeny. Retrieved from: https://carta.anthropogeny.org/events/imagination-and-human-origins

Bryant, J. & Miron, D. (2003). Excitation-Transfer Theory. In J. Bryant, D. Roskos-Ewoldsen & J. Cantor (Eds.), *Communication and Emotion: Essays in Honor of Dolf Zillman* (pp. 31–59). Mahwah, NJ: Erlbaum.

Bryant Quinn, J. (1995, 7 August). The Big Tease. *Newsweek*, pp. 64–65.

Bryner, J. (2008). Non-Voters: It's All in God's Hands. Live Science. Retrieved from: www.livescience.com/4974-voters-god-hands.html

Bulman, M. (2017, July). Brexit Sees Highest Spike in Religious and Racial Hate Crimes Ever Recorded. *The Independent*. Retrieved from: www.independent.co.uk/news/uk/home-news/racist-hate-crimes-surge-to-record-high-after-brexit-vote-new-figures-reveal-a7829551.html

Bupp, P. (2016, 20 December). The Dallas Cowboys Have a New Intimidation Coach. The Comeback. Retrieved from: http://thecomeback.com/nfl/the-dallas-cowboys-have-a-new-intimidation-coach.html

Burns, J.M. (1978). *Leadership*. New York: Harper Row.

Bush, L. (2018, 17 June). Laura Bush: Separating Children from Their Parents at the Border 'Breaks My Heart'. *The Washington Post*. Retrieved from: www.washingtonpost.com/opinions/laura-bush-separating-children-from-their-parents-at-the-border-breaks-my-heart/2018/06/17/f2df517a-7287-11e8-9780-b1dd6a09b549_story.html?utm_term=.ebd2278d633c

Cadwalladr, C. (2017a, May). The Great British Brexit Robbery: How Our Democracy Was Hijacked. *The Guardian*. Retrieved from: www.theguardian.com/technology/2017/may/07/the-great-british-brexit-robbery-hijacked-democracy

Cadwalladr, C. (2017b, 26 February). Robert Mercer: The Big Data Billionaire Waging War on Mainstream Media. *The Observer*. Retrieved from: www.theguardian.com/politics/2017/feb/26/robert-mercer-breitbart-war-on-media-steve-bannon-donald-trump-nigel-farage

Caprara, G., Schwartz, S., Capanna, C., Vecchione, M., & Barbaranelli, C. (2006). Personality and Politics: Values, Traits, and Political Choice. *Political Psychology*, 27, 1, 1–28.

Carré, J.M., & Putnam, S.K. (2010). Watching a Previous Victory Produces an Increase in Testosterone among Elite Hockey Players. *Psychoneuroendocrinology*, 35, 3, 475–479.

Caspi, A., McClay, J., Moffitt, T.E., Mill, J., Martin, J., Craig, I.W., ... Poulton, R. (2002). Role of Genotype in the Cycle of Violence in Maltreated Children. *Science*, 297, 5582, 851–854.

Cave, A. (2017, September). Deal that Undid Bell Pottinger: Inside Story of the South African Scandal. *The Guardian*. Retrieved from: www.theguardian.com/media/2017/sep/05/bell-pottingersouth-africa-pr-firm

CDC (Centers for Disease Control and Prevention). (2017). Opioid Overdose. Retrieved from www.cdc.gov/drugoverdose/index.html.

Chandler, D. (2009). War without End(s): Grounding the Discourse of 'Global War'. *Security Dialogue*, 40, 3, 243–262.

Changeux, J.P. (1997). *Neuronal Man: The Biology of Mind*. Princeton, NJ: Princeton University Press.

Channel 4. (2018, 20 March). Exposed: Undercover Secrets of Trump's Data Firm. Channel 4. Retrieved from: www.channel4.com/news/exposed-undercover-secrets-of-donald-trump-data-firm-cambridge-analytica

Charney, E. (2008). Genes and Ideologies. *Perspectives on Politics*, 6, 2, 299–320.

Chazan, D. (2018, 3 March). Emmanuel Macron's Popularity Sinks Ahead of Crunch Battle with Rail Unions. *The Telegraph*. Retrieved from: www.telegraph.co.uk/news/2018/03/03/emmanuel-macrons-popularity-sinks-ahead-crunch-battle-rail-unions/

Chen, S. (2010). Bolstering Unethical Leaders: The Role of the Media, Financial Analysts and Shareholders. *Journal of Public Affairs*, 10, 200–215.

Choic, J. (2006). A Motivational Theory of Charismatic Leadership: Envisioning, Empathy, and Empowerment. *Journal of Leadership & Organizational Studies*, 13, 24–43.

Chotikul, D. (1986). The Soviet Theory of Reflexive Control in Historical and Psychocultural Perspective: A Preliminary Study. US Naval Postgraduate School, Monterey, CA.

Christian, C.M., & Bennet, S. (1998). *Black Saga: The African American Experience: A Chronology*. New York: Basic Civitas Books. (Originally printed in 1850.)

Chrousos, G.P. (2009). Stress and Disorders of the Stress System. *Nature Reviews Endocrinology*, 5, 374–381.

CIA. (n.d.). *Manual for Psychological Operations in Guerrilla Warfare*. Edited by A.M. Nagy. CreateSpace Independent Publishing Platform.

Cikara, M., Botvinick, M.M., & Fiske, S.T. (2011). Us versus Them: Social Identity Shapes Neural Responses to Intergroup Competition and Harm. *Psychological Science*, 22, 3, 306–313.

Civitas. (2016, October). Hate Crimes: The Facts Behind the Headlines. Civitas Briefing Note. Retrieved from: www.civitas.org.uk/content/files/hatecrimethefactsbehindtheheadlines.pdf

Clark, D.M. (1986). A Cognitive Approach to Panic. *Behavior Research and Therapy*, 24, 461–470.

cnn (2018). Whistleblower: We Tested Trump Slogans in 2014. CNN Video. Retrieved from: https://edition.cnn.com/videos/cnnmoney/2018/03/20/christopher-wylie-cambridge-analytica-trump-slogans-2014-sot.cnn

cnn Money. (n.d.). What Is the Fear and Greed Index? cnn Money. Retrieved from: http://money.cnn.com/investing/about-fear-greed-tool/index.html

Coates, J.M., Gurnell, M., & Sarnyai, Z. (2010). From Molecule to Market: Steroid Hormones and Financial Risk-Taking. *Philosophical Transactions of the Royal Society B: Biological Sciences*, 365, 331–343.

Coccaro, E.F., McCloskey M.S., Fitzgerald D.A., & Phan K.L. (2007). Amygdala and Orbitofrontal Reactivity to Social Threat in Individuals with Impulsive Aggression. *Biological Psychiatry*, 62, 2, 168–178.

Cockburn, H. (2017, August). Nine-Year-Old among 24 Killed in Kenyan Election Riots. *The Independent*. Retrieved from: www.independent.co.uk/news/world/africa/kenya-election-riot-shooting-young-girl-kisumu-uhuru-kenyatta-raila-odinga-a7889471.html

Cohen, A., Pierce, J., Chambers, J., Meade, R., Gorvine, B.J., & Koenig, H. (2005). Intrinsic and Extrinsic Religiosity, Belief in the Afterlife, Death Anxiety, and Life Satisfaction in Young Catholics and Protestants. *Journal of Research in Personality*, 309, 3, 307–324.

Cohen, F., Solomon, S., Maxfield, M., Pyszczynski, T., & Greenberg, J. (2004). Fatal Attraction: The Effects of Mortality Salience on Evaluations of Charismatic, Task-Oriented, and Relationship-Oriented Leaders. *Psychological Science*, 15, 846–851.

Coleman, J.S. (1987). Families and Schools. *Educational Researcher*, 16, 32–38.

Confer, J.C., Easton, J.A., Fleischman, D.S., Goetz, C.D., Lewis, D.M., Perilloux, C., & Buss, D.M. (2010). Evolutionary Psychology: Controversies, Questions, Prospects, and Limitations. *The American Psychologist*, 65, 2, 110–126.

Confessore, N., & Yourish, K. (2016). $2 Billion Worth of Free Media for Donald Trump. *The New York Times*. Retrieved from: www.nytimes.com/2016/03/16/upshot/measuring-donald-trumps-mammoth-advantage-in-free-media.html

Corning, P.A. (2017, 13 March). The Evolution of 'Zoon Politikon' (The Political Animal). The Evolution Institute. Retrieved from: https://evolution-institute.org/the-evolution-of-zoon-politikon-the-political-animal/

Cosmides, L., & Tooby, J. (2000). Evolutionary Psychology and the Emotions. In M. Lewis & J.M. Haviland-Jones (Eds.), *Handbook of Emotions* (2nd ed.). New York: Guilford Press.

Crescat Capital. (2017, 24 January). Quarterly Investor Letter Q4.

Crockett, M.J., Clark, L., Hauser, M.D., & Robbins, T.W. (2010). Serotonin Selectively Influences Moral Judgement Behavior through Effects on Harm Aversion. *Proceedings of the National Academy of Sciences*, 107, 40, 17433–17438.

Cunningham, W.A., Raye, C.L., & Johnson, M.K. (2004). Implicit and Explicit Evaluation: fMRI Correlates of Valence, Emotional Intensity and Control in the Processing of Attitudes. *Journal of Cognitive Neuroscience*, 16, 1717–1729.

Curran, T., & Hill, A.P. (2018). Perfectionism Is Increasing and That's Not Good News. *Harvard Business Review*. Retrieved from: https://hbr.org/2018/01/perfectionism-is-increasing-and-thats-not-good-news

Curtis, C. (2017), May). UKIP Is a 'Gateway Drug' – But More Voters Are Going for the Hard Stuff. YouGov. Retrieved from: https://yougov.co.uk/news/2017/05/05/ukip-gateway-drug-more-are-going-straight-hard-stu/

Cymbalista, F. (2003, July). How Soros Knows What He Knows. Part 1: The Belief in Fallibility. *Stocks, Futures & Options*, 2, 7.

Dabbs, J.M., Jr (2000). Salivary Testosterone Measurements: Reliability across Hours, Days, and Weeks. *Physiology & Behavior*, 48, 83–86.

Dabbs, J.M., & Dabbs, M.G. (2000). *Heroes, Rogues and Lovers: Testosterone and Behaviour*. New York: McGraw-Hill.

Dahrendorf, R. (2003). Acht Anmerkungen zum Populismus. *Transit: Europäische Revue*, 25, 156–163.

Dal Zotto, E. (2017). Populism in Italy: The Case of the Five Star Movement. CIDOB Report No. 1. Accessible at: www.cidob.org/en/articulos/cidob_report/n1_1/pop ulism_in_italy_the_case_of_the_five_star_movement

Dalio, R., Kryger, S., Rogers, J., & Davis, G. (2017), 22 March). Populism: The Phenomenon. Bridgewater Daily Observations. Retrieved from: www.obela.org/system/files/Populism.pdf

Davis, H., & Yadron, D. (2016). How Facebook Tracks and Profits from Voters in $10bn US Election. *The Guardian*. Retrieved from: www.theguardian.com/us-news/2016/ja n/28/facebook-voters-us-election-ted-cruz-targeted-ads-trump

Dawes, C.T., & Fowler, J.H. (2009). Partisanship, Voting, and the Dopamine D2 Receptor Gene. *The Journal of Politics*, 71, 3, 1157–1171.

Dearden, L. (2017, October). Hate-Crime Reports Rise by Almost a Third in Year as Home Office Figures Illustrate EU Referendum Spike. *The Independent*. Retrieved from: www.independent.co.uk/news/uk/crime/hate-crimes-eu-referendum-spike-brex it-terror-attacks-police-home-office-europeans-xenophobia-a8004716.html

De Bondt, W., & Thaler, R. (1995). Does the Stock Market Overreact? *Journal of Finance*, 40, 793–807.

Decety, J., Pape, R., & Workman, C.I. (2017). A Multilevel Social Neuroscience Perspective on Radicalization and Terrorism. *Social Neuroscience*. https://doi.org/10.1080/17470919.2017.1400462

De Kloet, E.R. (2000). Stress in the Brain. *European Journal of Pharmacology*, 405, 1–3, 187–198.

De Martino, B., Kumaran, D., Seymour, B., & Dolan, R.J. (2009). Frames, Biases, and Rational Decision-Making in the Human Brain. *Science*, 313, 5787, 684–687/1–9 [online]. Retrieved from: www.ncbi.nlm.nih.gov/pmc/articles/PMC2631940/pdf/ukm uss-3681.pdf

De Neve, J. (2013). Personality, Childhood Experience, and Political Ideology. *Political Psychology*, 36, 1, 55–73.

de Quervain, D.J., Fischbacher, U., Treyer, V., Schellhammer, M., Schnyder, U., Buck, A. & Fehr, E. (2004). The Neural Basis of Altruistic Punishment. *Science*, 305, 5688, 1254–1258.

Derntl, B., Windischberger, C., Robinson, S., Kryspin-Exner, I., Gur, R.C., Moser, E., & Habel, U. (2009). Amygdala Activity to Fear and Anger in Healthy Young Males Is Associated with Testosterone. *Psychoneuroendocrinology*, 34, 5, 687–693. Devine, C., O'Sullivan, D., & Griffin, D. (2018, 16 May). How Steve Bannon Used Cambridge Analytica to Further His alt-Right Vision for America. CNN. Accessed at: https://edi tion.cnn.com/2018/03/30/politics/bannon-cambridge-analytica/index.html

De Vries, E.E., Roe, A.R., & Taillieu, T.C.B. (1999). On Charisma and the Need for Leadership. *European Journal of Work and Organizational Psychology*, 8, 109–133.

Dexter, E.G. (1899). Influence of the Weather upon Crime. *Popular Science Monthly*, 55. Accessible at: https://en.wikisource.org/wiki/Popular_Science_Monthly

Dichev, I. & Janes, T. (2001). Lunar Cycle Effects in Stock Returns. Accessible at: http://papers.ssrn.com/abstract=281665

Diesendruck, G. (2013). Essentialism: The Development of a Simple, but Potentially Dangerous, Idea. In M. Banaji & S. Gelman (Eds.), *Navigating the Social World: What Infants, Children, and Other Species Can Teach Us* (pp. 263–268). New York: Oxford University Press.

Dilts, E. (2017, January). Apple Says It Looks Out for Kids, as Investors Cite Phone 'Addiction'. Reuters. Retrieved from: www.reuters.com/article/us-apple-sharehol ders-children/apple-says-it-looks-out-for-kids-as-investors-cite-phone-addiction-idUSK BN1EW0WS

Dodd, M.D., Balzer, A., Jacobs, C.M., GruszczynskiM.W.SmithK.B., & Hibbing, J.R. (2012). The Political Left Rolls with the Good and the Political Right Confronts the Bad: Connecting Physiology and Cognition to Preferences. *Philosophical Transactions of the Royal Society of London B: Biological Sciences*, 367, 1589, 640–649.

Dodson, W. (2005). Pharmacotherapy of Adult ADHD. *Journal of Clinical Psychology*, 61, 589–606.

Dorn, D., & Sengmueller, P. (2009). Trading as Entertainment? *Management Science*, 55, 591–603.

Douglas, S. (2017). The Alabama Senate Race May Have Already Been Decided. *The New York Times*. Op-Ed. Retrieved from: www.nytimes.com/2017/12/11/opinion/roy-m oore-alabama-senate-voter-suppression.html

Doyen, S., Klein, S., Pichon, C-L., & Cleeremans, A. (2012), Behavioral Priming: It's All in the Mind, but Whose Mind? *PLOS One*. Retrieved from: https://doi.org/10.1371/ journal.pone.0029081

Dreber, A., Apicella, C.L., Eisenberg, D.T.A., Garcia, J.R., Zamore, R.S., Lum, J.K., … Campbell, B. (2009). The 7R Polymorphism in the Dopamine Receptor D4 Gene (DRD4) Is Associated with Financial Risk Taking in Men. *Evolution and Human Behavior*, 30, 85–92.

Drutman, L. (2018, 26 March). Why America's 2-Party System Is on a Collision Course with Our Constitutional Democracy. Vox. Retrieved from: www.vox.com/platfor m/amp/polyarchy/2018/3/26/17163960/america-two-party-system-constitutiona l-democracy

Durant, I., Cohn-Bendit, D., Hirsch, M., Schwan, G., De Waele, J-M., Hastings, M., … Pappas, T. (2013). *The Rise of Populism and Extremist Parties in Europe*. The Spinelli Group. Brussels: European Parliament.

DW. (2016). What Philosopher Hannah Arendt Would Say about Donald Trump. Retrieved from: www.dw.com/en/what-philosopher-hannah-arendt-would-say-about-donald-trump/a-36766400

Eatwell, R. (2006). Explaining Fascism and Ethnic Cleansing: The Three Dimensions of Charisma and the Four Dark Sides of Nationalism. *Political Studies Review*, 4, 263–278.

Eckett, T. (2017, 21 June). Soros: Brexit Is a 'Lose-Lose' Proposition for Britain and EU. Investment Week. Retrieved from: www.investmentweek.co.uk/investment-week/ news/3012352/soros-brexit-is-a-lose-lose-for-britain-and-eu

Eidelman, S., Crandall, C.S., Goodman, J.A., & Blanchar, J.C. (2012). Low-Effort Thought Promotes Political Conservatism. *Personality and Social Psychology Bulletin*, 38, 6, 808–820.

Eisenegger, C., Haushofer, J., & Fehr, E. (2011, June). The Role of Testosterone in Social Interaction. *Trends in Cognitive Sciences*, 15, 6, 263–271.

The Electoral Commission. (2017, 21 April). Electoral Commission Statement on Investigation into Leave. EU. Retrieved from: www.electoralcommission.org.uk/i-am-a/journalist/electoral-commission-media-centre/news-releases-referendums/electoral-commission-statement-on-investigation-into-leave.eu

Emmons, R.A. (1984). Factor Analysis and Construct Validity of the Narcissistic Personality Inventory. *Journal of Personality Assessment*, 48, 291–300.

Engelhaupt, E. (2016). How Human Violence Stacks Up Against Other Killer Animals. *National Geographic*. Retrieved from: https://news.nationalgeographic.com/2016/09/human-violence-evolution-animals-nature-science/

Engesser, S., Fawzi, N., & Larsson, A.O. (2017). Populist Online Communication: Introduction to the Special Issue. *Communication & Society*, 20, 9, 1279–1292.

Eres, R., Decety, J., Louis, W.R., & Molenberghs, P. (2015). Individual Differences in Local Gray Matter Density Are Associated with Differences in Affective and Cognitive Empathy. *NeuroImage*, 117, 305–310.

Evening Standard. (2008, 2 April). Boris Says Sorry over 'Blacks Have Lower IQs' Article in The Spectator. Retrieved from: https://www.standard.co.uk/news/mayor/boris-says-sorry-over-blacks-have-lower-iqs-article-in-the-spectator-6630340.html

Farhi, P. (2017, 27 March). Sean Hannity Thinks Viewers Can Tell the Difference between News and Opinion. Hold On a Moment. *The Washington Post*. Retrieved from: www.washingtonpost.com/lifestyle/style/sean-hannity-thinks-viewers-can-tell-the-difference-between-news-and-opinion-hold-on-a-moment/2017/03/27/eb0c5870-1307-11e7-9e4f-09aa75d3ec57_story.html

Faris, R.M., Roberts, H.Etling, B.Bourassa, N.Zuckerman, E.and Benkler ,Y. (2017). *Partisanship, Propaganda, and Disinformation: Online Media and the 2016 U.S. Presidential Election. Berkman Klein Center for Internet & Society Research Paper*. Retrieved from: https://dash.harvard.edu/bitstream/handle/1/33759251/2017-08_electionReport_0.pdf?sequence=9

Ferdman, R.A. (2015). Where People around the World Eat the Most Sugar and Fat. *The Washington Post*. Retrieved from: www.washingtonpost.com/news/wonk/wp/2015/02/05/where-people-around-the-world-eat-the-most-sugar-and-fat/?utm_term=.9e9a5ba0edaa

Fiske, S.T. (2002). What We Know about Bias and Intergroup Conflict: The Problem of the Century. *Current Directions in Psychological Science*, 11, 4, 123–128.

Fone, K.C., & Nutt, D.J. (2005). Stimulants: Use and Abuse in the Treatment of Attention Deficit Hyperactivity Disorder. *Current Opinion in Pharmacology*, 5, 87–93.

Ford, M. (2017, 16 June). Donald Trump Reports He's Getting Rich as President. *The Atlantic*. Retrieved from: www.theatlantic.com/politics/archive/2017/06/donald-trump-reports-hes-getting-rich-off-the-presidency/530718/

Fowler, J.H., & Dawes, C.Y. (2008). Two Genes Predict Voter Turnout. *Journal of Politics*, 70, 3, 579–594.

French, J.A., Smith, K.B., Alford, J.R., Guck, A., Birnie, A.K., & Hibbing, J.R. (2014). Cortisol and Politics: Variance in Voting Behavior Is Predicted by Baseline Cortisol Levels. *Physiology & Behavior*, 133, 61–67.

French, K., & Poterba, J. (1991). Investor Diversification and International Equity Markets. *American Economic Review*, 81, 222–226.

Friedman, J.P., & Jack, A.I. (2017). What Makes You So Sure? Dogmatism, Fundamentalism, Analytic Thinking, Perspective-Taking and Moral Concern in the Religious and Nonreligious. *Journal of Religion and Health*, 57, 1, 157–190.

Friedman, U. (2017, 27 February). What Is a Populist? And Is Donald Trump One? *The Atlantic*. Retrieved from: www.theatlantic.com/international/archive/2017/02/wha t-is-populist-trump/516525/

Friend, J.M., & Thayer, B.A. (2011). Brain Imaging and Political Behavior. In A. Somit& S.A. Peterson(Eds.), *Biology and Politics: The Cutting Edge*, 9, 231–255. Bingley, UK: Emerald Group Publishing Ltd.

Friend, J.M., & Thayer, B.A. (2013). Neuropolitics and Political Science: Providing a Foundation for the Study of Politics. In S.A. Peterson & A. Somit (Eds.), *The World of Biology and Politics: Organization and Research Areas*, 11, 71–90. Bingley, UK: Emerald Group Publishing Ltd.

Frydl, K. (2016). The Oxy Electorate. Medium. Retrieved from: https://medium.com/@ kfrydl/the-oxy-electorate-3fa62765f837

Fulford, T. (2004). Conducting and Vital Fluid: The Politics and Poetics of Mesmerism in the 1790s. *Studies in Romanticism*, 43, 1, 57–78.

Funk, M. (2016). Cambridge Analytica and the Secret Agenda of a Facebook Quiz. *The New York Times*. Retrieved from: www.nytimes.com/2016/11/20/opinion/cam bridge-analytica-facebook-quiz.html

Galbraith, J., & Sastre, D. (2009). The Generalized Minsky Moment. UTIP Working Paper No. 56. Austin: University of Texas.

Galbraith, J.K. (1954/1988). *The Great Crash, 1929*. Boston: Houghton Mifflin.

Galbraith, J.K. (1993). *A Short History of Financial Euphoria*. New York: Penguin.

Gallucci, J. (2018, 16 June). 1,995 Children Have Been Separated from Their Families by Border Patrol, DHS Confirms. *Fortune*. Retrieved from: http://fortune.com/2018/06/ 16/children-parents-separated-border/

Garber, M. (2017, 15 August). Joking After Charlottesville. *The Atlantic*. Retrieved from: www. theatlantic.com/entertainment/archive/2017/08/scaramucci-stephen-colbert/536901/

Gassendi, P. (1972). *The Selected Works of Pierre Gassendi*. C. B. Brush (Ed. & Trans.). New York: Johnson Reprint Corporation.

Ghoshal, D. (2018, 28 March). Mapped: The Breath-Taking Global Reach of Cambridge Analytica's Parent Company. Quartz. Retrieved from: https://qz.com/1239762/cam bridge-analytica-scandal-all-the-countries-where-scl-elections-claims-to-have-worked/

Gibb, J.W., Hanson, G.R., & Johnson, M. (1994). Neurochemical Mechanisms of Toxi-city. In A.K. Cho & D.S. Segal (Eds.), *Amphetamine and Its Analogs* (pp. 269–295). San Diego, CA: Academic Press.

Giroux, G. (2018, 22 June). Rep. Ted Lieu (D-California) Plays Audio from Child Detention Facility. C-Span. Retrieved from: www.c-span.org/video/?c4737014/rep -ted-lieu-plays-audio-child-detention-facility

Glenn, A.L., Raine, A., & Schug, R.A. (2009). The Neural Correlates of Moral Decision-Making in Psychopathy. *Molecular Psychiatry*., 14, 1, 5–6.

Goldberg, C. (2016). National Study: Teen Misuse and Abuse of Prescription Drugs up 33 Percent since 2008, Stimulants Contributing to Sustained Rx Epidemic. Partnership for Drug Free Kids. Retrieved from: https://drugfree.org/newsroom/news-item/nationa l-study-teen-misuse-and-abuse-of-prescription-drugs-up-33-percent-since-2008-stimula nts-contributing-to-sustained-rx-epidemic/

Gomez, B.T., Hansford, T.G., & Krause, G.A. (2007). The Republicans Should Pray for Rain: Weather, Turnout, and Voting in U.S. Presidential Elections. *The Journal of Poli-tics*, 69, 3, 649–663.

Goodstein, L. (2018). Conservative Religious Leaders Are Denouncing Trump Immigration Policies. *The New York Times*. Retrieved from: www.nytimes.com/2018/06/14/
us/trump-immigration-religion.html

Gottfried, J., & Anderson, M. (2014). For Some, the Satiric 'Colbert Report' Is a Trusted
Source of Political News. Fact Tank. Retrieved from: www.pewresearch.org/fact-tank/
2014/12/12/for-some-the-satiric-colbert-report-is-a-trusted-source-of-political-news/

Grabmeier, J. (2017). Not Just Funny: Satirical News Has Serious Political Effects. Ohio State
University. Retrieved from: www.sciencedaily.com/releases/2017/01/170123115741.htm

Graham, D.A. (2018a, 25 January). The Strange Cases of Anti-Islam Politicians Turned
Muslims. *The Atlantic*. Retrieved from: www.theatlantic.com/international/archive/
2018/01/far-right-politicians-convert-islam/551438/

Graham, D.A. (2018b, February). The Sharp Rise and Sudden Departure of Hope Hicks.
The Atlantic. Retrieved from: www.theatlantic.com/politics/archive/2018/02/the-sharp
-rise-and-sudden-departure-of-hope-hicks/554558/

Gray, J. A. (1972). The Psychophysiological Basis of Introversion-Extraversion: A Modification of Eysenck's Theory. In V.D. Nebylitsyn & J.A. Gray (Eds.), *The Biological
Bases of Individual Behaviour* (pp. 182–205). San Diego, CA: Academic Press.

Gray, J.A. (1981). A Critique of Eysenck's Theory of Personality. In H.J. Eysenck (Ed.), *A
Model for Personality* (pp. 246–277). Berlin, Germany: Springer.

Greenhill, L.L., Pliszka, S., Dulcan, M.K., Bernet, W., Arnold, V., Beitchman, J., …
American Academy of Child and Adolescent Psychiatry (2002). Practice Parameters for
the Use of Stimulant Medications in the Treatment of Children, Adolescents and
Adults. *Journal of the American Academy of Child and Adolescent Psychiatry*, 41, 26–49.

Greenspan, A. (1996, 5 December). Remarks by Chairman Alan Greenspan at the Annual
Dinner and Francis Boyer Lecture of The American Enterprise Institute for Public
Policy Research, Washington, D.C. Retrieved from: www.federalreserve.gov/boa
rddocs/speeches/1996/19961205.htm

Greven, T. (2016). *The Rise of Right-Wing Populism in Europe and the United States: A
Comparative Perspective*. Washington, DC: Friedrich Ebert Stiftung.

Griffin, R. (2017, September). The First Six Months: How Americans Are Reacting to the
Trump Administration. Democracy Fund Voter Study Group. Retrieved from: www.
voterstudygroup.org/publications/2017-voter-survey/first-six-months

Gruzelier, J.H. (2006). Frontal Functions, Connectivity, and Neural Efficiency Under-
pinning Hypnosis and Hypnotic Susceptibility. *Contemporary Hypnosis*, 23, 15–32.

Guimón, P. (2018, 27 March). Brexit Wouldn't Have Happened without Cambridge
Analytica. El País. Retrieved from: https://elpais.com/elpais/2018/03/27/inenglish/
1522142310_757589.html

Gu, L., Kropotov, V., & Yarochkin, F. (2017a). The Fake News Machine: How Propagandists Abuse the Internet. TrendLabs Research Paper. Trend Micro. Retrieved from:
https://documents.trendmicro.com/assets/white_papers/wp-fake-news-machine-how-p
ropagandists-abuse-the-internet.pdf

Gu, L., Kropotov, V., & Yarochkin, F. (2017b). Fake News and Cyber Propaganda: The Use
and Abuse of Social Media. Trend Micro. Retrieved from: www.trendmicro.com/vinfo/
us/security/news/cybercrime-and-digital-threats/fake-news-cyber-propaganda-the-abuse-
of-social-media

Guru Focus.com. (2016, March). Dr. Michael Burry of 'The Big Short' Holds Citigroup,
Bank of America in First Portfolio Filing since 2008. Forbes Investing. Retrieved from:

www.forbes.com/sites/gurufocus/2016/03/31/dr-michael-burry-of-big-short-holds-citi group-bank-of-america-in-first-portfolio-filing-since-2008/#3f3649ff66ec

Haidt, J. (2013). *The Righteous Mind*. London: Penguin Group.

Haidt, J., & Graham, J. (2007). When Morality Opposes Justice: Conservatives Have Moral Intuitions that Liberals May Not Recognize. *Social Justice Research*, 20, 98–116.

Haidt, J., & Hersh, M. (2001). Sexual Morality: The Cultures of Conservatives and Liberals. *Journal of Applied Social Psychology*, 31, 191–221.

Halberg, F., Cornélisson, G., Otsuka, K., Watanabe, Y., Katinas, G.S., Burioka, N., et. al. (2000). International BIOCOS Study Group: Cross-Spectrally Coherent 10.5- and 21-Year Biological and Physical Cycles, Magnetic Storms and Myocardial Infarctions. *Neuroendocrinology Letters, 21*, 233–258.

Hannity, S. (2016, 25 October). (@seanhannity). Tweet. Retrieved from: https://twitter.com/seanhannity/status/791132954298818561?lang=en

Harford, T. (2017). The Problem with Facts. *Financial Times*. Retrieved from: http://timharford.com/2017/03/the-problem-with-facts/

Harris, L.T., & Fiske, S.T. (2006). Dehumanizing the Lowest of the Low: Neuroimaging Responses to Extreme Out-Groups. *Psychological Science*, 17, 10, 847–853.

Hart, H.L.A. (1982). *Essays on Bentham: Jurisprudence and Political Philosophy* Oxford: Clarendon Press.

Hartelius, E.J., & Browning, L.D. (2003). The Application of Rhetorical Theory in Managerial Research: A Literature Review. *Management Communication Quarterly*, 22, 1, 13–39.

Hartog, D., & Verburg, R. (1997). Charisma and Rhetoric: Communicative Techniques of International Business Leaders. *The Leadership Quarterly*, 8, 355–391.

Harvard Medical School (2010). Humor, Laughter, and Those Aha Moments. *The Harvard Mahoney Neuroscience Institute Letter*, 16, 2. Retrieved from: https://hms.harvard.edu/sites/default/files/HMS_OTB_Spring10_Vol16_No2.pdf

Hatemi, P.K., Gillespie, N.A., Eaves, L.J., Maher, B.S., Webb, B.T., Heath, C., ... Martin, N.G. (2011). A Genome-Wide Analysis of Liberal and Conservative Political Attitudes. *Journal of Politics*, 73, 271–285.

Healy, A.J., Malhotra, N., & Hyunjung Mo, C. (2010). Irrelevant Events Affect Voters' Evaluations of Government Performance. *Proceedings of the National Academy of Sciences*, 107, 29, 12804–12809.

Hedges, C. (2002). *War Is a Force That Gives Us Meaning*. New York: Public Affairs.

Hedges, C. (2003, 6 July). 'What Every Person Should Know about War'. *The New York Times*. Retrieved from: www.nytimes.com/2003/07/06/books/chapters/what-every-person-should-know-about-war.html

Hegel, G. W. F. (1975). *Lectures on the Philosophy of World History: Introduction: Reason in History*. (Translated from the German Edition of Johannes Hoffmeister from Hegel papers assembled by H.B. Nisbet). New York: Cambridge University Press.

Hendrickse, J., Arpan, L.M., Clayton, R.B., & Ridgway, J.L. (2017). Instagram and College Women's Body Image: Investigating the Roles of Appearance-Related Comparisons and Intrasexual Competition. *Computers in Human Behavior*, 74, 92–100.

Heracleous, L., & Barrett, M. (2001). Organizational Change as Discourse: Communicative Actions and Deep Structures in the Context of Information Technology Implementation. *The Academy of Management Journal*, 44, 4, 755–778.

Heracleous, L., & Klaering, L.A. (2014). Charismatic Leadership and Rhetorical Competence: An Analysis of Steve Jobs' Rhetoric. *Group and Organization Management*, 39, 131–161.

Hermans, E.J., Ramsey, N.F., & van Honk, J. (2008). Exogenous Testosterone Enhances Responsiveness to Social Threat in the Neural Circuitry of Social Aggression in Humans. *Biological Psychiatry*, 63, 3, 263–270.

Hern, A. (2018a, 28 February). Bill Gates: Cryptocurrencies Have 'Caused Deaths in a Fairly Direct Way'. *The Guardian*. Retrieved from: www.theguardian.com/technology/2018/feb/28/bill-gates-cryptocurrencies-deaths-bitcoin-steve-wozniak-scam

Hern, A. (2018b, June). Arron Banks Walks Out as MPs' Questions on Brexit and Russia Run Late – As It Happened. *The Guardian*. Retrieved from:www.theguardian.com/uk-news/live/2018/jun/12/arron-banks-and-andy-wigmore-face-mps-leave-eu-brexit-russia-live?page=with:block-5b1f9ccee4b0a90d612a61e2

Hibbing, J.R. (2013). Ten Misconceptions Concerning Neurobiology and Politics. *Perspectives on Political Science*, 11, 2, 475–489.

Hillman, C.H., Erickson, K.I., & Kramer, A.F. (2008, January). Be Smart, Exercise Your Heart: Exercise Effects on Brain and Cognition. *Nature Reviews Neuroscience*, 9, 58–65.

Hills, C. (2016 , 4August). President Erdogan's Attempts to Silence Turkish Satirists: Not Working. PRI. Retrieved from: www.pri.org/stories/2016-08-04/president-erdogans-attempts-silence-turkish-satirists-not-working

Hinsliff, G. (2016, June). A Pyrrhic Victory? Boris Johnson Wakes Up to the Costs of Brexit. *The Guardian*. Retrieved from: www.theguardian.com/politics/2016/jun/24/a-pyrrhic-victory-boris-johnson-wakes-up-to-the-costs-of-brexit

Hirschfeld-Davis, D. (2018, 16 May). Trump Calls Some Unauthorized Immigrants 'Animals' in Rant. *The New York Times*. Retrieved from: www.nytimes.com/2018/05/16/us/politics/trump-undocumented-immigrants-animals.html

Hirshleifer, D. (2001). Investor Psychology and Asset Pricing. *Journal of Finance*, 4, 1533–1597.

Hirshleifer, D., & Shumway, T. (2003). Good Day Sunshine: Stock Returns and the Weather. Working Paper. University of Michigan Business School, Ann Arbor, MI.

Homeland Security. (2016, 7 October). Joint Statement from the Department of Homeland Security and Office of the Director of National Intelligence on Election Security. Retrieved from: www.dhs.gov/news/2016/10/07/joint-statement-department-homeland-security-and-office-director-national

Hooton, C. (2016, 24 June). Sadiq Khan's Brexit EU Referendum Response in Full: 'There Is No Need to Panic'. *The Independent*. Retrieved from: www.independent.co.uk/news/uk/sadiq-khans-brexit-eu-referendum-response-in-full-there-is-no-need-to-panic-a7100071.html

Horgan, J. (2014). *The Psychology of Terrorism* (2nd ed.). New York: Routledge.

House, R.J. (1977). A 1976 Theory of Charismatic Leadership. In J.G. Hunt & L.L. Larson (Eds.), *Leadership: The Cutting Edge* (pp. 189–207). Carbondale: Southern Illinois University Press.

House, R.J. (1996). Path-Goal Theory of Leadership: Lessons, Legacy, and a Reformulated Theory. *The Leadership Quarterly*, 7, 323–352.

House, R.J., & Howell, J.M. (1992). Personality and Charismatic Leadership. *The Leadership Quarterly*, 3, 81–109.

House, R.J., Spangler, W.D., & Woycke, J. (1991). Personality and Charisma in the US Presidency: A Psychological Theory of Leader Effectiveness. *Administrative Science Quarterly*, 36, 364–396.

Howard, P.N., Kollanyi, B., Bradshaw, S., & Neudert, L-M. (2017). Social Media, News and Political Information during the US Election: Was Polarizing Content

Concentrated in Swing States? COMPROP Data Memo 2017.8. Project on Computational Propaganda, Oxford, UK.

Howell, J.M. (1988). Two Faces of Charisma: Socialized and Personalized Leadership in Organizations. In I.J.A. Conger & K.N. Kanungo (Eds.), *Charismatic Leadership: The Elusive Factor in Organizational Effectiveness* (pp. 213–236). San Francisco: Jossey-Bass.

Howell, J.M., & Shamir, B. (2005). The Role of Followers in the Charismatic Leadership Process: Relationships and Their Consequences. *Academy of Management Review*, 30, 96–112.

Hsu, C. (2015). Media 'Fluff' Helped Hitler Rise to Power. University of Buffalo News Center. Retrieved from: www.buffalo.edu/news/releases/2015/08/034.html

Hu, X., Lipsky, R.H., & Zhu, G. (2006). Serotonin Transporter Promoter Gain-of-Function Genotypes Are Linked to Obsessive-Compulsive Disorder. *American Journal of Human Genetics*, 78, 5, 815–826.

Humphreys, J., Zhao, D., Ingram, K., Gladstone, J., & Basham, L. (2010). Situational Narcissism and Charismatic Leadership. A Conceptual Framework. *Journal of Behavioral and Applied Management*, 11, 118–136.

Inbar, Y., Pizarro, D.A., & Bloom, P. (2009). Conservatives Are More Easily Disgusted than Liberals. *Cognition and Emotion*, 23, 4, 714–725.

Inbar, Y., Pizarro, D.A., & Bloom, P. (2012). Disgusting Smells Cause Decreased Liking of Gay Men. *Emotion*, 12, 1, 23–27.

Ingraham, C. (2016). The Smoking Gun that Proves North Carolina Republicans Tried to Disenfranchise Black Voters. *The Washington Post*. Retrieved from: www.washingtonp ost.com/news/wonk/wp/2016/07/29/the-smoking-gun-proving-north-carolina-repub icans-tried-to-disenfranchise-black-voters/?utm_term=.32d5721528d2

IPA. (2017). Adults Spend Almost 8 Hours Each Day Consuming Media. IPA. Retrieved from: www.ipa.co.uk/news/adults-spend-almost-8-hours-each-day-consuming-m edia#.WzDTq6dKjIU

Isaac, M., & Ember, S. (2016, 8 November). For Election Day Influence, Twitter Ruled Social Media. *The New York Times*. Retrieved from:www.nytimes.com/2016/11/09/ technology/for-election-day-chatter-twitter-ruled-social-media.html

Jacobs, B. (2016). The Revenge of the 'Oxy Electorate' Helped Fuel Trump's Election Upset. Business Insider UK. Retrieved from: http://uk.businessinsider.com/trump -vote-results-drug-overdose-deaths-2016-11?r=US&IR=T

Jaipragas, B. (2018, April). Cambridge Analytica in Asia: Modern-Day Colonialism, or Empathy in the Digital Age? *South China Morning Post*. Retrieved from: www.scmp. com/week-asia/politics/article/2139719/cambridge-analytica-asia-modern-day-colonia lism-or-empathy

James, W. (1884). What Is an Emotion? *Mind*, 9, 34, 188–205.

James, W. (1910/2015). *The Moral Equivalent of War*. Whitefish, MT: Literary Licensing LLC.

Jarrett, C. (2018). Why Did Humans Evolve an Imagination? Science Focus. Retrieved from: www.sciencefocus.com/article/mind/why-did-humans-evolve-imagination

Jarzabkowski, P., Sillince, J., & Shaw, D. (2010). Strategic Ambiguity as a Rhetorical Resource for Enabling Multiple Interests. *Human Relations*, 63, 219–248.

Jia, Y., Van Lent, L.V., & Zeng, Y. (2014). Masculinity, Testosterone, and Financial Misreporting. *Journal of Accounting Research*, 52, 679–682.

Johansson, H. (2018). Timbro Authoritarian Populism Index 2017. Retrieved from: https://timbro.se/allmant/timbro-authoritarian-populism-index2017/

Jorion, P. (2006, April). Keeping Up with the Joneses: The Desire of Desire for Money. *Behavioral and Brain Sciences*, 29, 2, 187–188.

Joseph, A. (2016). Special Report: 26 Overdoses in Just Hours: Inside a Community on the Front Lines of the Opioid Epidemic. STAT. Retrieved from: www.statnews.com/2016/08/22/heroin-huntington-west-virginia-overdoses/

Jost, J.T.J., Glaser, A.W., Kruglanski, A.W., & Sulloway, F.J. (2003). Political Conservatism as Motivated Social Cognition. *Psychological Bulletin*, 129, 339–375.

The Juniper Center. (2017, 2 June). Can Watching Media Cause Symptoms of Trauma or PTSD? Retrieved from: www.thejunipercenter.com/1099-2/

Kaiser, E. (2012). 6 Facts about Crime and the Adolescent Brain. *MPR News*. Retrieved from: www.mprnews.org/story/2012/11/15/daily-circuit-juvenile-offenders-brain-development

Kalberg, S. (1980). Max Weber's Types of Rationality: Cornerstones for the Analysis of Rationalization Processes in History. *The American Journal of Sociology*, 85, 5, 1145–1179.

Kanai, R., Feilden, T., Firth, C., & Rees, G. (2011). Political Orientations Are Correlated with Brain Structure in Young Adults. *Current Biology*, 21, 677–680.

Kandel, E.R., & Kandel, D.B. (2014). A Molecular Basis for Nicotine as a Gateway Drug. *New England Journal of Medicine*, 371, 932–943.

Kashkin, H.B., & Kleber, H.D. (1989, 8 December). Hooked on Hormones? An Anabolic Steroid Production Hypothesis. *Journal of Applied Behavior Analysis*, 262, 22, 3166–3170.

Katz, R., & Kolodny, R. (1994). Party Organization as an Empty Vessel: Parties in American Politics. In R. Katz & P. Mair (Eds), *How Parties Organize* (pp. 23–50). London: Sage.

Keltner, D. (2004). The Compassionate Instinct. *Greater Good Magazine*. Greater Good Science Center at UC Berkeley. Retrieved from: https://greatergood.berkeley.edu/article/item/the_compassionate_instinct

Keneally, M. (2018, 20 June). Toddlers at a 'Tender Age' Facility Were Traumatized, Doctor Says. ABC News online. Retrieved from: https://abcnews.go.com/Politics/toddlers-tender-age-facility-traumatized-doctor/story?id=56026314

Kenning, P., & Plassmann, H. (2005). Neuroeconomics: An Overview from an Economic Perspective. *Brain Research Bulletin*, 67, 343–354.

Kessler, G., Rizzo, S., & Kelly, M. (2018). President Trump Has Made 3, 001 False or Misleading Claims So Far. *The Washington Post*. Retrieved from: www.washingtonpost.com/news/fact-checker/wp/2018/05/01/president-trump-has-made-3001-false-or-misleading-claims-so-far/?utm_term=.eb73d9e09579

Kets de Vries, M. (1988, January). The Dark Side of CEO Succession. *Harvard Business Review*. Retrieved from: https://hbr.org/1988/01/the-dark-side-of-ceo-succession

Kets de Vries, M.E.R. (2004). A Clinical Perspective on Organizational Dynamics. *European Management Journal*, 22, 183–200.

Keynes, J.M. (1936). *The General Theory of Employment, Interest and Money*. New York: Harcourt, Brace and Company.

Keynes, J.M. (1937). The General Theory of Employment. *Quarterly Journal of Economics*, 51, 209–223.,

Keynes, J.M. (2007). *The General Theory of Employment, Interest and Money*. London: Palgrave Macmillan.

Khalid, A. (2018). Republicans Might Want to Run Away from Trump this Year but Not in West Virginia. NPR. Retrieved from: www.npr.org/2018/04/15/601889282/republicans-might-want-to-run-away-from-trump-this-year-but-not-in-west-virginia

Kiewe, A. (1994). Introduction. In A. Kiewe (Ed.), *The Modern Presidency and Crisis Rhetoric* (pp. 15–37). Westport, CT: Praeger Publications.

Kinder, D. R. (2003). Communication and Politics in the Age of Information. In D. O. Sears, L. Huddy & R. Jervis (Eds.), *Oxford Handbook of Political Psychology* (pp. 357–393). New York: Oxford University Press.

Kinder, D. R. (2007). Curmudgeonly Advice. *Journal of Communication*, 57, 1, 155–162.

Kindleberger, C.P., & Aliber, R.Z. (2005). *Manias, Panics and Crashes: A History of Financial Crises* (5th ed.). London: Palgrave Macmillan.

King, C. (2016, 17 April). Chris King: Avoiding the Rabbit Hole. Young Minds Campaign. *The Sunday Times*. Retrieved from: www.thetimes.co.uk/article/8b133a 54-033d-11e6-a5f6-a676985ac2c5

Klapp, O.E. (1991). *Inflation of Symbols: Loss of Values in American Culture*. New Brunswick, NJ: Transaction Publishers.

Klarman, S. A. (1991). *Margin of Safety: Risk-Averse Value Investing Strategies for the Thoughtful Investor*. London: HarperCollins.

Klarman, S. A. (2017, 7 February). 2016 Year-End Letter. The Baupost Group, LLC.

Klein, E. (2018, 19 February). How Technology Is Designed to Bring Out the Worst in Us. Vox. Retrieved from: https://www.vox.com/technology/2018/2/19/17020310/ tristan-harris-facebook-twitter-humane-tech-time

Klein, K.J., & House, R.J. (1995). On Fire: Charismatic Leadership and Levels of Analysis. *Leadership Quarterly*, 2, 6, 183–198.

Kleiner Perkins. (2017). Internet Trends Report 2017. Retrieved from: www.kleinerp erkins.com/perspectives/internet-trends-report-2017

Knutson, B., & Bossearts, P. (2007, August). Neural Antecedents of Financial Decisions. *Journal of Neuroscience*, 27, 31, 8174–8177.

Knutson, B., Wimmer, G.F., Kuhnen, C.M., & Winkielman, P. (2008). Nucleus Accumbens Activation Mediates the Influence of Reward Cues on Financial Risk-Taking. *NeuroReport*, 19, 509–533.

Koerth-Baker, M. (2018, March). These Researchers Have Been Trying to Stop School Shootings for 20 Years. *ABC News* online. Retrieved from: https://fivethirtyeight.com/fea tures/school-shootings-are-still-rare-and-that-makes-them-hard-to-stop/

Kraft, P.W., Lodge, M., & Taber, C.S. (2015). Why People 'Don't Trust the Evidence': Motivated Reasoning and Scientific Beliefs. *The Annals of the American Academy of Political and Social Science*, 658, 121–133.

Kranz, M., & Gould, S. (2017, 3 November). These Maps Show that Counties Where Opioid Deaths and Prescription Rates Are Highest Are also Places Where Trump Won Big in 2016. Business Insider UK. Retrieved from: http://uk.businessinsider.com/map s-counties-where-opioid-deaths-are-high-trump-2016-crisis-2017-10

Krivelyova, A., & Robotti, C. (2003). Playing the Field: Geomagnetic Storms and International Stock Markets. Working Paper No. 2003–2005a, Federal Reserve Bank of Atlanta.

Kruger, J., & Dunning, D. (1999). Unskilled and Unaware of It: How Difficulties in Recognizing One's Own Incompetence Leads to Self-Inflated Self-Assessments. *Journal of Personality and Social Psychology*, 77, 6, 1121–1134.

Kteily, N., Hodson, G., & Bruneau, E. (2016). They See Us as Less than Human: Meta-Dehumanization Predicts Intergroup Conflict via Reciprocal Dehumanization. *Journal of Personality and Social Psychology*, 110, 3, 343–370.

Kurtzleben, D. (2015, August). 2016 Campaigns Will Spend $4.4 Billion on TV Ads, but Why? NPR. Retrieved from: www.npr.org/sections/itsallpolitics/2015/08/19/432759311/2016-campaign-tv-ad-spending?t=1529691232137

Kurzban, R.J., Tooby, R.J., & Cosmides, L. (2001). Can Race Be Erased? Coalitional Computation and Social Categorization. *Proceedings of the National Academy of Sciences*, 98, 15387–15392.

Kuss, D.J., & Griffiths, M.D. (2017). Social Networking Sites and Addiction: Ten Lessons Learned. *International Journal of Environmental Research and Public Health*, 17, 14, 3.

LaBouff, J., Rowatt, W., Shen, M., & Finkle, C. (2012). Differences in Attitudes toward Outgroups in Religious and Nonreligious Contexts in a Multinational Sample: A Situational Context Priming Study. *The International Journal for the Psychology of Religion*, 22, 1–9.

Laignee, B. (2018, 20 June). Corey Lewandowski Mocks Story about 10-Year-Old with Down Syndrome Separated from Her Mother at the Border. *Time Magazine*. Retrieved from: http://time.com/5316822/corey-lewandowski-womp-womp/

Lakoff, G., & Wehling, E. (2016). *Your Brain's Politics*. Exeter: Imprint Academic.

Lapowsky, I. (2017). The Real Trouble with Trump's 'Dark Post' Facebook Ads. Wired. Retrieved from: www.wired.com/story/trump-dark-post-facebook-ads/

Lavandera, E., Morris, J., & Simon, D. (2018, 14 June). She Says Federal Officials Took Her Daughter While She Breastfed the Child in a Detention Center. CNN. Retrieved from: https://edition.cnn.com/2018/06/12/us/immigration-separated-children-southern-border/index.html

Lawrence Smith, E. (1939). *Tides in the Affairs of Men*. New York: The Macmillan Co.

Lea, S.E.G., & Webley, P. (2006). Money as a Tool, Money as a Drug: The Biological Psychology of a Strong Incentive. *Behavioral and Brain Sciences*, 29, 161–209.

Lefevre, C.E., Lewis, G.J., Perrett, D.I., & Penke, L. (2013). Telling Facial Metrics: Facial Width Is Associated with Testosterone Levels in Men. *Evolution & Human Behavior*, 34, 273–279.

Lenihann, M. (2018). Obesity Rates among American Adults Continue to Rise. WGBH. Retrieved from: www.wgbh.org/news/2018/03/28/news/obesity-rates-among-american-adults-continue-to-rise.

Leri, F. (2017). Sugar in the Diet May Increase Risks of Opioid Addiction. The Conversation. Retrieved from: https://theconversation.com/sugar-in-the-diet-may-increase-risks-of-opioid-addiction-85313

Leung, A.K., & Lemay, J.F. (2003). Attention Deficit Hyperactivity Disorder: An Update. *Advances in Therapy*, 20, 305–318.

Levy Economics Institute of Bard College. (2008, May). Book Series: Stabilizing an Unstable Economy. Retrieved from: www.levyinstitute.org/publications/stabilizing-an-unstable-economy

Levy, G. (2015, 21 January). How Citizens United Has Changed Politics in 5 Years. *US News & World Report*. Retrieved from: www.usnews.com/news/articles/2015/01/21/5-years-later-citizens-united-has-remade-us-politics#close-modal

Lewis, G.J., Lefevre, C.E., & Bates, T.C. (2012). Facial Width-to-Height Ratio Predicts Achievement Drive in US Presidents. *Personality and Individual Differences*, 52, 855–857.

Lewis, M. (2011). *The Big Short: Inside the Doomsday Machine*. New York: Penguin.

Li, J., & Tang, Y. (2010). CEO Hubris and Firm Risk-Taking in China: The Moderating Role of Managerial Discretion. *Academy of Management Journal*, 53, 45–68.

Lifton, R.J. (1961/1989). *Thought Reform and the Psychology of Totalitarianism*. Chapel Hill: University of North Carolina Press.

Lillenfeld, W.S.O., Waldman, I.D., Landfield, K., Watts, A.L., Rubenzer, S., & Fashingbauer, T.R. (2012). Fearless Dominance and the US Presidency: Implications of Psychopathic Personality Traits for Successful and Unsuccessful Political Leadership. *Journal of Personal and Social Psychology*, 103, 489–505.

Lin, L.Y., Sidani, J. E., Shensa, A., Radovic, A., Miller, E., Colditz, J. B., ... Primack, B. A. (2016). Association between Social Media Use and Depression among U.S. Young Adults. *Depression and Anxiety*, 33, 4, 323–331.

Livingstone Smith, D. (2011). *Less than Human: Why We Demean, Enslave, and Exterminate Others*. New York: St. Martin's Griffin.

Lo, A.W. (2005). Reconciling Efficient Markets with Behavioral Finance: The Adaptive Markets Hypothesis. *The Journal of Investment Consulting*, 7, 2, 21–44.

Lodge, M., & Taber, C.S. (2013). *The Rationalizing Voter*. New York: Cambridge University Press.

Loewenstein, G.F., Weber, E.U., Hsee, C.K., & Welch, N. (2001). Risk as Feelings. *Psychological Bulletin*, 127, 2, 267–286.

Lopez-Leon, S., Janssens, A., & Ladd, A. (2008). Meta-Analyses of Genetic Studies on Major Depressive Disorder. *Molecular Psychiatry*, 13, 772–785.

Maccoby, M. (2000). Narcissistic Leaders: The Incredible Pros, the Inevitable Cons. *Harvard Business Review*, 78, 68–77.

Maccoby, M. (2003). *The Productive Narcissist*. New York: Broadway Books.

Mackay, C. (1841). *Extraordinary Popular Delusions and the Madness of Crowds*. London: Richard Bentley.

MacLean, P. (1990). *The Triune Brain in Evolution: Role in Paleocerebral Function*. New York: Plenum Press.

Madfis, E. (2014). Triple Entitlement and Homicidal Anger: An Exploration of the Intersectional Identities of American Mass Murderers. *Men and Masculinities*, 17, 1, 67–86.

Madsen, D. (1985). A Biochemical Property Related to Power Seeking in Humans. *American Political Science Review*, 79, 448–457.

Magno, C.N. (2010). Crime as Political Capital in the Philippines. Doctoral dissertation. Department of Criminal Justice, Indiana University, USA.

Marketdata Enterprises. (2017, August). *The Market for Self-Improvement Products & Services* (12th ed.). Tampa, FL: Marketdata Enterprises Inc.

Markets & Markets (2009). Global Weight Loss and Diet Managment Market (2009–2014). Markets & Markets Report. Accessible at: www.marketsandmarkets.com/Market-Reports/global-weight-loss-and-gain-market-research-28.html

Markiewicz, L., & Weber, E.U. (2013). DOSPERT's Gambling Risk-Taking Propensity Scale Predicts Excessive Stock Trading. *The Journal of Behavioral Finance*, 14, 65–78.

Masters, R.D. (1990). Evolutionary Biology and Political Theory. *The American Political Science Review*, 84, 1, 195–210.

Masters, R.D., & McGuire, M.T. (Eds). (1994). *The Neurotransmitter Revolution: Serotonin, Social Behavior, and the Law*. Carbondale: Southern Illinois University Press.

Mazur, A., & Booth, A. (1998). Testosterone and Dominance in Men. *Behavioral and Brain Sciences*, 21, 353–363. Discussion, 363–397.

McCann, U.D., & Ricaurte, G.A. (2004). Amphetamine Neurotoxicity: Accomplishments and Remaining Challenges. *Neuroscience and Biobehavioral Review*, 27, 821–826.

McClelland, D.C. (1970). The Two Faces of Power. *Journal of International Affairs*, 24, 29–47.

McClosky, H. (1958). Conservatism and Personality. *American Political Science Review*, 52, 27–45.

McDermott, R. (2004). The Feeling of Rationality: The Meaning of Neuroscientific Advances for Political Science. *Perspectives on Politics*, 2, 4, 691–706.

McDermott, R. (2009). The Case for Increasing Dialogue between Political Science and Neuroscience. *Political Research. Quarterly*, 62, 571–583.

McDermott, R., Johnson, D., Cowden, J., & Rosen, S. (2007). Testosterone and Aggression in a Simulated Crisis Game. *Annals of the American Academy of Political and Social Science*, 614, 15–33.

McEwen, B. (1998). Stress, Adaptation and Disease: Allostasis and Allostatic Load. *Annals of the New York Academy of Sciences*, 840, 33–44.

McEwen, B.S. (2000). Allostasis And Allostatic Load: Implications for Neuropsychopharmacology. *Neuropsychopharmacology*, 22, 2, 108–124.

McLaughlin, D., & Moritz, S. (2018, 11 May). How AT&T's Desperate Hunt for Trump Insight Led to Cohen Fiasco. Bloomberg. Retrieved from:www.bloomberg.com/news/articles/2018-05-11/at-t-says-in-memo-hiring-michael-cohen-was-big-mistake

McLean, C.Y., Reno, P.L., Polen, A.A., Bassan, A.I., Capellini, T.D., Guenther, C., … Kingsley, D.M. (2011). Human-Specific Loss of Regulatory DNA and the Evolution of Human-Specific Traits. *Nature*, 471, 7337, 216–219.

McNair, D. (2003). Celebrity Culture in America: Has Personality Finally Replaced Reality? The Rutherford Institute. Retrieved from:www.rutherford.org/publications_resources/oldspeak/celebrity_culture_in_america_has_personality_finally_replaced_reality

McNamee, R. (2017a, 10 August). I Invested Early in Google and Facebook. Now They Terrify Me. *USA Today*. Retrieved from: www.usatoday.com/story/opinion/2017/08/08/my-google-and-facebook-investments-made-fortune-but-now-they-menace/543755001/

McNamee, R. (2017b, 11 November). How Facebook and Google Threaten Public Health – and Democracy. *The Guardian*. Retrieved from: www.theguardian.com/commentisfree/2017/nov/11/facebook-google-public-health-democracy

Mehta, P.H., & Beer, J. (2010). Neural Mechanisms of the Testosterone-Aggression Relation: The Role of Orbitofrontal Cortex. *Journal of Cognitive Neuroscience*, 22, 10, 2357–2368.

Menand, L. (2004, 30 August). The Unpolitical Animal. *The New Yorker*. Retrieved from: www.newyorker.com/magazine/2004/08/30/the-unpolitical-animal

Milazzo, C., & Mattes, K. (2016). Looking Good for Election Day: Does Attractiveness Predict Electoral Success in Britain? *The British Journal of Politics & International Relations*, 18, 1, 161–178.

Miller, M.A., Bershad, A.K., & de Wit, H. (2015). Drug Effects on Responses to Emotional Facial Expressions: Recent Findings. *Behavioural Pharmacology*, 26, 6, 571–579.

Miller, Z.J. (2017, February). President Trump Held a Re-Election Rally after Just a Month on the Job. *Time*. Retrieved from: http://time.com/4676011/donald-trump-melbourne-florida-rally/

Mills, M., Gonzalez, F.J., Giuseffi, K., Sievert, B., Smith, K.B., Hibbing, J.R., & Dodd, M.D. (2016). Political Conservatism Predicts Asymmetries in Emotional Scene Memory. *Behavioral Brain Research*, 306, 1, 84–90.

Minsky, H.P. (1975). *John Maynard Keynes*. New York: Columbia University Press.

Minsky, H.P. (1986). *Stabilizing an Unstable Economy*. New Haven, CT: Yale University Press.

Mio, J.S., Riggio, R.E., Levin, S., & Reese, R. (2005). Presidential Leadership and Charisma: The Effects of Metaphor. *The Leadership Quarterly*, 16, 287–294.

Mischkowski, D., Crocker, J., & Way, B.M. (2016). From Painkiller to Empathy Killer: Acetaminophen (Paracetamol) Reduces Empathy for Pain. *Social Cognitive and Affective Neuroscience*, 11, 9, 1345–1353.

Mitchell, J.P., Banaji, J.R., & Macrae, C.N. (2005). General and Specific Contributions of the Medial Prefrontal Cortex to Knowledge about Mental States. *NeuroImage*, 28, 4, 757–762.

Mondak, J. (2010). *Personality and the Foundations of Political Behavior*. Cambridge: Cambridge University Press.

Montague, P.R. (2007, October–December). Neuroeconomics: A View from Neuroscience. *Functional Neurology*, 22, 4, 219–234.

Morrison, P.D., Allardyce, J., & McKane, J.P. (2002). Fear Knot. Neurobiological Disruption of Long-Term Fear Memory. *British Journal of Psychiatry*, 180, 195–197.

Mortimer, C. (2015). Synthetic Drug Ravaging Blackpool and Turning People's Empathy Off. *The Independent*. Retrieved from: www.independent.co.uk/news/uk/home-news/synthetic-drug-ravaging-blackpool-and-turning-peoples-empathy-off-a6726211.html

Mudde, C. (2016, November/December). Europe's Populist Surge: A Long Time in the Making. Foreign Affairs (Council on Foreign Relations).

Mullen, L. (2018, 15 June). The Fight to Define Romans 13. *The Atlantic*. Retrieved from: www.theatlantic.com/politics/archive/2018/06/romans-13/562916/

Müller, J-W. (2016). Trump, Erdoğan, Farage: The Attractions of Populism for Politicians, the Dangers for Democracy. *The Guardian*. Retrieved from: www.theguardian.com/books/2016/sep/02/trump-erdogan-farage-the-attractions-of-populism-for-politicians-the-dangers-for-democracy

Müller, J-W. (2017). *What Is Populism?*London: Penguin Random House.

Muraven, M., & Baumeister, R.F. (2000). Self-Regulation and Depletion of Limited Resources: Does Self-Control Resemble a Muscle? *Psychological Bulletin*, 126, 2, 247–259.

Mutz, D. C. (2007). Political Psychology and Choice. In R.J. Dalton & H-D. Klingemann (Eds.), *The Oxford Handbook of Political Behavior* (pp. 80–99).New York: Oxford University Press..

NBC Sports Bay Area Staff. (2017, 22 September). Trump to Anthem Protesters: 'Get that Son of a B—— Off the Field'. NBC Sports. Retrieved from: www.nbcsports.com/bayarea/49ers/trump-anthem-protesters-get-son-b-field

Nell, E., & Lees, C. (2018). Brexit Vote Two Years On: Survation for Good Morning Britain. Survation. Retrieved from: http://survation.com/brexit-vote-two-years-on-survation-for-good-morning-britain/

Newkirk, V.R.II (2017, 29 September). Football Has Always Been a Battleground in the Culture War. *The Atlantic*. Retrieved from: www.theatlantic.com/politics/archive/2017/09/football-is-the-culture-war/541464/

Nisbet, E.C., Cooper, K.E., & Garrett, R.K. (2015). The Partisan Brain: How Dissonant Science Messages Lead Conservatives and Liberals to (Dis)Trust Science. *Annals of the American Academy of Political and Social Science*, 658, 36–66.

Ocasio-Cortez, A. (2018, May). *The Courage to Change*. Campaign video. Retrieved from: www.youtube.com/watch?v=rq3QXIVR0bs

Ohler, N. (2016). *Blitzed. Drugs in Nazi Germany*. London: Allen Lane.

Olfsen, M., Marcus, S.C., Druss, B., Pincus, H.A., & Weissman, M.W. (2003). Parental Depression, Child Mental Health Problems, and Health Care Utilization. *Medical Care*, 41, 6, 716–721.

Oosterhoff, B., Shook, N.J., & Ford, C. (2018). Is that Disgust I See? Political Ideology and Biased Visual Attention. *Behavioral Brain Research*, 336, 227–235.

OpenSecrets. (2017). Mercer, Robert, L: Donor Detail. OpenSecrets.org. Retrieved from: www.opensecrets.org/outsidespending/donor_detail.php?cycle=2016&id= U0000003682&type=I&super=S&name=Mercer%2C+Robert+L

Ott, B.L. (2017). The Age of Twitter: Donald J. Trump and the Politics of Debasement. *Critical Studies in Media Communication*, 34, 1, 59–68.

Owen, J., & Lloyd, L. (2018, March). Costing Brexit: What Is Whitehall Spending on Exiting the EU? Institute for Government. Retrieved from: www.instituteforgovernm ent.org.uk/publications/costing-brexit-what-whitehall-spending-exiting-eu

Oxley, D.R., Smith, K.B., Alford, J.R., Hibbing, M.V., & Miller, J.L. (2008). Political Attitudes Vary with Physiological Traits. *Political Science*, 26. Accessible at: http://digita lcommons.unl.edu/poliscifacpub/26

Padilla, A., Hogan, R., & Kaiser, R.B. (2007). The Toxic Triangle: Destructive Leaders, Susceptible Followers, and Conducive Environments. *The Leadership Quarterly*, 18, 176–194.

Papadimitriou, D.B., & Wray, L. R. (1999). Minsky's Analysis of Financial Capitalism (Working Paper No. 275). Annandale-on-Hudson, NY: The Jerome Levy Economics Institute.

Papadimitriou, D.B., & Wray, L.R. (Eds.). (2011). *The Elgar Companion to Hyman Minsky*. Cheltenham, UK: Edward Elgar.

Parkin, S. (2018, 4 March). Has Dopamine Got Us Hooked on Tech? *The Guardian*. Retrieved from: www.theguardian.com/technology/2018/mar/04/has-dopamine-go t-us-hooked-on-tech-facebook-apps-addiction

Parsons, T. (1965). Introduction to Max Weber. In T. Parsons, *The Sociology of Religion* (pp. xix–lxvii). London: Methuen.

PBS. (2016, December). 16 Memorable Quotes from the 2016 Campaign Trail. Washington Week. PBS. Retrieved from: www.pbs.org/weta/washingtonweek/blog-p ost/16-memorable-quotes-2016-campaign-trail

Pegg, D., & Campbell, I. (2018, May). Arron Banks Company Provided £12m of Services to Leave.EU. *The Guardian*. Retrieved from: www.theguardian.com/politics/2018/ma y/09/arron-banks-company-provided-12m-of-services-to-leaveeu

Pengelly, M. (2018, 15 June). Trump Praises Kim on Fox & Friends: 'I Want My People to Do the Same'. *The Guardian*. Retrieved from: www.theguardian.com/us-news/ 2018/jun/15/antsy-and-bored-trump-nearly-left-kim-summit-in-peril-report-says

Perkins, A., & Quinn, B. (2018, April). May's Immigration Policy Seen as 'Almost Reminiscent of Nazi Germany'. *The Guardian*. Retrieved from: www.theguardian.com/ uk-news/2018/apr/19/theresa-may-immigration-policy-seen-as-almost-reminiscen t-of-nazi-germany

Perraudin, F. (2018). Seaside Towns Are Hotspots for Heroin Deaths Says ONS. *The Guardian*. Retrieved from: www.theguardian.com/politics/2018/apr/04/seaside- towns-are-hotspots-for-heroin-deaths-says-ons

Persinger, M.A. (1987). Geopsychology and Geopsychopathology: Mental Processes and Disorders Associated with Geochemical and Geophysical Factors. *Experientia*, 43, 1, 92–104.

Petersen, J. (2016). Trump's Twitter Followed by Millions of Inactive or Fake Accounts. *The Washington Free Beacon*. Retrieved from: http://freebeacon.com/politics/trump s-twitter-followed-millions-inactive-fake-accounts/

Peterson, E., Moler, A., Doudet, D.J., Bailey, C.J., Hansen, K.V., Rodell, A., … Gjedde, A. (2010). Pathological Gambling: Relation of Skin Conductance Response to

Dopaminergic Neurotransmission and Sensation-Seeking. *European Neuropsychopharmacology*, 20, 766–775.

Peyser, M. (2012). The Truthiness Teller. *Newsweek* online edition. Retrieved from: www.newsweek.com/truthiness-teller-112951

Phelps, E.A. (2001). Faces and Races in the Brain. *Nature Neuroscience*, 4, 8, 775–776.

Phelps, E.A., O'Connor, K.J., Gatenby, J.C., Gore, J.C., Grillon, C., & Davis, M. (2001). Activation of the Left Amygdala to a Cognitive Representation of Fear. *Nature Neuroscience*, 4, 4, 437–441.

Phillips, A. (2018, 4 April). Democrats Just Won Another Big Race in Wisconsin — and Republicans Are Panicking. *The Washington Post*. Retrieved from: www.washingtonpost.com/news/the-fix/wp/2018/04/04/democrats-just-won-another-big-race-in-wisconsin-and-republicans-are-panicking/?noredirect=on&utm_term=.9ac3fd738a30

Pillai, R., & Meindl, J.R. (1998). Context and Charisma: A "Meso" Level Examination of the Relationship of Organic Structure, Collectivism, and Crisis to Charismatic Leadership. *Journal of Management*, 24, 5, 643–671.

Popper, M. (2002). Narcissism and Attachment Patterns of Personalized and Socialized Charismatic Leaders. *Journal of Social and Personal Relations*, 19, 798–809.

Porzecanski, K. (2017, 22 March). Ray Dalio Says Populism Might Be a Bigger Deal than Monetary and Fiscal Policy. Bloomberg Business. Retrieved from: www.bloomberg.com/news/articles/2017-03-22/dalio-says-populism-may-be-stronger-than-fiscal-monetary-policy

PRCA. (2018). Bell Pottinger Case Study. Summary accessible at:www.prca.org.uk/campaigns/ethics/bell-pottinger-case-study

Pyeongseon, O. (2016). Horse-Race Coverage Includes Candidates' Policy Positions. *Newspaper Research Journal*, 37, 1, 34–43.

Quinn, E., & Young, C. (2015, 15 January). DC Influencers Spend More on Advertising and PR than Lobbying. Center for Public Integrity. *Time*. Retrieved from: http://time.com/3668128/lobbying-advertising-public-relations/

Rada, P., Mark, G.P., & Hoebel, B.G. (1998). Galanin in the Hypothalamus Raises Dopamine and Lowers Acetylcholine Release in the Nucleus Accumbens: A Possible Mechanism for Hypothalamic Initiating of Feeding Behaviour. *Brain Research*, 798, 1–2, 1–6.

Raghanti, M.A., Stimpson, C.D., Marcinkiewicz, J.L., Erwin, J.M., Hof, P.R., & Sherwood, C.C. (2008). Cortical Dopaminergic Innervations among Humans, Chimpanzees, and Macaque Monkeys: A Comparative Study. *Neuroscience*, 155, 1, 203–220.

Raines, J.P., & Leathers, C. (2010). Behavioral Finance and Post-Keynesian-Institutionalist Theories of Financial Markets. *Journal of Post-Keynesian Economics*, 33, 539–553.

Reference Website. (n.d.). What Is the Purpose of Politics? Retrieved from: www.reference.com/government-politics/purpose-politics-2f742bd7c0fff5c9

Renshom, J., Lee, J.J., & Tingley, D. (2015). Physiological Arousal and Political Beliefs. *Political Psychology*, 36, 5, 569–585.

Reuters Staff. (2016, 8 November). More First-Time Voters, Late-Deciders in U.S. Presidential Race. Reuters. Retrieved from: www.reuters.com/article/us-usa-election-voters-poll/more-first-time-voters-late-deciders-in-u-s-presidential-race-reuters-ipsos-idUSKBN1332RY

Ricuarte, G.A., Mechan, A.O., Yuan, J., Hatzidimitriou, G., Xie, T., Mayne, A.H., & McCann, U.D. (2005). Amphetamine Treatment Similar to That Used in the Treatment of Adult Attention-Deficit/Hyperactivity Disorder Damages Dopaminergic Nerve

Endings in the Striatum of Adult Nonhuman Primates. *Journal of Pharmacology and Experimental Therapeutics*, 315, 1, 91–98.

Rijsenbilt, A., & Commandeur, H. (2012). Narcissus Enters the Courtroom: CEO Narcissism and Fraud. *Journal of Business Ethics*, 117, 413–429.

Ripley, A. (2017, 11 January). Trump's Facial Characteristics May Predict Leadership Style. City University of London. Retrieved from: www.city.ac.uk/news/2017/january/trumps-facial-characteristics-may-predict-leadership-style

Roberts, H. (2018, May). The Dark Side of Italy's Five Star Movement. *The New European*. Retrieved from: www.theneweuropean.co.uk/top-stories/the-dark-side-of-five-star-italian-movement-1-5493911

Robison, L.M., Sclar, D.A., Skaer, T.L., & Galin, R.S. (2004). Treatment Modalities among US Children Diagnosed with Attention-Deficit Hyperactivity Disorder: 1995–1999. *International Clinical Psychopharmacology*, 19, 17–22.

Rodrik, D. (2017a). Economics of the Populist Backlash. VOX CEPR Policy Portal. Retrieved from: https://voxeu.org/article/economics-populist-backlash

Rodrik, D. (2017b). Populism and the Economics of Globalization. CEPR Discussion Paper No. 12119.

Rosenthal, S.A., & Pittinsky, T.L. (2006). Narcissistic Leadership. *The Leadership Quarterly*, 17, 617–633.

Rucker, P. (2018, 15 June). 'Dictator Envy': Trump's Praise of Kim Jong Un Widens His Embrace of Totalitarian Leaders. *The Washington Post*. Retrieved at: www.washingtonpost.com/gdpr-consent/?destination=%2fpolitics%2fdictator-envy-trumps-praise-of-kim-jong-un-marks-embrace-of-totalitarian-leaders

Rutchick, A.M. (2010). Deus ex Machina: The Influence of Polling Place on Voting Behavior. *Political Psychology*, 31, 209–225.

Sáez, I., Zhu, L., Set, E., Kayser, A., & Hsu, M. (2015). Dopamine Modulates Egalitarian Behavior in Humans. *Current Biology*, 25, 7, 912–919.

Salmon, P. (2001). Effects of Physical Exercise on Anxiety, Depression, and Sensitivity to Stress: A Unifying Theory. *Clinical Psychology Review*, 21, 1, 33–61.

Samuels, L. (2018, May). Is Donald Trump's Dictator Envy Fueling US Economy – Or Just Repression? *Newsweek*. Retrieved from: www.newsweek.com/2018/07/13/donald-trump-dictators-strongmen-fueling-us-economy-repression-aggression-1010200.html

Sanders, S., Munro, D., & Bore, M. (1998). Maslow's Hierarchy of Needs and Its Relationship with Psychological Health and Materialism. *South Pacific Journal of Psychology*, 10, 2, 15–25.

Sankowsky, D. (1995). The Charismatic Leader as Narcissist: Understanding the Abuse of Power. *Organizational Dynamics*, 23, 57–71.

Sapra, S.G., Beavin, L., & Zak, P.J. (2012). A Combination of Dopamine Genes Predicts Success by Professional Wall Street Traders. *PLOS ONE*, 7, 1–7.

Saxe, R., & Haushofer, J. (2008). For Love or Money: A Common Neural Currency for Social and Monetary Rewards. *Neuron*, 58, 164–165.

Schjoedt, U. (2009). The Religious Brain: A General Introduction to the Experimental Neuroscience of Religion. *Method and Theory in the Study of Religion*, 21, 310–339.

Schjoedt, U., Stødkilde-Jørgensen, H., Geerts, A., Lund, T., & Roepstorff, A. (2011). The Power of Charisma: Perceived Charisma Inhibits the Frontal Executive Network of Believers in Intercessory Prayer. *SCAN*, 6, 119–127.

Schjoedt, U., Støkilde-Jørgensen, H., Geertz, A.W., & Roepstorff, A. (2008). Rewarding Prayers. *Neuroscience Letters*, 443, 165–168.

Schleifer, A. (2012). Psychologists at the Gate: A Review of Daniel Kahneman's Thinking Fast, and Slow. *Journal of Economic Literature*, 50, 1–12.

Schrand, C., & Zechman, S. (2012). Executive Overconfidence and the Slippery Slope to Financial Misreporting. *Journal of Accounting and Economics*, 53, 311–329.

Schreiber, D., Fonzo, G., Simmons, A.N., Dawes, C.T., Flagan, T., Fowler, J.H., & Paulus, M.P. (2013). Red Brain, Blue Brain: Evaluative Processes Differ in Democrats and Republicans. *PLOS One*, 8, 2, e52970.

Schreiber, D.M. (2012). Throwing a Big Party? Neurocorrelates of Membership in the Major Political Parties. APSA 2012 Annual Meeting Paper. Available at SSRN: https://ssrn.com/abstract=2105167

Schwartz, H.S. (2010). Narcissism Project and Corporate Decay. *Business Ethics Quarterly*, 1, 249–268.

Science Daily. (2006 31 January). Emory Study Lights Up the Political Brain. Retrieved at: www.sciencedaily.com/releases/2006/01/060131092225.htm

Settle, J.E., Dawes, C.T., Christakis, N.A., & Fowler, J.H. (2010). Friendships Moderate an Association between Dopamine Gene Variant and Political Ideology. *Journal of Politics*, 72, 4, 1189–1198.

Shamir, B., Arthur, M.B., & House, R.J. (1994). The Rhetoric of Charismatic Leadership: A Theoretical Extension, A Case Study, and Implications for Research. *The Leadership Quarterly*, 5, 25–42.

Shamir, B., House, R.J., & Arthur, M.B. (1993). The Motivational Effects of Charismatic Leadership: A Self-Concept Based Theory. *Organization Science*, 5, 577–594.

Shen, F.X., & Gromet, D.M. (2015). Red States, Blue States, and Brain States: Issue Framing, Partisanship, and the Future of Neurolaw in the United States. *Annals of the American Academy of Political and Social Science*, 658, 1, 86–101.

Shenkman, R. (2016). *Political Animals*. New York: Basic Books.

Shermer, M. (2006, 1 July). The Political Brain. *Scientific American*. Retrieved from: www.scientificamerican.com/article/the-political-brain/

Shook, N.J., & Fazio, R.H. (2009). Political Ideology, Exploration of Novel Stimuli, and Attitude Formation. *Journal of Experimental Social Psychology*, 45, 4, 995–998.

Siever, L. (2008). Neurobiology of Aggression and Violence. *American Journal of Psychiatry*, 165, 4, 429–442.

Sinclair, E. (2013). *Volatility Trading* (2nd ed.). Hoboken, NJ: John Wiley and Sons.

Sloane, G. (2017, 9 November). Sean Parker Says Facebook Was Designed to Be Addictive. *AdAge*. Retrieved from: http://adage.com/article/digital/sean-parker-worries-facebook-rotting-children-s-brains/311238/

Slothuus, R., & de Vreese, C.H. (2010). Political Parties, Motivated Reasoning, and Issue Framing Effects. *The Journal of Politics*, 72, 3, 630–645.

Smircich, L., & Morgan, G. (1982). Leadership. The Management of Meaning. *The Journal of Applied Behavioral Science*, 18, 257–273.

Smith, K.B., Oxley, D., Hibbing, M.V., Alford, J.R., & Hibbing, J.R. (2011). Disgust Sensitivity and the Neurophysiology of Left-Right Political Orientations. *PLOS ONE*, 6, 10, e25552.

Smith, K.E., Porges, E.C., Norman, G.J., Connelly, J.J., & Decety, J. (2014). Oxytocin Receptor Gene Variation Predicts Empathic Concern and Autonomic Arousal while Perceiving Harm to Others. *Social Neuroscience*, 9, 1, 1–9.

Snelders, S., & Pieters, T. (2011). Speed in the Third Reich: Metamphetamine (Pervitin) Use and a Drug History from Below. *Social History of Medicine*, 24, 3, 686–699.

Soat, M. (2015). Social Media Triggers a Dopamine High. American Marketing Association. Retrieved from: www.ama.org/publications/MarketingNews/Pages/feeding-the-a ddiction.aspx

Solon, O., & Laughland, O. (2018, 2 May). Cambridge Analytica Closing After Facebook Data Harvesting Scandal. The Cambridge Analytica Files. *The Guardian*. Retrieved from: www.theguardian.com/uk-news/2018/may/02/cambridge-analytica-closing-down-after-facebook-row-reports-say

Somit, A., & Peterson, S.A. (2013). Biology and Politics: An Introduction. In S.A. Peterson & A. Somit (Eds.), *The World of Biology and Politics: Organization and Research Areas*. Research in Biopolitics,11, 1–11. Bingley, UK: Emerald Group Publishing Ltd.

Spiker, J.A. (2012). Palin, Bachmann, Tea Party Rhetoric, and American Politics. *International Journal of Humanities and Social Science*, 2, 1–12.

Springer. (2016). Drug Use May Hamper Moral Judgement. Springer. Retrieved from: www.springer.com/gp/about-springer/media/research-news/all-english-research-news/drug-use-may-hamper-moral-judgment/10369578

Spruill, I.J., Coleman, B.L., Powell-Young, Y.M., Williams, T.H., & Magwood, G. (2014). Non-Biological (Fictive Kin and Othermothers): Embracing the Need for a Culturally Appropriate Pedigree Nomenclature in African-American Families. *Journal of the National Black Nurses Association*, 25, 2, 23–30.

Stahl, L. (2018, 10 June). Facebook 'Embeds' Russia and the Trump Campaign's Secret Weapon. CBS News. Retrieved from: www.cbsnews.com/news/facebook-embed s-russia-and-the-trump-campaigns-secret-weapon-60-minutes/

Stanton, S.J., Beehner, J.C., Saini, E.K., Kuhn, C.M., & LaBar, K.S. (2009). Dominance, Politics, and Physiology: Voters' Testosterone Changes of the Night of the 2008 United States Presidential Election. *PLOS ONE*, 4, 10, e7543.

Stein, A. (2017). *Terror, Love and Brainwashing*. New York: Routledge.

Stein, C. (2017, January 11). Trump Effect Triples ETF Inflows Even Before He Takes Office. Bloomberg News.

Steinberg, L. (2010). A Dual-Systems Model of Adolescent Risk-Taking. *Developmental Psychobiology*, 52, 216–224.

Stelter, B., (2018, 13 June). After Meeting with North Korean Dictator, Trump calls Press America's 'Biggest Enemy'. CNN online edition. Retrieved from: http://money.cnn.com/2018/06/13/media/trump-tweet-media/index.html

Stieglitz, S., & Dang-Xuan, L. (2013). Social Media and Political Communication: A Social Media Analytics Framework. *Social Network Analysis & Mining*, 3, 4, 1277–1291.

Stokes, S. (2011). Political Clientelism. In R.E. Goodin (Ed.), *The Oxford Handbook of Political Science*. Oxford Handbooks Online. Retrieved from: www.oxfordhandbooks.com/view/10.1093/oxfordhb/9780199604456.001.0001/oxfordhb-9780199604456-e-031

Strasel, K.A. (2016, November). Steve Bannon on Politics as War. *Wall Street Journal*. Retrieved from: www.wsj.com/articles/steve-bannon-on-politics-as-war-1479513161

Stetka, B. (2018). Cocktail of Brain Chemicals Might Be Key to What Makes Us Human. *Scientific American*. Retrieved from: www.scientificamerican.com/article/cocktail-of-bra in-chemicals-may-be-a-key-to-what-makes-us-human/

Stewart, R. (2017). US Political Ad Spend Hit Record High in 2016 but TV Lost Momentum Thanks to Donald Trump. The Drum. Retrieved from: www.thedrum.com/news/2017/01/04/us-political-ad-spend-hit-record-high-2016-tv-lost-mom entum-thanks-donald-trump

Student Loan Hero. (2018). A Look at the Shocking Student Loan Debt Statistics for 2018. Retrieved from: https://studentloanhero.com/student-loan-debt-statistics/

Sullivan, A. (2016). Democrats Sue Trump for Alleged Voter Intimidation in 4 States. Reuters. Retrieved from: www.reuters.com/article/us-usa-election-intimidation/dem ocrats-sue-trump-for-alleged-voter-intimidation-in-four-states-idUSKBN12V28G

Sullivan, T. (2018). Class Action Suits over Opioid Epidemic Ramping Up. Policy & Medicine. Retrieved from: www.policymed.com/2017/10/class-action-suits-over-op ioid-epidemic-ramping-up.html

Sumner, C., Byers, A., Boochever, R., & Park, G.J. (2012). Predicting Dark Triad Personality Traits from Twitter Usage and a Linguistic Analysis of Tweets. Proceedings of the 2012 11th International Conference on Machine Learning and Applications, 2, 386–393.

Swartz, J. (2018). Mary Meeker: The 'Privacy Paradox' of Tech & Personal Data. Barron's. Retrieved from: www.barrons.com/articles/mary-meeker-the-privacy-paradox-of-tech-and-personal-data-1527709813

Szegedy-Maszak, M. (2005). Competition Freaks. Los Angeles Times. Retrieved from: http://articles.latimes.com/2005/nov/28/health/he-competition28

Talhelm, T., Haidt, J., Shigehiro, O., Zhang, X., Miao, F., & Chen, S. (2012). Liberals Think More Analytically (More 'Weird') than Conservatives. Social Science Research Network Working Paper. Retrieved from: http://papers.ssrn.com/sol3/papers.cfm? abstract_id=2111700.

Tanner, A. (2016). How Data Brokers Make Money Off Your Medical Records. Scientific American. Retrieved from: www.scientificamerican.com/article/how-data-brokers-ma ke-money-off-your-medical-records/

Tau, B., & Orden, E. (2018, 26 March). White House Probes Loans to Kushner's Business. The Wall Street Journal, Politics Section. Accessed at: www.wsj.com/articles/white-house-probes-loans-to-kushners-business-1522101516

Taylor, S. (2014). Sport and the Decline of War. Psychology Today. Retrieved from: www. psychologytoday.com/gb/blog/out-the-darkness/201403/sport-and-the-decline-war

Tenhouten, W.D. (2016). The Emotions of Powerlessness. Journal of Political Power, 9, 1, 83–121.

Terrizzi, J.A., Shook, N.J., & Ventis, L. (2010). Disgust: A Predictor of Social Conservatism and Prejudicial Attitudes toward Homosexuals. Personality and Individual Differences, 49, 587–592.

Thirthalli, J., Naveen, G., Rao, M., Varambally, S., Christophe, R., & Gangadhar, B. (2013). Cortisol and Antidepressant Effects of Yoga. Indian Journal of Psychiatry, 55, 7, 405.

Thirthalli, J., & Benegal, V. (2006). Psychosis among Substance Users. Current Opinion in Psychiatry, 19, 3, 239–245.

Thompson, G. (2018). Listen to Children Who've Just Been Separated from Parents at Border. ProPublica. Retrieved from: www.propublica.org/article/children-separated-from-parents-border-patrol-cbp-trump-immigration-policy

Thoroughgood, C.N., Padilla, A., Hunter, S.T., & Tate, B.W. (2012). The Susceptible Circle: A Taxonomy of Followers Associated with Destructive Leadership. The Leadership Quarterly, 23, 897–917.

Times of Israel Staff and Agencies. (2018, 19 June). Sessions Says Border Policy Not Nazi-Like: 'They Were Keeping Jews from Leaving'. The Times of Israel. Retrieved from: www.timesofisrael.com/sessions-says-border-policy-not-nazi-like-they-were-keeping-je ws-from-leaving/

Tingley, D. (2007). Evolving Political Science: Biological Adaptation, Rational Action, and Symbolism in Political Science. *Politics and Life Sciences*, 25, 1, 23–41.

Tingley, D. (2011). Neurological Imaging and the Evaluation of Competing Theories. In A. Somit& S.A. Peterson(Eds.), *Biology and Politics: The Cutting Edge*. Research in Bio-politics,9, 187–204. Bingley, UK: Emerald Group Publishing Ltd.

Tobeña, A. (2009). Lethal Altruists: Itineraries Along the Dark Outskirts of Moralistic Pro-Sociality. *Annals of the New York Academy of Sciences*, 1167, 5–15.

Todorov, A., Mandisodza, A.N., Goren, A., & Hall, C.C. (2005). Inferences of Compe-tence from Faces Predict Election Outcomes. *Science*, 308, 10, 1623–1626.

Tooby, J., & Cosmides, L. (1988). Groups in Mind: The Coalitional Roots of War and Morality. In H. Hogh-Olesen (Ed.), *Human Morality and Sociality: Evolutionary and Comparative Perspective* (pp. 191–234). New York: Palgrave-Macmillan.

Trefis Team, Great Speculations. (2018, 15 November). Is BlackRock Losing Its Edge in the ETF Industry? Forbes. Retrieved from: www.forbes.com/sites/greatspeculations/2018/11/15/is-blackrock-losing-its-edge-in-the-etf-industry/

Tripp, K. (2018, 25 June). 'Dumb, Stupid' Family Separations Harm Children Says Detention Camp Manager. *The Guardian*. Retrieved from: www.theguardian.com/us-news/2018/jun/25/family-separations-donald-trump-harm-children-camp-manager

Trump, D.J. (2015, 19 June). (@realDonaldTrump). Tweet. Retrieved from: https://twitter.com/realdonaldtrump/status/612083064945180672?lang=en

Trump, D.J. (2017, 17 June). (@realDonaldTrump). Tweet. Retrieved from: https://twitter.com/realdonaldtrump/status/837996746236182529?lang=en

Trump, D.J. (2018, 17 June). (@realDonaldTrump). Tweet. Retrieved from: https://twitter.com/realdonaldtrump/status/1008510118395293699

Tuncdogan, A., Acar, O.A., & Stam, D. (2017). Individual Differences as Antecedents of Leader Behavior: Towards an Understanding of Multi-Level Outcomes. *The Leadership Quarterly*, 28, 1, 40–64.

Tusk, D. (2018, June). Invitation Letter by President Donald Tusk to the Members of the European Council Ahead of Their Meetings on 28 and 29 June 2018. European Council. Council of the European Union. Retrieved from: www.consilium.europa.eu/en/press/press-releases/2018/06/27/invitation-letter-by-president-donald-tusk-to-the-members-of-the-european-council-ahead-of-their-meetings-on-28-and-29-june-2018/

Turner, S. (2003). Charisma Reconsidered. *Journal of Classical Sociology*, 3, 5–26.

Uhls, Y.T., Michikyan, M., Morris, J., Garcia, D., Small, G.W., Zgourou, E., & Greenfield, P. M. (2014). Five Days at Outdoor Education Camp without Screens Improves Preteen Skills with Nonverbal Emotion Cues. *Computers in Human Behavior*, 39, 387–392.

UK Addiction Treatment Centres. (2016, September). Blackpool Mental Health Issues and the Need Its Drug Addiction. UK Addiction Treatment Centres. Retrieved from: www.ukat.co.uk/drugs/blackpool-mental-health-issues-need-drugs/

United States of America vs. Internet Research Agency. (2018). United States of America vs. Internet Research Agency LLC A/K/A mediasintez LLC a/K/A Glavset LLC A/K/A Mixinfo LLC A/K/A Azimut LLC A/K/A Novinfo LLC, Concord Management and Consulting LLC, Concord Catering, Yevgeniy Viktorovich Prigozhin, Mikhail Ivano-vich Bystrov, Mikhail Leonidovich Burchik A/K/A Mikhail Abramov, Aleksandra Yuryevna Krylova, Anna Vladislavovna Bogacheva, Sergey Pavlovich Polozov, Maria Anatolyevna Belyaeva, Robert Sergeyevich Bovda, Dzheykhun Nasimi Ogly Aslanov A/K/A Jayhoon Aslanov A/K/A Jay Aslanov, Vadim Vladimirovich Podkopaev, Gleb

Igorevich Vasilchenko, Irina Viktorovna Kaverzina, Vladimir Venkov. Case 1:18-cr-00032-DLF. Filed 02/16/18. Retrieved from: www.justice.gov/file/1035477/download

University of Glasgow. (2015). Pressure to Be Available 24/7 on Social Media Causes Teen Anxiety and Depression. University of Glasgow. Retrieved from: www.gla.ac.uk/news/archiveofnews/2015/september/headline_419871_en.html

University of Oxford. (2018, 6 February). Trump Supporters and Extreme Right 'Share Widest Range of Junk News'. University of Oxford. Retrieved from: www.ox.ac.uk/news/2018-02-06-trump-supporters-and-extreme-right-share-widest-range-junk-news#

US Department of Justice. (1994, September). Fact Sheet: Drug-Related Crime. NCJ–149286 .US Department of Justice, Office of Justice Programs, Bureau of Justice Statistics. Retrieved from: www.bjs.gov/content/pub/pdf/DRRC.PDF

US District Court N.D. of Alabama. (2017, 6 November). Greater Birmingham Ministries vs. John Merrill. Civil Case No.: 2:15-cv-02193-LSC. Retrieved from: www.naacpldf.org/files/about-us/255%20CORRECTED%20Pls%20Opp%20MSJ_GBMvAL.pdf

Valentino, N.A., Brader, T., Groenendyk, E.W., Gregorowicz, K., & Hutchings, V.L. (2011). Election Night's Alright for Fighting: The Role of Emotions in Political Participation. *The Journal of Politics*, 73, 1, 156–170.

Van Zee, A. (2009). The Promotion and Marketing of OxyContin: Commercial Triumph, Public Health Tragedy. *American Journal of Public Health*. Retrieved from: https://ajph.aphapublications.org/doi/abs/10.2105/AJPH.2007.131714

Vazire, S., Naumann, L.P., Rentfrow, P.J., & Gosling, S.D. (2008). Portrait of a Narcissist: Manifestations of Narcissism in Physical Appearance. *Journal of Research in Personality*, 42, 1439–1447.

Veblen, T. (1898). Why Is Economics Not an Evolutionary Science? *The Quarterly Journal of Economics*, 12, 4, 373–397.

Vincent, J. (2017, 11 December). Former Facebook Exec Says Social Media Is Ripping Apart Society. The Verge. Retrieved from: https://www.theverge.com/2017/12/11/16761016/former-facebook-exec-ripping-apart-society

Viner, J. (1958). *The Long View and the Short: Studies in Economic Theory and Policy*. Glencoe, IL: Free Press.

Vis, B. (2017, 25–30 April). Do Politicians Use Cognitive Heuristics like the Rest of Us? ECPR Joint Sessions. Workshop on 'The Politics of Information. How Political Elites Select and Process Information'. University of Nottingham, Nottingham, UK.

Viser, M. (2017, 5 May). Trump Has Been Sued 134 Times in Federal Court since Inauguration. *The Globe*. Retrieved from: www.bostonglobe.com/news/politics/2017/05/05/trump-has-been-sued-times-federal-court-since-inauguration-day/E4AqZBYaKYHtzwfQ3k9hdM/story.html

Volkow, N.D., & Insel, T.R. (2003). What Are the Long-Term Effects of Methylphenidate Treatment? *Biological Psychiatry*, 54, 1307–1309.

Wagner, M.W., Deppe, K.D., Jacobs, C.M., Friesen, A., Smith, K.B., Hibbing, J.R. (2015). Beyond Survey Self-Reports: Using Physiology to Tap Political Orientations. *International Journal of Public Opinion Research*, 27, 3, 303–317.

Wakefield, J. (2018, 10 February). Is Social Media Causing Childhood Depression? BBC News. Retrieved from: www.bbc.co.uk/news/technology-42705881

Walt, V. (2017, 7 November). At Home in the World. *Time*. Retrieved from: http://time.com/emmanuel-macron-president-france-interview/

Walters, J. (2017, October). America's Opioid Crisis: How Prescription Drugs Sparked a National Trauma. *The Guardian*. Retrieved from: www.thegardian.com/us-news/2017/oct/25/americas-opioid-crisis-how-prescription-drugs-sparked-a-national-trauma

Warner, J., & McGraw, P. (2012). Scientifically Speaking, Who's Funnier: Democrats or Republicans? *Wired*. Retrieved from: www.wired.com/2012/10/humor-democrats-vs-republicans/

Wasserman, D., & Flinn, A. (2017, 7 April). Introducing the Cook Political Partisan Voter Index. The Cook Political Report. Cook Partisan Voter Index for the 115th Congress.

Watt, D.F. (2005). Social Bonds and the Nature of Empathy. *Journal of Consciousness Studies*, 12, 8–10, 185–209.

Watts, A.L., Lilienfeld, S.O., Smith, S.F., Milller, J.D., Campbell, W.K., Waldman, I. D., ... Faschingbauer, T.J. (2013). The Double-Edged Sword of Grandiose Narcissism: Implications for Successful and Unsuccessful Leadership among U.S. Presidents. *Psychological Science*, 24, 12, 2379–2389.

Wayman, E. (2012). When Did the Human Mind Evolve to What It Is Today? Smithsonian.com. Retrieved from: www.smithsonianmag.com/science-nature/when-did-the-human-mind-evolve-to-what-it-is-today-140507905/#ze6Xu7HHu163uQJu.99

Wearden, G., & Fletcher, N. (2016, 24 June). Brexit Panic Wipes $2 Trillion Off World Markets – As It Happened. *The Guardian*. Retrieved from: www.theguardian.com/business/live/2016/jun/24/global-markets-ftse-pound-uk-leave-eu-brexit-live-updates

Weaver, M. (2016, 28 September). 'Horrible Spike' in Hate Crime Linked to Brexit Vote, Met Police Say. *The Guardian*. Retrieved from: www.theguardian.com/society/2016/sep/28/hate-crime-horrible-spike-brexit-vote-metropolitan-police

Weber, B., Rangel, A., Wibral, M., & Falk, A. (2009). The Medial Prefrontal Cortex Exhibits Money Illusion. *Proceedings of the National Academy of Sciences*, 106, 13, 5025–5028.

Weber, M. (1864–1920/1954). *Max Weber on Law in Economy and Society*. Cambridge, MA: Harvard University Press.

Weber, M. (1904/1958). *The Protestant Ethic and the Spirit of Capitalism*. New York: Charles Scribner's Sons.

Weber, M. (1924/1947). *The Theory of Social and Economic Organizations*. (T. Parsons, Trans.). New York: Free Press.

Weber, M. (1958/1965). *From Max Weber: Essays in Sociology*. H. Gerth & C. Wright.Mills (Eds.). New York: Oxford University Press.

Weber, M. (1968). *Economy and Society: An Outline of Interpretive Sociology*. G. Roth & K. Wittich (Eds.). New York: Bedminster Press.

Weber, M. (1978). *Economy and Society: An Outline of Interpretive Sociology*. G. Ross & C. Wittich (Eds.). Berkeley: University of California Press.

The Week. (2018, 2 June). Is Mike Pence the Most Repulsive Figure in US Politics? News Section, p. 16.

Weisberg, J. (2010, 27 September). A Tea Party Taxonomy. *Newsweek*, 156, 13, 32–33.

Weller, C. (2018, 5 February). A Group of Former Facebook and Apple Employees Are Teaming Up to Warn Kids about Tech Addiction. Business Insider UK. Retrieved from: http://uk.businessinsider.com/ex-facebook-and-google-employees-launch-anti-tech-addiction-campaign-2018-2

Westen, D. (2007). *The Political Brain*. New York: Public Affairs.

Westen, D., Blagov, P.S., Harenski, K., Kilts, C., & Hamann, S. (2006). Neural Bases of Motivated Reasoning: An FMRI Study of Emotional Constraints on Partisan Political

Judgement in the 2004 US Presidential Election. *Journal of Cognitive Neuroscience*, 18, 11, 1947–1958.

Wharton University of Pennsylvania. (2008, 10 December). CEOs and Market Woes: Is Poor Corporate Governance to Blame? Retrieved from: http://knowledge.wharton.upenn.edu/article/ceos-and-market-woes-is-poor-corporate-governance-to-blame/

White, A.E., & Kenrick, D.T. (2013, 1 November). Why Attractive Candidates Win. Op-Ed. *The New York Times*. Retrieved from: www.nytimes.com/2013/11/03/opinion/sunday/health-beauty-and-the-ballot.html

White, A.E., Kenrick, D.T., & Neuberg, S.L. (2013). Beauty at the Ballot Box: Disease Threats Predict Preferences for Physically Attractive Leaders. *Psychological Science*, 24, 12, 2429–2436.

Wilens, T.E., Faraone S.V., & Biederman, J. (2004). Attention-Deficit/Hyperactivity Disorder in Adults. *Journal of the American Medical Association*, 292, 619–623.

Wiley, N.F. (1983). The Congruance of Weber and Keynes. *Sociological Theory*, 1, 30–56.

Willingham, A.J. (2016, 20 July). When Bad News Gets to Be Too Much. CNN. Retrieved fromwww.https.//edition.cnn.com/2016/07/20/health/how-to-deal-with-traumatic-news-trnd/index.html

Winter, D.G. (1973). *The Power Motive*. New York: Free Press.

Wong, E.M., Ormiston, M.E., & Haselhuhn, M.P. (2011). A Face Only an Investor Could Love: CEOs' Facial Structure Predicts Their Firms' Financial Performance. *Psychological Science*, 22, 1478–1483.

Yates, E. (2017, 25 March). What Happens to Your Brain When You Get a Like on Instagram. Business Insider UK. Retrieved from: http://uk.businessinsider.com/what-happens-to-your-brain-like-instagram-dopamine-2017-3

Young, S.M., & Pinsky, D. (2006). Narcissism and Celebrity. *Journal of Research in Personality*, 40, 463–471.

Zajonc, R.B. (1984). On the Primacy of Affect. *American Psychologist*, 39, 2, 117–123.

Zakharov, I.G., & Tyrnov, O.F. (2001). The Effect of Solar Activity on Ill and Healthy People under Conditions of Nervous and Emotional Stresses. *Advances in Space Research*, 28, 4, 685–690.

Zauzmer, J., & MacMillan, K. (2018, 15 June). Sessions Cites Bible Passage Used to Defend Slavery in Defense of Separating Immigrant Families. *The Washington Post*. Retrieved from: www.washingtonpost.com/news/acts-of-faith/wp/2018/06/14/jeff-sessions-points-to-the-bible-in-defense-of-separating-immigrant-families/?utm_term=.8d9a518d7eb3

Zehndorfer, E. (2014). *Leadership: A Critical Introduction*. New York: Routledge.

Zehndorfer, E. (2015). *Charismatic Leadership: The Role of Charisma in the Global Financial Crisis*. New York: Routledge.

Zehndorfer, E. (2018). *The Physiology of Emotional and Irrational Investing: Causes and Solutions*. New York: Routledge.

Ziegbe, M. (2010). Jon Stewart Speech Closes Rally to Restore Sanity and/or Fear. MTV online. Retrieved from: www.mtv.com/news/1651165/jon-stewart-speech-closes-rally-to-restore-sanity-andor-fear/

Zillmann, D. (1998) The Psychology of Portrayals of Violence. In J. Goldstein (Ed.), *Why We Watch: The Attractions of Violent Entertainment* (pp. 179–209). New York: Oxford University Press.

Zillmann, D. (2006). Dramaturgy for Emotions from Fictional Narration. In J. Bryant & P. Vorderer (Eds.), *Psychology of Entertainment* (pp. 215–238). Mahwah, NJ: Erlbaum.

Zweig, J. (2007a). Your Money and Your Brain. *Money Magazine*. Retrieved from: http s://money.cnn.com/2007/08/14/pf/zweig.moneymag/index.htm?postversion= 2007082313

Zweig, J. (2007b). *Your Money and Your Brain*. New York: Simon & Schuster.

INDEX

Turkey, electoral violence 86
turn out, low 38
Turnbull, M. 5
Tusk, D. 119
tweets: Trump's 74, 84; US Presidential
  Election (2016) 40; weaponizing 73–74
Twitter 61–62, 68, 72, 73, 81; Trump's
  account 74, 81, 84, 99–100, 109
two-party state 1

UKIP 23–24
uncertainty 11
United Kingdom Independence Party
  (UKIP) 23–24, 59
United Kingdom (UK), Prime Minister 46
United States of America (USA):
  Constitution threats 1; Southern Baptist
  Convention 85; Stock Market record
  overvalued and overdue for bear market
  101; *versus* Internet Research Agency
  (IRA) 71–72
US Presidential Election (2008) 38
US Presidential Election (2012) 88
US Presidential Election (2016): advertising
  52, 58, 67n4, 119; campaign press
  coverage 117–118; donations 52, 88,
  120n8; invocation of populism 22;
  Russian interference 1, 14, 71–72, 76;
  sensation seeking engagement 43; social
  media 62; tweets 40
us/them 32–33

Van Der Bellen, A. 95
vaping 64–65
Veblen, T. 103
Venezuela, electoral violence (2017) 86
vicarious traumatization 43–44
Viner, J. 100
violence: campaign rallies 26; electoral
  85–86; incitement 107; PTSD 43–44;
  rallies 23; teen 31; testosterone 14

vision 25
VIX Volatility Index 102
voter manipulation service
  (Siguldin) 77
voters: affiliation 1–2; ambiguity-tolerant
  12; intimidation of 55; right-wing
  populist 13; suppression 12, 54–55;
  turnout 14, 38
voting: behaviors 105–106;
  emotional 2; location 14; opting out 35;
  preference 37; weather 34

war: elixirs 52–53; human death toll 51;
  political 105
warfare: guerrilla 105; psychological
  74–75, 115
Washington, G., Presidential Farewell
  Address (1796) 1
wealth 22
weather 36, 50n3; and voting 34–35
Weber, M. 22, 28, 84, 92–93; charismatic
  authority 69
Weibosu 77
Westen, D. 2–4, 10, 11, 16–18, 34;
  et al. 6
white control 54–55
Wigmore, A. 79
Wikileaks 40
Willingham, A.J. 44
winner effect 108–109
Woods, D. 11; *Biko* 12
World Health Organization
  (WHO) 40
Wrangham, R. 51
Wylie, C. 58, 59, 78, 114

YouTube 73

Ziegbe, M. 30
Zuckerberg, M. 79–80
Zweig, J. 104